Indo-Tibetan Studies Series-III

HISTORY OF RELIGION IN TRIPURA

Projit Kumar Palit

2004

Kaveri Books

New Delhi - 110 002

First Published in 2004

ISBN 81-7479-064-0

Published by : Rakesh Goel
Kaveri Books
4697/5-21 A, Ansari Road,
New Delhi - 110 002 (India).
Tel.: 2 328 8140, 2 324 5799
e-mail: kaveribooks@vsnl.com

Laser Typesetting by : Aarti Computers, Delhi - 110 009.

Printed at : Chawla Offset Printers, Delhi - 110 052

PRINTED IN INDIA

Dedicated to

Prof. Pranabananda Jash

&

Mrs. Sikha Jash

as a

token of love and respect

VISVA-BHARATI

FOUNDED BY

RABINDRANATH TAGORE

ACHARYA
INDER KUMAR GUJARAL
UPACHARYA
DILIP KUMAR SINHA

• বিশ্বভারতী •
শান্তিনিকেতন

SANTINIKETAN—731 235
WEST BENGAL, INDIA

PROLOGUE

The Department of Indo-Tibetan Studies is a centre for Studies in Indological research in general and Buddhism in particular. This Department is first of its kind to introduce Area Study in the University system under the guidance of Dr. Prabodh Chandra Bagchi. The Department is regularly publishing research works on various subjects related to Indo-Tibetan Studies. I am happy that Kaveri Books is going to publish the third volume of the Indo-Tibetan Studies Series entitled 'History of Religion in Tripura'. I do hope the volume will attract the notice of the academicians.

NDash

Narendra K. Dash
Head
Dept. of Indo-Tibetan Studies
Visva-Bharati, Santiniketan
West Bengal - 731 235

Foreword

It is with pleasure that I introduce this book, *History of Religion in Tripura*, by Sri Projit Kumar Palit. This work covers the period from early times to c. 1775 A.D., which marks practically the end of the Manikya dynasty when Mr. Ralph Leak was appointed the first British Resident of Tripperah. Formerly known as Hill Tripperah during the British rule, Tripura is popularly known as the land of *Chaturdasa Devata* (i.e., fourteen gods and goddesses), and it has been a confluence of diverse religious and cultural traditions with traces of Brahmanism of various hues, as also later Buddhism and indigenous tribal religions. This has been substantiated by the discovery of innumerable archaeological artefacts, sculptural representations, and numismatic illustrations.

Buddhism—in particular the Mahayana form of it—has held sway over this region since the first decade of the sixth century A.D., as has been revealed in the religious practices of the tribals. Since the eighth century Tantric Buddhism, an offshoot of Mahayana Buddhism, has become quite popular, especially among the tribal folk of the Chakmas and Maghs. Then immigration of people from the plains brought in Brahmanism of various shades, and thus Saivism, Vaisnavism, Saktism, and other minor sects flourished there, though each invariably bore a conspicuous regional imprint. The interplay of these historical forces during the medieval period greatly influenced the folk literature and traditions. Besides this, the rites and ritual practices and faiths of the tribals flowed down the stream of time almost unchanged. These two co-existent streams markedly influenced the culture of Tripura. And though after that, the socio-political situation in Tripura became rather muddled, the religious spirit of the people remained strong, even as Islam, Christianity, and Brahmoism came in. This period needs serious study now.

I hope this work, with its painstaking research, will be well received by all, particularly by scholars of Indological studies.

Swami Prabhananda
Secretary
Ramakrishna Mission
Institute of Culture,
Gol Park, Kolkata - 29

Contents

LIST OF ABBREVIATIONS

ABORI	:	Annals of the Bhandarkar Oriental Research Institute, Poona
AR, ASB	:	Annual Report of Archaeological Survey of Burma
ASI	:	Archaeological Survey of India
ASI-AR	:	Archaeological Survey of India - Annual Report
ASR	:	Archaeological Survey Report
EHI	:	Elements of Hindu Iconography
EI	:	Epigraphia Indica
IAR	:	Indian Archaeology - A Review
IC	:	Indian Culture
IHQ	:	Indian Historical Quarterly
ISS	:	In The Sylvan Shadows
JAIH	:	Journal of Ancient Indian History, Calcutta University
JAS	:	Journal of the Asiatic Society
JASB	:	Journal of the Asiatic Society of Bengal
JNSI	:	Journal of the Numismatic Society of India
JBORS	:	Journal of the Bihar and Orissa Research Society, Patna
JRASB	:	Journal of the Royal Asiatic Society of Bengal
JRASB(L)	:	Journal of the Royal Asiatic Society of Bengal: Letters
Maha	:	Mahānārāyaṇa Upaniṣad
MASI	:	Memoirs of the Archaeological Survey of India
Mbh/	:	Mahābhārata
PA	:	Pakistan Archaeology
PIHC	:	Proceedings of Indian History Congress

System of Transliteration

Roman equivalents of Devanāgari Letters

a	अ	ka	क	da	द
ā	आ	kha	ख	dha	ध
i	इ	ga	ग	na	न
ī	ई	gha	घ	pa	प
u	उ	ṅ	ङ	pha	फ
ū	ऊ	ca/cha	च	ba	ब
ṛ	ऋ	cha/chha	छ	bha	भ
e	ए	ja	ज	ma	म
ai	ऐ	jha	झ	ya	य
o	ओ	ñ	ञ	ra	र
au	औ	ṭa	ट	la	ल
		ṭha	ठ	va	व
		ḍa	ड	śa	श
		ḍha	ढ	ṣa/sha	ष
		ṇa	ण	sa	स
		ta	त	ha	ह
		tha	थ	ṁ	ं
				ḥ	ः

INTRODUCTION

Tripura, the land of *'Chaturdaśa-devatā'* (fourteen Gods and Goddesses) in the north-eastern India with its capital at Agartala is located between 20°56' and 24°32' north latitude and 91°10' and 91°21' east longitude measuring 10,477 square kilometres. It is a small state with a population 3191168 of whom 29 per cent belong to the tribal communities. It is bounded in the north, west, south-east by the international boundary of Bāṅglādesh in the present districts of Sylhet, Comilla, Noakhali, Chittagong and Chittagong Hill Tracts. In the east it has a common boundary with the Cachar district of Assam and Mizo district of Mizoram. The geographical continuity with the Indian mainland is maintained only in the north-east by an outlet through Cachar district of Assam. The region is rich in natural resoures and ethnologically interesting as a habitat of several tribal communities such as Tripuris, Riangs, Hālāms, Maghs, Jāmātias, Chākmās, etc. The present state of Tripura was known as "Hill *Tripperah*" in the British period. It was ruled by the lunar dynasty of members with Māṇikya ending names since the beginning of 15th century A.D. The British Government gave 'Tripura' the status of "Native State" under the general supervision of a Political agent. It merged with India on October 15, 1949 and became a full-fledged state on January 21, 1972.

It is not known how and when this land was named as Tripura. A common belief is that the name has originated from "*Tripurasundarī*", the presiding goddess of the land, who was installed by the king Dhaṇya Māṇikya (śaka 1412-37/1490-1515 A.D.) According to some, the name Tripura is much older than *Tripurasundarī* and one of them sought to derive the name Tripura from the word *"Tuipsra"* which means "places adjoining water". However, the word Tripura is met with for the first time on the coins of Dhaṇya Māṇikya carrying *Tripurendra* as the royal epithet. And the name is not known to have been in use until the reign of Dhaṇya Māṇikya. It is reasonable to hold that the name of this state is the Sanskritized form, the Tripura, a name borne by a well-known Tribe of the land.

This state has a rich cultural and religious background. But unfortunately no comprehensive and systematic study of all the religious sects of Tripura like Buddhism, Brahmanism and various indigenous tribal religions from the early times to the time of Māṇikya dynasty has so far been attempted. The region has flourished as repository of ancient religion and sculpture for centuries. It has archaeological evidence to show the presence of various religious sects of Tripura at one time or the other in its history. The fact Buddhism flourished in different parts of Tripura from very early times has been attested by the discovery of various archaeological materials. The immigration of the plain people, marked the rise of Brahmanism and its diverse sectarian beliefs and practices in Tripura. The religious history of Tripura prior to the twelfth century A.D. is mixed up with the religious history of ancient Sylhet, Samataṭa, Noakhali and Chittagong. Brahmanism is the earliest religion of Tripura and its various sects in their fullfledged form flourished here for long.

The main obstacle in the study of religion of Tripura, as in most cases in regard to other parts of India, is the problem of determining the date of undated sculptures. As regards the religious sculptures, not a single specimen with any dedicatory inscription on it, has so far been found in Tripura. Still, an attempt has been made to ascertain the period mainly on the basis of some archaeological evidences: first, the style of the relevant sculpture and secondly, where available, its affiliation with allied fields (sometimes dated) hailing from the neighbouring regions like Assam, West Bengal, etc. or from the neighbouring countries like Bāṅglādesh and Burma. We are in a better position, however, as regards temples and monuments where dedicatory inscriptions having dates of the foundation of the shrines as well as names of the founders are engraved on the walls of the majority of the temples of the land.

The present dissertation consists of four chapters covering a period from the earliest times till c.1775 A D. The first chapter deals with the geographical and socio-ethnic background of Tripura. Geographically Tripura is located in areas where in diverse civilizations, religions and cultures met in the past. Lying at the cross-roads of Assam and Bengal, it was probably connected with Burma, via land-routes through Gomati, Surmā and Cāchār valley, Lushai hills and Manipur on the one hand and via Chittagong, Arākān on the other. Perhaps it was through the latter route in the eleventh-twelfth centuries A.D. that the kingdoms of Paṭṭikera and Burma maintained relations among themselves. Although the city of Paṭṭikera cannot be identified, it must have been situated within the district of Tripura, for an important place near Maināmati hills is still known as Paitkora, which had been under the administration of the Māṇikya rulers of Tripura even before the partition of India. Tripura's link with Arākān appears to have been effected via Chittagong and Govinda Māṇikya (1661-67 A D), a ruler of Tripura is said to have taken shelter in Arākān court due to turmoil in his motherland and he most probably used the same route. From the north through Assam valley came the Chinese as well as different tribal immigrants of Indo-Mongoloid race of whom the Bodo speaking group deserves a special mention. They spread over the whole of Brahmaputra valley and extended to Tripura in the shape of Tripura tribe. Bengal had a happy cultural relation with Burma and probably it was through the passes of Tripura, this cultural religious trend migrated. Morever, where colonization and trade linked together parts of south-east Asia or Buddhist missionaries came from the said region via sea routes to visit Bodhgayā, they had to pass through land routes via Tripura to reach the destination. As a result, apart from other factors, this both way assimilation of elements with the local idioms gave rise to a regional mixed culture and religion of Tripura which is an important phase towards the development of religion, art and culture of north eastern India.

The second chapter traces the political background of the pre-Māṇikya period and its development and progress in the Māṇikya period till 1775 A.D. The archaeological evidences found in the region prove the fact that a large portion of the region, particularly south-western part of the present state of Tripura, was politically attached to the kingdoms of eastern Bengal known as Samataṭa, Vaṅga and Harikela.

The second phase of Māṇikya dynasty begins with the establishment of political power by a successor of eneong-Phā, during the later half of the fifteenth century A.D. The king of Gauḍa entitled him by "Māṇikya". From that time the kings of this dynasty have been using the title permanently. According to historical chronology the king of Gauḍa Sultan Ruknuddin Barbak Shah (1455 A.D. to 1476 A.D.) of Bengal was the contemporary of Ratna Māṇikya. From Ratna Māṇikya upto the death of Kṛṣṇa Māṇikya, Tripura passed through constant political turmoil caused by internal and external factors and the socio-religious condition in that time suffered a serious setback in consequence.

The third chapter deals with religion in Tripura. From the early time, people of the plains and the royal family appear to have remained within the fold of Buddhism and Brahmanism. Side by side, tribal religion with its faiths and beliefs, rites and rituals appear to have flourished in Tripura. This kind of assimilation in religions is reflected in various kinds of evidences, both literary and archaeological, which are mainly found from this tiny state. In order to make the investigation critically and comprehensively the present chapter is divided into the following sub titles:

(a) Buddhism

Tripura and its adjoining regions became an important centre of Buddhism since the period of Aśoka and continued to be so for several centuries thereafter. A copper-plate of Gunaigar proves that Buddhism flourished here around 507-508 A.D. Before the sixth century A.D. the *Mahāyāna* form of Buddhism had found its way all over Tripura. Hiuen Tsang on a visit to Samataṭa noticed thrity Buddhist monasteries with 2000 priests, all of the *Sthavira* school. Another Chinese pilgrim Sen-chi noticed that *Mahāyāna* Buddhism had been established in different parts of Samataṭa mainly through the patronage of the Khaḍga dynasty. It is from the eighth century A.D. onwards that Tantric Buddhism flourished and it became the most widely prevalent and popular religion of this region, especially with the Chākmā and the Magh tribes of Tripura.

(b) Śaivism

Śaivism also attained a predominant position along with Vaiṣṇavism in Tripura during the sixth century A.D. The copper-plate inscription from Gunaigar in Comilla informs that the cult of Śiva had secured royal patronage in Tippera region. Śaivism as identified in the above inscription is a federation of cults, which had combined in it the various cults of *Rudra,* Śiva and *Liṅga.* So far as Tripura is concerned, a collection of antiquities dating from c. 700-1200 A.D. have come to light from *Unakoti, Pilāk* and some other parts of Tripura.

(c) Vaiṣṇavism

Vaiṣṇavism was the most widely prevalent and popular religion in Tripura region from the sixth century A.D. A copper-plate inscription of Gunaigar in Comilla speaks of a temple of *Pradūmneśvara* in Tippera. The discovery of a copper-plate of Lokanātha from Tippera proves that the worship of Ananta Nārāyaṇa was prevalent in Tripura region during the seventh century A.D. Another copper-plate inscription of Kailan also indicates that Śrīdharaṇarata a king of Tippera during the seventh century A.D. was a *Paramavaiṣṇava* and a worshipper of *Purushottama*. Therefore, Viṣṇu in his different forms represents the existence of Vaiṣṇava sect in this region from the sixth and seventh centuries A.D.

The development of Vaiṣṇavism was unchecked during the next couple of centuries as a large number of Viṣṇu images of the Pāla-Sena periods have been discovered in different parts of Tripura. The nature of early Vaiṣṇavism during its formative period was probably influenced by Viṣṇu of the Vedic Brahmanism, Nārāyaṇa of the Pāñcharātras and Kṛṣṇa-Vāsudeva of the *Sāttvatas*. The earliest image of Rādhā-Kṛṣṇa in Tripura dates back to seventeenth century A.D. only. Almost all the aspects of later Vaiṣṇavism were prevalent as known from the sculptural representations.

(d) Śaktism

Śakti worship prevailed originally among the Indo-Mongoloid race of Tripura as Mataikātārmā. In the religious history of Tripura Śakti seems to be the active goddess who enjoyed wide popularity during seventh century A.D. onwards. An excellent bronze image of

Śarvānī has been discovered in Tripura and it belongs to early centuries of the Christian era. A large number of sculptures, found in Tripura bear evidence to the various manifestations of the Śākta cult. The famous image of the four-handed goddess Kālī, locally called *Tripurasundarī* is worshipped in the temple at Udaipur. Evidence of Śakti cult or the mother goddess worship has come to light from Uṅakoti, Pilāk and other parts of Tripura.

(e) Other Minor Sects

The worship of Gaṇapati or Gaṇeśa was not unknown to the people of Tripura. Four images of Gaṇeśa of the 11th-12th centuries A.D., were found at *Unakoti*. Of them, the two *Ṣaḍa-bhūja* and rest of *Aṣṭabhūja* Gaṇeśa deserve attention. These sculptural representations do not bear any conspicuous features. Similarly, there is also ample evidence to the popularity of the Sūrya worship in Tripura. The Sun cult appears to have come from north India. The inscribed image of Sūrya discovered from Deulbāḍi in Tripura belongs to the seventh century A.D. There are several other images of this deity, which evidently show his popularity during the medieval period.

In the last chapter, an attempt has been made to throw some light on the various aspects of the tribal religion. A large number of people in Tripura are still the followers of nature worship or spirit and ancestors worship. In fact, their religious beliefs and practices may be characterised as polytheistic. This chapter describes beliefs connected with origins of some of their pūjās, the systems of these and role of the Ochais of different categories and the classifications of their deities. It also describes the origin of the Garia Pūjā, Ker Pūjā, Kharchī Pūjā, Lamprā Pūjā etc. The construction of the images of deities with green bamboo and the specific customs in the arrangement of the bamboo sticks for specific deities are also important aspects of these pūjās. The mantras they chant in their traditional pūjās are quite interesting. Of course, there is no specific cult centered round these worships but the people of non-Brahmanical fold are the main votaries of this type of worship.

The present book 'History of Religion in Tripura' is primarily a revised text of my work. It is my pious responsibility to acknowledge the valuable help I received from different quarters without which it would not have been possible to present the work in the form.

Words fail to express my deep regard and gratitute to Swami Prabhananda Maharaj, Secretary, Ramakrishna Mission Institute of Culture, Golpark, Kolkata, for his valuable 'Foreword'.

In course of research work, I have the opportunity to receive blessings and advice from Swami Sarvabhutananda Maharaj, Ramakrishna Mission Institute of Culture, Golparak, Kolkata, Swami Sumedhananda Maharaj, Swami Sarvadhebananda Maharaj and Swami Debapriyananda Maharaj, Ramakrishna Mission, Viveknagar, Tripura.

I express my deep regards to Professor Pranabananda Jash, Department of Ancient Indian History, Culture & Archaeology, Visva-Bharati, who has kindly supervised me to complete the work for my Ph.D degree from Visva-Bharati.

I express my sense of gratitude to Prof. G. Subbiah, Dr. Bikash Mukherjee and Dr. Ananda Chandra Sahoo, Department of Ancient Indian History Culture & Archaeology, Visva-Bharati, Prof. Samir Mukherjee, Calcutta University, Mr. Bijoy Kumar Debbarman, former Director, Archaeological Survey of India, Prof. Mahadev Chakraborty and Prof. Sirajuddin Ahamed, Tripura University, Dr. Juthika Bhowmik, former Publication Officer, Govt. of Tripura, Dr. Ratna Das, former Curator, Govt. Museum of Tripura, Mr. Ratan Acharjee, Tribal Research Institute, Govt. of Tripura, for their advice and suggestions in different time.

I must acknowledge my sincere gratitude to Dr. Narendra Kumar Dash, Department of Indo-Tibetan Studies, Visva-Bharati, who has taken interest for the publication of the work under Indo-Tibetan Studies Series.

I am thankful to my wife Susmita, my daughter Poulomi and my friend Indraneel, who encouraged and assisted me to complete this work.

I am also thankful to the authorities of the Ramakrishna Mission Institute of Culture, Golpark, Kolkata, for providing me partial financial grant for the completion of my research work.

Thanks are also due to the staff members of different libraries like, Visva-Bharati; Tripura University (Agartala); Tribal Research Institute (Agartala); National Library (Kolkata); The Ramakrishna

Mission Institute of Culture (Kolkata); The Asiatic Society (Kolkata); and Museums like, Indian Museum (Kolkata); Tripura Govt. Museum (Agartala); Tribal Research Institute Museum (Agartala); etc. for their valuable help during the course of research.

1

Historical Geography of Tripura, Pre-Historic Objects, People and Socio-Religious Background

Tripura, the land of *'Chaturdaśa-devatā'* (fourteen Gods and Goddesses) in the north-eastern India with its capital at Agartala is located between 20° 56' and 24°32' north latitude and 91°10' and 91°21' east longitude. Bordered by Bāṅgladesh on three sides, Tripura is connected to the main land through the eastern frontier which is adjacent to the Cachar district of Assam and the State of Mizoram. The districts of Sylhet, Comilla (erstwhile Tippera), Noakhali, Chittagong, and Chittagong Hill Tracts in Bāṅglādesh share a common boundary with Tripura on the north, west, south and south-east direction respectively.

The present day international boundary has its basis in 1854 when Tippera (now Comilla, Bāṅglādesh) was demarcated from Hill Trippera (now Tripura state, India).

The eastern boundary of the state separating the Lushai hills and the Chittagong Hill Tracts is formed by the river Langai between the Haichek and Jampai ranges to its source in the Betling sub peak. The line then runs in an irregular fashion upto the Dolājari, and then along the Sardeng range and the river Fenny till the latter enters into the Noakhali district of Bāṅgladesh. This eastern boundary was fixed as a provisional 'inner line' in the early seventies of the last century for strategic reasons when the Lushais were increasingly showing their raiding propensities. It was nevertheless acknowledged that the princely state of Tripura had bonafide control over the entire Lushai hills upto the river Dhaleśwari, thirteen miles east of the present boundary. But when the Lushai disturbances were over, the British Indian Government unilaterally fixed the boundary along the Langai river, the present boundary, without the slightest reference to the Tripura Durbār. Since the times of Birchandra Māṇikya (1862-96 A.D.) repeated representations were made to the then Government of eastern Bengal and Assam and also the Government of India stated that they "see no sufficient reason for reconsidering the previous orders" and that "they are unable to accede to the Durbār's request.[1]" Tripura was thus deprived of a considerable portion of territory that rightfully belonged to her.

The state embraces an area of 10,49,169 square kilometres according to State Department of Land Records and Settlement[2]. Geologically, the territory is not very old. It seems to have risen from the sea-bed in the late tertiary age about forty million years ago. It is a part of Assam — Arākān geological province. Originally this province was a basin. Topographically, the whole territory can be divided into the following divisions of physical features — Hill, Hillock, River Valley, Lunga, Tilla, Flat lands and Lakes. The climate of Tripura is generally dry and humid with plenty of rains. The state lies within the south-west Monsoon belt and rainfall is quite moderate. The annual temperature ranges from 10'4°C to 35'2°C.

The early history of the present state of Tripura is still shrouded into obscurity. No records in the shape of documents or monuments of the autochthonous people of the land belonging to the pre-historic or proto-historic periods have survived. The physiographical aspect of eastern India is dominated by the basins of the Ganges in Bihar, the Brahmaputra in Assam and their joint deltaic formation in Bengal. The Bengal Delta described as one of the seven natural divisions in which eastern India is generally divided, is again sub-divided into five main parts by the present river system. Of these parts, south east Bengal extends to the east of the river Meghnā. "Here the rivers rise from the eastern Tertiary Hills of Tripura and Chittagong and flow in a west or south-west direction. There are three important river valleys in this region, which cut through Tertiary ranges. The Surmā valleys, incorporating the district of Sylhet, separates the Tipperah hills from a fringe of the Tertiary rocks bordering the southern edge of the Shillong plateau. The Gomti river, rising in the Tipperah hills, encircles the lateritic deposit of the Lālmāi - Maināmati hill on three sides. The deposit is made up of slightly micaceous, yellow-coloured sand stone and ferruginous concretions which when decomposed colour the top of the hill brick-red. The sand stone is not very compact and appears to be in horizontal beds. There are, also, horizontal intercalcations of clay, only a few inches thick and occasional bands of a argillaceous nodules. The most striking feature here is the abundant occurrence of fossil world"[3]. Though old alluvium could be traced in the red lateritic soil of the Lālmāi-Maināmati range in Comilla (old Tipperah) district of Bāṅglādesh, adjoining the plains of hill Tripura and near Sītākundu in Chittagong district "nothing has so far been discovered about the early man in this region".

It is interesting that some neolithic fossil tools[4] such as scrapers or hoe made of chert and grinder made of silicised fossil wood have been found at Nandannagar, Agartala while digging a tank. In addition to its quite a good number of fossil wood, boulders of different shape and size are found in Sonāmurā subdivision of west Tripura district. The scrapers beautifully polished, are now preserved in Agartala Museum. All these tools might belong to the same culture complex.

The earliest inhabitants of north eastern India, were very probably of the Austric stock. They were the pre-Dravidian aborigines who are now represented by the Monkhmer Khāsīs and Syntengs of Assam. These Austric people were supplanted by the Dravidians who belonged to the Chalocolithic Age. Then came the Indo-Mongoloids who "belonged to the Tribe to Burman family of the Indo-Chinese group and their representatives of the present day are the Kacharis, Koches, Rabhas, Meches, Mikirs, Lalungs, Gāros, Nāgās, Kūkis, and Chūtias. Of these, the tribes speaking the Bodo (Boro) language seems to have occupied the plains of Assam for a very long time. These Bodo people were no doubt the Kirātas and Mlechhas spoken of in the Mahābhārata."[5]

The Bodos "who spread over the whole of Brahmaputra valley and north Bengal as well as east Bengal forming a solid block in north eastern India, were the most important Indo-Mongoloid people in eastern India, and they formed one of the main bases of the present day population of these tracts... From Nowgong district in Assam their area of occupation extended to Cachar district (Particularly in the north Cachar hills) and into Sylhet and from Cachar and Sylhet they extended further to the south to Tripura State, where there is still a Bodo speaking block in the shape of the Tripura tribe which founded the state and from Tripura they spread into Comilla and possibly also Noakhali districts, and thus they occupied the mouth of the Gaṅgās by the eastern Sea."[6] But the Rājmālā[7], (the verse Chronicle of the ruling dynasty of Tripura) claims, Tripura king descended from Yayātī, the sixth descendant of the lunar dynasty, who is stated to have ruled over India from the capital city of Pratisthana situated at the confluence of the Gaṅgā and the Jamunā somewhere near modern Allahābād.

One of his descendants is said to have come to Assam and established his kingdom at Tribeg on the bank of the river Kapilī in the present Nowagong district of Assam. He ruled there for many years. The period of the rulers from Dhruhya to Yujarphā, the 72nd king, according to the Rājmālā, may be called the purāṇic or mythical period of the history of Tripura.

Based on the legendary account given in the Rājmālā, perhaps one of the oldest specimens of Bengali composition extant, Captain W.L. Samuells, who was then officiating as Political agent sent a report to the Government of Bengal in 1875 A.D. In this report Samuells sums up the legendary account thus :

"The present raja (Birchandra Māṇikya) claims descent from Dhruhya, son of Yayātī, one of the lunar race of kings; from him the succession is traced down in a direct line, including thirty-eight reigns, to his descendent Daity... (who) is said to have left his father's dominions after the battle of Kurukṣetra, in which his two elder brothers were killed, and to have fled with his widowed mother to the country now called Tipperah, which then included the hill country to the east, as far as the borders of Burma. In his new home a son and heir was born to him, who succeeded him under the name of Tripura. Tripura so harassed his subjects that they fled in a body to Hirambā (Cachar). After the lapse of five years they returned as votaries of the God Śiva, who promised them a ruler by the widow of Tripura. The promised prince, named 'Trilochan or the three eyed' was born in due course. He married the daughter of the Hirambā rājā, who is called Hiramba raja of Kāmrup. Trilochan conquered many countries and died at an advanced age, leaving 12 sons."[8]

In the *Mahābhārata* Trilochana is mentioned as a king of Tripura.[9] Trilochana's eldest son who was adopted by the rājā of Cachar, eventually inherited the kingdom of Cachar, and thereafter soon claimed his father's kingdom on legal grounds. Consequently, a war broke out between him and his brothers on this issue. Dakṣin one of Trilochana's sons, was defeated and had to retreat to the south along with his other brothers and followers. He is believed to have established a kingdom on the banks of the river Barak with headquarters at Kholongmā in the north Cachar hills. (now known as Khorongmā).[10]

During the reign of Pratita, 69th rājā of Tripura, a war broke out between him and the king of Cachar. Being defeated, Pratita had to leave Kholongmā and proceed further south, and ultimately to Dharmanagar on the banks of the river Juri. He built his new headquarters there.[11] The river Barak was the boundary between Cachar and Tripura during the reign of Pratita who later entered into a treaty with the king of Cachar to prevent any boundary disputes. Captain Samuells observes that Tripura remained at peace with Cachar for a pretty long time. Marriage alliance was also established between the two royal families.[12]

Rāngāmāti (the present Udaipur in south Tripura) was annexed by Yujārphā the 72nd rājā of Tripura, from the rājā of Likā[13] who opposed the move and led a disciplined army of 10,000 men. Rāngāmāti was then made the capital of the kingdom. Long afterwards the name was changed to Udaipur, perhaps by rājā Udai Māṇikya.

It is almost impossible to define the limits of this ancient land at any particular point of time. At various times throughout its history, the kingdom seemed to have gained through conquests and possession areas that spread from the Sunderbans in the west and from Kamrup in the north to Burma in the south and east. It is described in the Rājmālā :

"Kirāt nagare Rājābidhir gathan
Rājyer sīmānā kahī sūnaha vachan
Uttare Tairaṅga nadī Dakṣin Rasaṅga

Pūrve Mekhali sīmā Paśchime Kachbaṅga

Tribeg thanete Rājā karila ek purī

Nānāmata Nirmaila Purīr Chauri"[14]

The state was bounded by Mekhali kingdom (Manipur) in the east and Koch, Vaṅga in the west. In the northern frontiers is river Tairaṅga (Brahmaputra), while Ācharaṅga or Rāshaṅga (Arākān), is the southern extreme.

A geneological list of the Māṇikya dynasty is given in the Rājmālā[15].

1. Dhruhya	2. Babru	3. Setu
4. Anarta	5. Gandharā	6. Dharma
7. Dhnia	8. Drumad	9. Praceta
10. Praci	11. Prabasu	12. Parishad
13. Arijit	14. Sujit	15. Pururaba
16. Bibarna	17. Purusen	18. Meghabarna
19. Bikarna	20. Basuman	21. Kirti
22. Kanian	23. Pratisraba	24. Pratisha
25. Satrujit	26. Pratardhan	27. Pramath
28. Kalinda	29. Krama	30. Mitrari
31. Baribarha	32. Karmuk	33. Kaliṇaga
34. Bhishan	35. Bhanumitra	36. Citrasen
37. Citrarath	38. Citrayudha	39. Daitya
40. Tripur	41. Trilocan	42. Dakṣin
43. Taydakṣin	44. Sudakṣin	45. Tardakṣin
46. Dharmataru	47. Dharmapal	48. Sadharmā
49. Tarbanga	50. Debanga	51. Naranjit
52. Dharmangal	53. Rukamangal	54. Somangal
55. Nauyogray	56. Trjung	57. Rajdharma
58. Hamrāj	59. Birrāj	60. Śrirāj
61. Śriman	62. Lakṣmitaru	63. Rupbān
64. Lakṣmibān	65. Nageśvara	66. Jogeśvara
67. Nildhawaj	68. Basurāj	69. Dhānrajta
70. Harihar	71. Chandraṣekhar	72. Candrarāj
73. Tripali	74. Śūmanta	75. Rupabanta
76. Tarhom	77. Harirāj	78. Kasirāj
79. Madhav	80. Candrarāj	81. Gajeśvara
82. Birrāj	83. Nagesvara	84. Śikhirāj

85. Devrāj
86. Dhusharaṅga
87. Barakirti
88. Sagarfā
89. Malaychandra
90. Sūryanarayan
91. Indra Kirti
92. Birsinhā
93. Sūrendra
94. Bimar
95. Kumar
96. Sukumar
97. Bircandra
98. Rajyeśvara
99. Nageśvara
100. Taichangfā
101. Narendra
102. Indrakirti
103. Biman
104. Jasorāj
105. Banga
106. Gangarāj
107. Citrasen
108. Pratit
109. Marici
110. Gagan
111. Kirti
112. Himti
113. Rajendra
114. Partha
115. Sevray
116. Dharmafā
117. Ramchandra
118. Niriṣingha
119. Lalitray
120. Mukundafā
121. Kamalray
122. Kṛṣṇdas
123. Josarāj
124. Uddhav
125. Sadhuray
126. Pratapray
127. Viṣnuprasad
128. Baneṣvara
129. Birbahu
130. Samrat
131. Campakeṣvar
132. Meghrāj
133. Dharmadhar
134. Kirtidhar
135. Acangfā
136. Khicangfā
137. Dangarfā
138. Rājāfā
139. Ratna Maṇikya
140. Pratap Maṇikya
141. Mukul Maṇikya
142. Mahā do
143. Dharma do
144. Pratap do
145. Dhaṇya do
146. Dhwaja do
147. Dev do
148. Indra do
149. Vijay do
150. Ananta do
151. Uday do
152. Jay do
153. Amar do
154. Rajdhar do
155. Jasodhar do
156. Kalyāṇa do
157. Govinda do
158. Chatra do
159. Ramdev do
160. Ratna II do
161. Narendra do
162. Mahendra do
163. Dharma II do
164. Mukunda do
165. Jay do
166. Indra II do
167. Vijay II do
168. Kṛṣṇa do
169. Rajdhar do
170. Ramganga do
171. Durgā do
172. Kasicandra do
173. Kṛṣṇakisor do
174. Iśān do
175. Birchandra do
176. Radhakisor do
177. Birendra Kisor do
178. Bir Bikram do
179. Kirit Bikram do

However, the historicity of the ruling dynasty of Tripura given in the Rājmālā can hardly stand the test of history. The claim of the Rājmālā is based on questionable geneology, and a sober and unruffled history would dismiss much of the accounts of fiction and legendary. What seems more probable, however is that a dominating tribe, the Tripuris, was able to carve out a small principality and in course of time the tribal chief, looked up to always by the rank and file with almost religious veneration got himself transformed into Rājā or Chief of a particular territory.

Earliest references to Tripura are found in the *Mahābhārata* and the Purāṇas and Gupta pillars where Tripura has been referred to as a Frontier Kingdom. But the account tracing the beginning of the dynasty to the epic of *Mahābhārata*, is not historically acceptable to all. The identification of Tripura is not mentioned in any old literary or epigraphical record. Attempts to identify 'Tripura' with '*Traipura'* of the Mahābhārata[16] or to trace it in the Allahabad pillar inscription of Sumudra-gupta (335-75 A.D.)[17] is not beyond doubt. The Chinese traveller Hiuen Tsang who had reached Kāmarūpa in 642-43 A.D.[18], noted the names of almost all the contemporary kingdoms situated in north eastern India. He did not mention the name of Tripura. Had there been such a powerful kingdom as Tripura, it would not have missed the notice of a keen observer like Hiuen Tsang.

The earliest archaeological relic that has been discovered within the limits of ancient Samataṭa is a fragmentary image with an inscribed pedestal, the exact find spot being Silua. The inscription is in Brahmi of about the second century B.C.[19] But nothing definite can be deduced from this epigraphic record about the prevalence of Tripura as an independent geographical unit during this period. It is thus possible to think that Tripura had not formed at that time. No other archaeological record from the Samataṭa region between the second century B.C. and the end of the fifth century A.D. has been reported so far. A copper plate charter found at Gunaighar (Comilla, Bāṅglādesh) of the year 188 of the Gupta Era (A.D. 507-8) proves the rule of a certain Mahārājā Vaiṇya-Gupta in the Tripura region, who was most probably a member of the imperial Gupta family. So it may quite reasonably be inferred that there was no kingdom named Tripura over the tract between Kāmarupa and Samataṭa till last half of the fifth century A.D.

In the British official records Tripura was usually known as 'Parbatya Tripura' (Hill Tipperah) and sometimes as 'Independent Tipperah'[20]. It was uniterruptedly ruled by a lunar dynasty of members with Māṇikya-ending names since the beginning of the fifteenth century A D. The British Government gave Tripura the status of

'Native State' under the general supervision of a Political agent. It merged with India on October 15, 1949 and became a fulfledged state on January 21, 1972.

The origin of the name "Tripura" cannot be conclusively traced back to any recorded source of history. According to Captain Lewin, the "origin of the name of Tipperah is doubtful".[21] Attempts in this regard were lost in the mist of legends and traditions. A common belief is that the name Tripura has originated from 'Tripurasundarī'—the presiding deity of the land.[22] Hunter remarks, "the name Tripura was probably given to the country in honour of the temple at Udaipur, which still exists. This temple now ranks as the second Tirtha, or sacred shrine. It was dedicated either to Tripurdana, the sun God or to Tripureśvari, the mistress of the three worlds"[23]. But it is not correct. The country had been known as Tripura even before the installation of the deity which took place at the time of Mahārājā Dhaṇya Māṇikya in the first half of the sixteenth century A D. What is more probable is that the deity took the name of the land.

According to the Rājamālā, after the death of Daitya, Tripur became the king of the land. Possibly the state came to be known in the name of its king, a situation maintained by his lineage.[24]

"Tripura is the land of the God Śiva who is also known as Tripurāri or Tripureśvara. The people who settled in the land of Tripureśvara Śiva came to be known as Tripuri and the land as Tripura".[25] But the famous Śaiva centre of Tripura is Unakotiśvara and not Tripureśvara.

An interesting tradition that is still prevalent among older generation of Tripuris, is that in ancient time three families (i.e. Tripura) settled in the present land. The name of this state owe to the three family or Tripura. *(Tri* means—three and *Pārā* means—community).[26]

Analysing the name etymologically some researchers have found it to be a combined form of two Tripuri words, 'tui' and 'pārā'. In Tripuri language 'tui' means water and 'pārā' means near. It is believed that originally the land was known as Tripura, meaning a land adjoining the waters. It is a fact that in the days of yore the boundaries of Tripura extended upto the Bay of Bengal when its rulers held sway from the Gāro hill to Arākān.[27] It might be that the name appropriately derived its origin from its nearness to water. This Tripura has subsequently been corrupted into Tipra and from Tipra to Tripura. It is relevant to note that even to day the hill people pronounce the word as Tripra and not Tripura. Of all the views on the origin of the name Tripura, the last one offered by Kailash Chandra Singha appears to be quite probable and appropriate.[28]

Tripura is one of those strategically located areas where in diverse civilizations, religions and cultures met in the past. Lying at the cross-roads of Assam and Bengal, it was probably connected with Burma via land-routes through Gomati, Surmā and Cachar valley, Lushai hills and Manipur on the one hand and via Chittagong, Arākān on the other.[29] It was more or less the same route which the Buddhist monk Buddhagupta followed while travelling from Buntavarta (Puṇḍravardhana ?) to Bālgu (Pegu) via, Tripura (high lands), Kasaranga or Devikoṭa Rak'an (Arākān), Haribhanja and Bak'an (Papan).[30]

Perhaps it was through the latter route in the eleventh-twelfth centuries A.D. kingdoms of Paṭṭikera and Burma maintained relations among themselves.[31] Although the city of Paṭṭikera can not be definitely identified, it must have been situated within the district of Tripura (modern Comilla District, Bāṅglādesh), for an important place near Maināmati hills is still known as Paitkora,[32] which had been under the administration of the Māṇikya rulers of Tripura even before the partition of India. Captain T H Lewin in the later half of nineteenth century A.D.[33] suggested that Govinda Māṇikya (1661-1667 A.D.), the ruler of Tripura possibly had used the Chittagong-Arākān route on his exile following political turmoil of the state.[34]

On the banks of river Mainee in Hill Tract of Chittagong are found ruins of old mason by buildings. Some tradition attributes these ruins to a former ruler of hill Tripura who is said to have been driven away from his land and again was forced to leave the new area by some hillmen.[35] Colonization, trade and also the Buddhist mission towards Bodh Gayā had linked different parts of South East Asia. It was certain that the land route via Tripura was in use.

From the north through the Assam Valley came the Chinese Pilgrims[36] as well as different tribal immigrants of Indo-Mongoloid race who belonged to the Tribe to Burman family of Indo-Chinese group, of whom the Bodo speaking group deserves a special mention.

They settled down at the confluence of the great rivers namely Twiyung (Brahmaputra), Sengrongmā (Gaṅga) and Borok Twima (Barak).[37] They extended to Tripura in the shape of Tripra tribe. In Kokbork, river confluences are called Twibupra or Twipra or later on Tripura. Those Boro people who were later known as Boroks, believed rivers to be incarnation of a goddess and hence they count themselves to be the children of the rivers. Since then, the Tripuris call themselves Twibupranibwsa, in short Twiprasa, Triprasa, Tipra or Tripuri.[38] People of ethnically similar groups assembled in the Nowagong-Cachar districts of Assam for habitation and they maintained contact with Bengal, particularly with the Śrīhaṭṭa sector which considerably influenced the religious and cultural history of Tripura. Bengal had a happy cultural relation with Burma and the Bengal-Burmese style of art seems to have an out come of religious factor. Moreover, where colonization and trade linked together parts of South-east Asia, or Buddhist missionaries came from the said region via sea-routes to visit Bodhgayā and other sacred places, they had to pass from or to Bengal through land routes via Tripura to reach the destination.[39] Being situated in such cross roads of different religious and cultural waves, Tripura experienced the blending of Bengal and south-east Asian (particular Burmese) culture on its soil. As a result, apart from other factors, this both way assimilation of extraneous elements with the local idiom gave rise to a regional mixed culture, typical of Tripura which is an important phase towards the development of art, culture and religion of eastern India.

The boundaries of the state in the ancient period lay between the river Brahmaputra in the north and Acharang to the southern part contiguous with Udaipur, from the kingdom of Manipur on the east to the Koch kingdom and Bengal on the west.[40] The southern boundary of ancient Tripura sometimes even extended to Rashang (Arākān).[41] It is impossible to define the limits of the ancient kingdom of Tripura at any particular point of time, because it emerged as a recognised political power in the south eastern part of Bengal in the sixteenth century A.D. In the period of consolidation its rulers were involved in active conflict with the neighbouring powers, not only in the hills but also in the plains and sometime across the Meghnā. Tripura made conquests and gained or regained possessions at varying period of medieval times, which extended its territories from Chittagong and

Bhulua in the south-east to the river Meghnā on the west, and to Thanangchi province lying on the east of Tripura and Lushai hills bordering Burma.

In later period, through its unguarded western (including north western and south-western) gates Muslims entered Tripura and attacked it on many occasions. But physical features and natural factors like mountain vastness and dense forests, unsuitable climate, excessive rains and floods and consequent difficulties in movement helped the Tripura rulers in offering resistance to the alien aggressors and impeded the latter in staying here for a substantial period.[42.]

As a result these Muslims could not effect the Tripuri cultural and religious life very much, as they did in religion and cultures of many other parts of India. So, the local lunar dynasty survived and ruled till recently in Tripura, where culture and religion flourished owing to the royal patronage.

According to 1991 census the total population of Tripura is 27,57,205. The total population may broadly be classified into tribals (scheduled tribes) and non-tribals (Bengalees mainly and Manipuries and others). Out of this 8,53,345 are tribals. The tribals have their origin in the Indo-Mongoloid group and their ancestors came from the Bodo nome in Central Asia.

No doubt, it is a melting pot of ethnic diversity. Even though the tribals have so many groups, they seem to have similar ethnological characteristics. According to the order of the President of India in 1956 on the scheduled castes and scheduled tribes in Tripura, there are nineteen scheduled tribes in Tripura. These tribes are — Tripuri, Reang, Jāmātia, Noatiā, Hālam, Chākmā, Magh, Lushai, Kuki, Gāro, Chaimāl, Khasia, Bhutia, Mundā, Orang, Lepcha, Santal, Bhil, Uchai. Of these tribes the Tripras constitute the most numerous sections with the Riangs coming next. These two tribes in fact comprises the earliest inhabitants of Tripura, other are supposed to be the later migrants. However, subsequently the Bengalees from the plains belonging mostly to different Brahmanical sects started taking refuge in the hilly region of Tripura. This movement of people become more and more intense after the partition of India in 1947. It has been observed that the Tripras are divided into two groups namely the Puran Tripras and the Deshi Tripras. The Deshi Tripras seem to have originated as a result of admixture between the Bengalees and Tripras.[43] Ethnologically, the Jāmātias and Tripras belong to one and undivided group. According to the census report of 1981, the Jāmātia belongs to Hinduism. The Noatiās are believed to be mixed tribe. They are supposed to be mixed with Tripras and Jāmātias. They are Hindu by religion. The Chākmā, the fourth largest tribal group migrated to Tripura from Chittagong hill tracts.[44] Buddhism is their popular religion. The Maghs claimed that they had descended from the same line of Kṣatriyas in which Lord Buddha was born. In Tripura, they migrated from Arākān. Magh was the local name of the Arākānese in Chittagong. They are devout Buddhists.

The tribal population of Tripura has a distinct and independent cultural existence over an extensive area by means of its natural position and they still maintain their indigenous tribal religious behaviour patterns along with other higher religion. In the field of religion and culture they are conservative and try to preserve their customs and beliefs which they inherited from their predecessors. But matrimonial relation of the royal family of Tripura with different states of India made this land culturally a part of Indian mainland, and paved the way for the transmission of different elements in its religion and culture. Various racial and cultural elements of other parts of India are discernible in the cultures in both hills and plains of Tripura. For instance, the people of Tripura like most Indians have a spirit of religious toleration and members of the royal family of the land who adopted Bengali language, gave it the prestige of state language and even today it is serving as a great cementing force, without suppressing the linguistic variety of the tribals. Immigrants like Manipuris, Nāgās, Gāros etc. while adopted many local customs and beliefs, also offered some of their cultural traits to the people of Tripura. In short, the population being a composite one, the culture of the land has been heterogenous in content, but with the passage of time and growth of the spirit of toleration, an ideal of homogenity has laced the complex life, religion and culture of Tripura.

It is not known as to when exactly Aryans influenced the religion of Tripura. The religion now prevailing is a form of Hindu idolatry, but it is said that before the accession of Trilochana,[45] they worshipped no idols but objects of nature, e.g. trees, stones, animals etc. A trace of this is noticed in their present practice of sticking a bamboo in the ground during religious festivals and worshipping it.[46] Bamboo is literally the staff of the life of the tribes and deified probably from the earliest period. Majority of the clans of this tract offer worship to bamboo. It is to them merely an impersonation of the deity of forest (Vanakumarī), but it is interesting to note that no artistic representation of bamboo tree has come to our notice as yet, even in the art of later period. Lack of archaeological evidences from Tripura proper makes it difficult to say anything about the condition of Buddhism or Brahmanism in Tripura during the early centuries of Christian era. Icono-plastic art recovered from this land provides data about the prevelance of these faiths since earlier part of 7th century A.D. This tide of Brahmanical faith also came to Tripura during this period which is corroborated by large number of Brahmanical images belonging to the 7th - 8th century A.D. Tripura was also a seat of Buddhism which is evidenced by the Buddhist icons and remains found at Pilāk. But Buddhist and Hindu ideas of religion and philosophy are usually put forward in support of the tribal religion. The religion may be called Hill Hinduism or Hill Buddhism.[47] But no clear tribal philosophy can be assumed as there is no tribal literature as yet with philosophical contents. So at this stage, no one can expect much in the name of philosophy of the tribals of Tripura. The idea of a number of gods and goddesses, or good and evil spirits is there in the religion of tribals. Moreover there is the belief in a great God called Matai Katar. Human soul is admitted under the name Falā, Rebirth is also admitted. This is obviously due to the fact that both the Hindus and the Buddhists have same belief. Such faiths and beliefs under the influence of Brahmanism seemingly testified to by the well established practice of worshipping fourteen gods, the antiquity of which has been pushed back to the time of Ratna-māṇikya-I.[48] The original association of the fourteen gods with the tribal people survives in the practice of performing the relevant rites of non-Aryan nature connected with their worship by the tribal priest like Chantais and Debhais. The fourteen gods, identified with members of Brahmanical pantheon are as follows : Hara, Umā, Hari, Mā, Bānī, Kumar, Gaṇeśa, Brahmā, Pṛithivī, Gaṅgā, Aditi, Agni, Kāma and Himālaya.[49]

This mixed type of socio-ethnic and religious pattern of life influenced in a greater degree towards the development of religion of Tripura. In the earlier period, the religious stream of Tripura is mainly influenced by mainstream of Indian religion, partly as a result of domination of inferior civilization by the superior in respect of higher standard of attainment in the field of culture and their rich earlier tradition and partly by the geographical influence. Thus it has been a heaven for co-existence of several religious sects and denominations such as Vaiṣṇavism, Śaivism, Śaktism, Buddhism along with their respective cults of animatism, animism, magic and fertility etc.

References

1. *Tripura State Memorandum for the Indian State Enquiry Committee,* (Financial), No.2, 1932, Appendix IX, Exhibit CI.
2. *State Report on World Agricultural Census,* (1970-71). In Tripura, Land Records and Settlement Directorate, Government of Tripura, Agartala, 1974, p.4.
3. Dani, A.H., *Pre-History and Proto-History of Eastern India,* Calcutta, 1960, pp.9-10.
4. Menon, K.D., *Tripura District Gazetteers,* Agartala, 1975, p.477, plate I.
5. Dani, A.H., *op cit.* pp.13-14; The Mahābhārata, Calcutta, 1384 B S 2nd *"Sungānāmādhipañchaiba ye cha Sāgar Bāsira. Sarbabān Mlechchhagananshaichaba bijigeya Bharatasarcbḥa"* Sabhāparba, 5th khanda, page 256, 23 no. Śloka (line). K.C. Sinha also advocated this view. The tribe Mlechhas which is mentioned in the Mahābhāratas they lived in sea side. They were probably coastal tribe, but Bodos are entire hill tribes. They live in entire hilly region of Northeastern India. So they should not be identified with tribe Mlechhas of Mahābhārata.
6. Chatterjee, S.K., Kirata jano kriti *J.O. A.S.B,* Letters, vol.XVI, 1950, no.2, Calcutta, pp.172-73.
7. Long, James, considered the first part of the Rājmālā a literary work of the early 15th century. According to him "We may consider this as the most ancient work in Bengali that has come down to us, as the *Chaitanya Charitāmrita* was not written before 1557 and Kirthibās subsequently translated the *Rāmāyaṇa.* The Rājmālā of the Tipperah family which bears all the marks of antiquity is kept with the greatest care. I have every reason to believe it to be a genuine record of the Tipperah family", "Analysis of Rājmālā", *J.A.S.B.*, Vol. X, IX, 1850, Calcutta, pp.533-57. But the Rājmālā is not as old as it was believed by Long. According to Prof. S.K. Chatterjee, "The historical value of this chronicle (Rājmālā) is not much for the period prior to

the fifteenth century A.D.". (*Kirata Jana Kriti*, p.131, 1974 Calcutta). The Rājmālā was not composed before the close of the eighteenth century A.D. In regard to the earlier part, "the compilers must have relied on traditions recorded or unrecorded and their own imaginations". See, D.C. Sircar, *Some Epigraphic Records of the Medieval period from Eastern India,* Delhi, 1979, p.89. Kaliprasanna Sen, a compiler of the Rājmālā, admits his difficulty in utilising the epigraphic material available to him, presumably because he could not "reconcile the evidence of inscriptions with the details supplied by the Rājmālā .... There are cases where the author is silent about the expert opinion". [Comment by D.C. Sircar in the *Journal of Asiatic Society of Bengal,* Vol.XVII. No.2, 1951, pp.76-77]. According to a set scholars, the modern editions of Rājmālā were redacted at the beginning of the nineteenth century A.D. and hence this chronicle is not of much value as a source of the history of Tripura. It is mixed with mythologies and legends which need verification from other sources. For details see Prof. N.R. Roy, Introduction of *Rājmālā Bā Tripurār Itibritha,* 1984, Agartala.

8. Report dated 19th September, 1875 submitted to the Lt. Governor of Bengal by Captain W.L. Samuells, acting Political Agent, quoted in W.W. Hunter, *Statistical Account of Bengal*, (Delhi Reprint 1973), Vol.VI, pp.463-64.
9. Hunter *op.cit.* pp.463-64.
10. At Khorongma ruins of old forts and moats have been found. Tripura District Gazetteers, see p.71.
11. *Ibid.*
12. Hunter *op.cit,* p.464.
13. Hunter *Ibid.* spells the name as Nikka.
14. Singha, K.P., *Rājmālā*, p.9.
15. Singha, K.P., *op.cit* pp.39-43.
16. *Mahābhārata*, Calcutta, 1384 B S, 2nd ed., *"Vatsa bhūming Vinirjitya keralaṅg Mithikabtima. Mohanaṅg Paṭṭaṅg Chaiba Tripuriṅg Koshalaṅg Tathā"*. Vanaparva, 10th Kāṇḍa, 210 Chapter, 10 Śloka (line), p.2213. Tripuring mentioned in the Mahābhārata, should not be identified with the modern Tripura, Tripuring was near Koshala in the neighbourhood of the modern Jabalpur.
17. Sinha, K.C., advocated this view. The country in question which acknowledged the supremacy of Samudra Gupta was Katripura, and should not be identified with the modern Tripura. Kartipura has been variously identified with Kartarpur in Jallundur district,

Panjab; Katuria in Kumaon, Garhwal and Rohilkhand districts, Uttaranchal and Kahror, between Multan and Lohni, Pakistan.

18. Majumdar, R.C., *History of Ancient Bengal*, 1971, Calcutta, p.8.
19. *ASI, AR,* Part I, 1930-34, pp.38-39.
20. Erstwhile Tripura district (modern Comilla) of East Pakistan, now Bāṅglādesh, was known as 'Plain Tipperah'. As the name suggests the land is not undulating like the present State of Tripura and is bathed by large watery viens like Meghnā and Titas. It was directly ruled by the British, a part being the Zamindary of the kings of Tripura.
21. Lewin, T.H., *The Hill Tracts of Chittagong and the Dwellers therein*, Calcutta, 1869, p.79.
22. Menon, K.D., *Tripura District Gazetteers,* Agartala, 1975, p.1.
23. Hunter, W.W., *op.cit* pp.357-58.
24. Singha, K.C., *Rājmālā Bā Tripurar Itibritha,* Agartala, 1984, Reprint edition, p.8.
25. Deb Barman, D.P., *Treatise on Traditional Social Institutions of Tripura Community,* Tribal Research Institute, Govt. of Tripura, Agartala, 1983, p.3
26. *Ibid,* p.4.
27. Menon, K.D., *op.cit,* p. 1.
28. Singha, K.C., *op.cit*, p.8.
29. Das, Ratna, *Archaeological Sources of the History of Tripura* (monumental remains) [ed. N.R. Ray], Cal, 1982, p.458.
30. Mukherjee, B.N., *External Trade of Early North Eastern India,* New Delhi, 1992, p.24.
31. Ray, N.R., *Bāṅgālīr Itihās* (in Bengali) Calcutta, 1949, p.119.
32. Shamsul Alam, A.K.M., *Maināmati*, Dhākā, 1982, pp.21-24.
33. Lewin, T.H., *op.cit,* p.6.
34. Sen, K.P. (ed), *Śrī Rājmālā,* IV, 1927, Agartala, pp.7-9.
35. Das, Ratna, *Art & Architecture of Tripura,* Agartala, 1997, p.1.
36. Dani, A.H., *op.cit*, pp.13-14.
37. Deb Barman, Binoy, *Anglo Kakbark Dictionary*, 1996, Agartala, p.VII.
38. *Ibid,* p.VII.
39. Mukherjee, B.N., *op.cit*, p.24.
40. *Rājmālā,* (Bangiya Sahitya Parishad Manuscript Version), Education Directorate, Govt. of Tripura, Agartala, 1967, pp.1-2.
41. Uzir, Durgamoni, *Rājmālā,* Vol. 1, Agartala, 1901, p.1, K.P. Sen, *op.cit,* p.6, Singha, K.C., *op.cit*, p.9.

42. Das, Ratna, *op.cit*, p.2.
43. Bhattacharjee, Priyabrata, *Tribal Pujas and Festivals in Tripura*, Tribal Research Institute, Govt. of Tripura, Agartala, 1994, p.3.
44. Singha, K.C., *op.cit*, p.25.
45. Trilochana, the 47th king of Tripura who settled his kingdom in present land of Tripura introduced the worship of fourteen gods, *Rājmālā*-1, pp.281-82.
46. Delton, E.T., *op.cit*, p.110.
47. Bhowmik, Dr. Dwijendra, *Tribal Religion of Tripura*, Agartala, 1997, p.1.
48. Chowdhury, Vasanta and Ray, Parimal "Representation of the Chaturdaśadevatās on a coin of Ratna-māṇikya deva of Tripura" *JNSI*, vol.XXXVII, 1975, Parts I-II, pp.111-113.
49. Sen, K.P., *op.cit*, pp.31-32.

2

Political History of Tripura upto the Māṇikya Dynasty

The reconstruction of political history of ancient Tripura poses a formidable problem owing to dearth of reliable records of the early periods. One of the major sources of the history of Tripura is a dynastic account of the local kings with the names ending with Māṇikya. While the earlier part of this account tracing the beginning of the dynasty to the epic hero Yudhiṣhṭhira, is difficult to accept historically, but the latter part of the account especially from the middle of the fifteenth century A.D. onwards can be taken for consideration.

Presumably the present state of Tripura did not exist as such from the earliest times to the thirteenth century A.D. Hence the history of Tripura in the pre-Māṇikya period is interwinded with that of ancient Samataṭa, a region roughly corresponding to the present districts of Sylhet, Noakhali and Chittagong. As a kingdom under the early Māṇikya rulers it also included Tippera (now Comilla, Bāṇglādesh) and portions of Sylhet and in an extended sense it comprised the districts of Noakhali and Chittagong. So the southern part of Tripura integrally belonged to the domains of more substantial rulers of south-eastern Bengal, while the northern hilly sector was governed by the semi-nomadic primititve tribes who have left no records of their activities, political as well as cultural, for the posterity. Their land was gradually but slowly Aryanised and this process of acculturation could not make much headway in the northern region due to its impregnable geographical position.

The major corpus of the materials indispensable for drawing an authentic account of the ancient history of Tripura consists of those gleaned from the epigraphic records of the Khaḍgas, the Devas, the Chandras and a few others who ruled in the Tripura region of ancient Samataṭa.[1] The earliest archaeological record was a copper-plate charter of the year 188 of the Gupta era (507-08 A.D.). It proves the rule of Mahārājā Vaiṇya Gupta in the Tripura region.[2] Of the places mentioned in this epigraphic record, the name of *'Joari Kshetram'* appears to us to be interesting. We may identify it with modern Jolāibaḍi in south Tripura, situated on the border of the Comilla and Noakhali districts of Bāṇglādesh and not far from its find spot. In fact, the Jolāibaḍi-Pilāk region of Tripura, has yielded a relatively rich religious zone whose relics are datable from the seventh-eighth centuries of the Christian era.

Mahārājā Vaiṇyagupta, a member of the dynasty of Imperial Guptas, ruled over Samataṭa and granted lands in Tripura. The seat of his kingdom was situated in or near the Tripura region. At first he was a local governor under an imperial Gupta monarch, but subsequently he became an independent ruler. After Vaiṇyagupta, Gopachandra, Dharmāditya and Samāchāradeva ruled Samataṭa between 525 - 575 A.D. It appears that these three kings ruled from a place, where from Vaiṇyagupta also had ruled before them. This locality was somewhere either in the eastern Dacca, or in northern Tippera district which formed the central part of the kingdom of these monarchs.[3]

Hiuen Tsang who visited India in the first half of the seventh century A.D. referred to the kingdom of Samataṭa which included the major part of Vaṅga proper. According to his account, it included within its political boundaries a part of the central Bengal in addition to region of the district Tippera.[4] Hiuen Tsang also tells that a line of Brahmin kings ruled there in the first half of the seventh century A.D.

It may be mentioned in this context of the Tippera copper-plate of a feudatory chief called Lokanātha (the plate was discovered somewhere in the district of Tripura, now a part of Bāṇglādesh) which records that a family of four or five chiefs (Lokanātha being the fourth) ruled in the Tippera (perhaps including a part of modern Tripura) in about the late seventh century A.D. (the period is indicated by the palaeography), but unfortunately the lineage lord of Lokanātha is not mentioned in the plate, and it records a grant of land in the forest region *(aṭavibhū-khaṇḍa)* for construction of a temple of Ananta-Nārāyaṇa.[5]

This forest might be under the control of Lokanātha of Tripura and may be identified with a portion of Hill Tripura. It is said that even before fifty years ago, a brick-temple, locally called as the temple of Nārāyaṇa was visible in the Thākurānibāḍi area of Pilāk.[6] Now a days debris of large sized bricks, some decorated (stylistically similar to those from Maināmati) are being stacked there and a massive Nrisiṁha image was recovered from the region. It is tempting to suggest that this portion of modern Tripura might be the control of Lokanātha.[7]

The Asrāfpur plates[8] and Deulbāḍi[9] Śarvānī image inscription (Asrāfpur and Deulbāḍi are in the Dacca and Comilla districts respectively) have revealed that family of four rulers, Khaḍgodyama, Jāta-khaḍga, Devakhaḍga and Rājarājabhaṭṭa[10] used to rule in the Dacca, Noakhali, Tippera and on the basis of palaeography of these inscriptions, these Khaḍga kings have been placed in the last three quarters of seventh century A.D.[11] From the Chinese evidences it appears that the Khaḍga dynasty comprised nearly the whole of the Eastern and Southern Bengal including Tripura.[12] Two copper-plate grants of Devakhaḍga, were issued from the royal camp of Karmanta Vasaka which was their capital. This city has been identified with modern Baḍakamta[13] situated twelve miles west of Comilla. The above mentioned Śarvānī image and an image of Sūrya from the same spot may be treated as the fore runners of stele-carved Pāla sculptures and in this respect have a large contribution towards the growth of eastern school of medieval Indian art. The Khaḍgas were also Buddhists.

Another copper-plate discovered at Kailān[14] (13 miles west of the Lālmāi railway station, Comilla) discloses that Jivadhārana was the lord of Samataṭa and his son Śrīdharāna received from him the sovereignty over Samataṭa. From this record it is known that the Rātas had the headquarters of Devaparvata which was encircled by the river Kshirodā (probably the Khirā or Khirnai, a dried up river, course of the Gomati still traceable, just west of the Comilla town).

The river surrounds the southern end of the Maināmati hills, where the ancient hill-fort of Devaparvata seems to have been situated.[15] On palaeographic ground this inscription may be placed in the second half of the 7th century A.D.[16] Jivadhārana Rāta, father of Śridharāna may possibly be identified with Jivadhārana of the Tippera copper-plate of Lokanātha. The next important epigraphic document is the copper-plate of Mahārājādhirāja Bhavadeva from Devaparvata.[17] From this plate we come to know that a new family of kings with Deva name ending ruled in this area. The land-grant of Bhavadeva refers to one Virā Deva as the founder of the family. Another Buddhist kingdom also flourished in this land, as is known from an incomplete copper plate hailing from Chittagong,[18] palaeographically datable to the ninth century A.D. mentions, 'Harikela maṇḍala'. The geographical connotation of the name Harikela may be taken to denote originally an area now included in the Chittagong district of Bāṅglādesh[19] — and the Sabrum subdivision of Tripura which are collateral territories and topographically, ethnologically and culturally similar with each other, though politically separated now a days, these might have been included into Harikela-maṇdala. This record supplies the names of three members of this Buddhist family, each being the son of his predecessor : Bhadra Data (Bhadra Datta), Dhana Datta and Kānti Deva who issued the charter.

Apart from the epigraphic records of this period, mention is to be made of the coins found in south Tripura as well as the Comilla and Chittagong districts of Bāṇglādesh. Broadly divisible into two groups, the first of them consists of debased gold coins closely imitating the issue of the Imperial Gupta kings in respect of device and metrology and was dated by Allan to the middle of 7th century A.D.[20] A large number of same type of coins have been recorded from the vicinity of the Jolāibadi-Pilāk of south Tripura. Though the lack of stratigraphic information on the coins forbids us to deduce any definite conclusion, we may infer or suggest reasonably that atleast the southern part of Tripura was under the same political power as was in south-eastern Bengal after the decline of the Guptas.

The second group consists of thin silver coins, stylistically and metrologically connected with the coins of the Chandra dynasty of Arākān (bearing recumbent bull and tripartite symbol on them) found in plenty in and around Sābrum and Belonia areas of south Tripura (adjacent to Chittagong of Bāṅglādesh). They bear on them the legend Harikela.[21]

It has been assigned to the seventh century A.D. on the basis of the palaeographic evidence of Sandoway inscription of Arākān of the same period[22] and the legend Harikela suggests the existence of a kingdom Harikela in the Chittagong district and its adjacent areas which is contiguous to Arākān and might be influenced by the more dominating mint-masters of Arākān of that period. Most probably the Sābrum area, the southern most part of Tripura, where numerous such coins are being found, was included in, or otherwise connected with, the kingdom of Harikela during the 7th - 8th century A.D. The Maināmati copper-plates mention land-grants at Samataṭa maṇḍala by the rulers of Chandra dynasty and suggest that these Chandras originated from Rohitagin (identified as Lālmāi hills of erstwhile Tripura district and modern Comilla district of Bāṅglādesh) and this Rohitagiri enjoyed the position of royal seat of Chandras. In earlier period Samataṭa was probably the kingdom of the Chandra dynasty.

It is interesting to note in this connection that one Chandra dynasty was also ruling in the Arākān kingdom. We do not know whether the Chandras of Arākān had any relation with the Chandras of the east Bengal. From the coins and inscriptions found in Arākān it is proved that about twenty kings of the Chandra dynasty ruled in Arākān. Whether these Chandras extended their political influence in Tripura or its adjoining regions before the establishment of the Chandra dynasty of east Bengal is not certain.

Another dynasty with personal names suffixed by the word 'Chandra' ruled in eastern Bengal from about 900 A.D. to 1050 A.D.[23] The source of information about the Chandras is their own inscriptions. From the Bharella inscription of Laḍaha Chandra,[24] Ramapāla copper-plate,[25] Kedarpur copper-plate,[26] Dhulia copper-plate[27] and Edilbur copper-plate[28] of Śrī Chandra has constructed the reign of the Chandra dynasty in Bengal.[29] According to these plates Pūrṇa Chandra was succeeded by his son Suvarṇa-Chandra. Suvarṇa-Chandra's next successor was his son Trailokya-Chandra who was succeeded by his son Śrī Chandra. Two other names of Laḍaha-Chandra and Govinda-Chandra had also been deciphered from some image inscriptions.[30] Their names could not be connected with the Chandra genealogy for nearly half a century. But the recent discovery of some new plates have given us the connected political narrative of the Chandra dynasty.[31] Two copper plates of Laḍaha Chandra and one of Govinda Chandra were discovered in 1956 from Charpatra Mūra of Maināmati.[32] These three copper-plates are presently known as Maināmati plates[33] of the Chandras.

From these records their genealogy has been established. It runs thus :

Pūrṇa-Chandra
Suvarṇa-Chandra
Trailokya-Chandra
Śrī-Chandra
Kalyāṇa-Chandra
Laḍaha-Chandra
Govinda-Chandra[34]

They also supply us with the following maximum reigning years of the Chandra kings :

Śrī-Chandra	46 years	in Madanpur plate
Kalyāṇa-Chandra	24 years	in Dacca plate
Laḍaha-Chandra	18 years	in Bharella image inscription
Govinda-Chandra	23 years	in Pāikpārā image inscription

We are, thus, able to establish the continuous rule of the Chandras in east Bengal for at least one hundred and eleven years. Vikrampura was their headquarters. The chronology of the Chandra kings is further clear from the Tirumalai inscription of the Rajendra-Cola.[35] It refers to Govinda-Chandra as the ruler of Bāṇgalā-deśa in 1021-23 A.D. Further light has been thrown by the Śabda-Pradīpa of Śūreśvara (or Śūrapala). His father Bhadreśvara served Vaṅgeśvara Ramapāla, apparently of the Pāla dynasty. His period of reign is given as 1077-1120 A.D. Bhadreśvara's father Devagana was a court physician of Govinda-Chandra. Govinda-Chandra was none other than the Chandra ruler of that name. Thus, there was hardly a gap of one generation between Govinda-Chandra and the Pāla ruler Ramapāla.

The Tirumālāi inscription records the early career of Govinda Chandra. His reign may be placed from 1020 A.D. to 1050 A.D. We can, thus fix the date of Laḍaha-Chandra from 1000 A.D. to 1020

A.D., and Kalyāṇa-Chandra from 975 A.D. to 1000 A.D., and Śrī-Chandra from 929 A.D. to 975 A.D. The date of Śrī-Chandra is also corroborated from a Dacca plate.[36] Śrī Chandra reinstated Gopāla who was apparently Gopāla II on the Pāla throne. He ruled from 940 A.D. to 960 A.D. The reign of Trailokya-Chandra may be placed at 900 A.D. Two other Chandra rulers, viz, Suvarṇa Chandra and Pūrṇa-Chandra ruled east Bengal before 900 A.D., although they were merely subordinate chieftains ruling under the authority of the Pāla kings.[37] Thus, the Chandras ruled the Vaṅga country from at least 900 A.D. to 1050 A.D.

The Bāghāurā image inscription and another inscription engraved on an image of Gaṇēśa discovered in the village of Nārāyaṇpur[38] in the Tippera district shows that some portions of Tripura were included in Samataṭa, which itself was under the suzerainty of Mahipāla I. Probably, he wrested it from Laḍaha Chandra.

Damodaradeva, grandson of Madhumāthenadeva (founder of an independent kingdom in the eastern region of the river Meghnā) was a powerful ruler whose kingdom comprised of the district of Tripura, Noakhali and Chittagong.[39] These rulers might had some contact with the southern part of Tripura. In this connection mention may be made of an Umā-Maheśvara image inscription (the icon is now in worship at Agartala) of Taraṅga Chandradeva, identification of whom has not yet been known. The image was recovered from the Khandal Paragana[40] (Noakhali district of Bāṅglādesh). Taraṅga Chandradeva might be a member of this family and have a close relation with southern portion of Tripura. Stylistically the image is assignable to the late eleventh century A.D. and the dating is supported by the palaeography of the accompanying inscription.[41]

The existence of the small kingdom of Paṭṭikerā[42] in the district of Tippera may be traced back to the eleventh century A.D. The Burmese Chronicles may contain references to this kingdom. According to the Hmannan (a text of the Burmese Chronicles), the kingdom of the Burmese king Anaratha (1044-1077 A.D.) was bounded on the west by Paṭṭikerā. The same text narrates a romantic story of love between the prince of Paṭṭikerā and Sweinthi, the daughter of the king of Burma. There was an intimate intercourse between the kingdoms of Burma and Paṭṭikerā during the 12th century A.D. The origin of the Paṭṭikerā kingdom can be traced in the accounts of the Burmese chronicles which state that the Shans invaded Arākān in the tenth century A.D., and northern Arākān was conquered by Anaratha. At this time of political turmoil, the Chandras were ousted from Arākān and a branch of them settled at Paṭṭikerā. The existence of the kingdom of Paṭṭikerā in the thirteenth century is proved by an inscription engraved on a copper-plate found in the neighbourhood of Comilla. It records a grant of land in favour of Buddhist monastery built at Paṭṭikerā, by Dhadi-ebā, the Chief Minister of Śrī Harikeladeva Rānavankamallā in 1220 A.D., which was the seventeenth year of his reign. Harikeladeva Rānavankamallā, who ascended the throne in 1203-04 A.D. and ruled till 1220 A.D., was undoubtedly an independent ruler. The name of the father of Dhadi-ebā was recorded as Mamhedi-ebā and the name of the writer of the grant was Madeni-ebā. The ending suffix "ebā" in the names indicates their Burmese origin. Whether king Harikeladeva Rānavankamallā belonged to the old royal family of Paṭṭikerā or to Deva family, is not known and after him there is no mention of the name of the kingdom of Paṭṭikerā. It was most probably absorbed in the growing kingdom of the Deva family. The Māṇikya rulers of Tripura upto the 15th century A.D. had been bearing the word "phā"[43] as their name endings. It is tempting to suggest a connection between the respectable Burmese family of Paṭṭikerā on the one hand and the families of Tripura and Ahom rulers on the other and it is expected that discovery of some new data in near future may substantiate our suggestion.[44] Whatever be the relation, the Māṇikya rulers of Tripura were influenced by the Burmese cultural tradition, which is evidenced, interalia, by examples of religious architecture of the land (Tripurasundarī temple, Udaipur).[45] The discovery of same types of coins and sculptural art in south-eastern Bengal and in southern part of the present state of Tripura also seems to indicate that at least the latter area was governed by or somehow rather politically connected, with Harikela, Samataṭa and Paṭṭikerā in pre-Muhammadan days[46] and same stream of religious activity was current in both the regions probably under the same type of royal patronage.

The nature of relation of the Māṇikya rulers, with the ruling dynasties of Bengal as mentioned above, can not be ascertained in the absence of some more positive documents in the present land of

Tripura. It seems probable, that after the fall of the Devas (family of Damodara-deva), the predecessors of the Māṇikyas became powerful and formed an independent kingdom. Alternatively it may be suggested that due to political turmoil in Hindu and Buddhist kingdoms of south-eastern Bengal, a certain noble family of that reign who was somehow connected with those kingdoms, sought the help of the Muslim invaders and formed a new kingdom in the present land of Tripura.[47] It is equally probable that the successors of any of the above mentioned Hindu and Buddhist royal families were forced to take shelter in the Hilly regions of Tripura due to turmoils caused by the Muslim invasions and with the alliance of the autochthonous people of this land, they were able to form a kingdom in the land lying between Chittagong in the south and Sylhet in the north.

It has already been mentioned that the Rājmālā gives an account of a lunar dynasty since very ancient period, but evidences so far discovered, do not substantiate its claim earlier than the 15th century A.D. At the beginning of the 15th century A.D., Tripura came into contact with the Jālāl-ud-Din Muhammad Shah (1415-31 A.D.), who annexed a portion of Tippera and issued a type of coinage having a figure of grotesque lion on the reverse, which was prevailing in the contemporary State of hill Tipperah and perhaps this was done in order to make the currency acceptable to the people of a portion of Tripura conquered by the Sultan.[48]

No numismatic or epigraphic evidences is available yet for the period prior to 1464 A.D. to substantiate the existence of Māṇikyas as independent rulers. But the Rājmālā narrates that king Cheong-phā (who was the great grandfather of Ratna Māṇikya, the first datable king of this lunar line) had a fight with king of Gauḍa.[49] This king of Gauḍa may be identified with Jālāl-ud-Din and Cheongphā may be placed on the earlier part of the 15th century A.D. Some scholars are of opinion that Ratna Māṇikya was not the first ruler to assume the title Māṇikya. According to this school Cheong-phā was the first Māṇikya king whose Sanskritized name is Mahā Māṇikya[50] and he was the grandfather of Ratna Māṇikya (not great grandfather as stated by the Rājmālā). The latest accepted genealogy of Māṇikya rulers of Tripura as corroborated by numismatic and epigraphic evidences (as sometimes supported by the Rājmālā) are as follows :

1. Mahā-Māṇikya alias Cheon-phā
2. Dharma-Māṇikya alias Dangar-phā
3. Ratna Māṇikya Śaka 1386-89*

4. Vijaya-Māṇikya I Śaka 140*
5. Mukuta-Māṇikya Śaka*
6. Pratāpa-Māṇikya Śaka 1412*
7. Dhaṇya-Māṇikya* ⌘
8. Deva-Māṇikya Śaka 1442-52*
9. Indra-Māṇikya
10. Vijaya-Māṇikya II Śaka 1454-85* ⌘
11. Ananta-Māṇikya Śaka 1487*
12. Udaya-Māṇikya Śaka 1489*
13. Jayā-Māṇikya Śaka 1495*
14. Amara-Māṇikya Śaka 1499-1508*
15. Rājdharā-Māṇikya Śaka 1508-21*
16. Īśvara-Māṇikya
17. Yaśo-Māṇikya Śaka 1522*
18. Kalyāṇa-Māṇikya Śaka 1548-78* ⌘
19. Govinda-Māṇikya Śaka 1578-82, 1589-95 * ⌘
20. Chatra-Māṇikya Śaka 1583-88 *
21. Rāma-Māṇikya Śaka 1595-1607 * ⌘
22. Ratna-Māṇikya II Śaka 1607-34 *
23. Mahendra-Māṇikya Śaka 1634 *
24. Dharma-Māṇikya Śaka 1436 *
25. Mukunda-Māṇikya Śaka 1651-61
26. Indra-Māṇikya Śaka 1666-68 *
27. Jaya-Māṇikya
28. Vijaya-Māṇikya III
29. Kṛṣṇa-Māṇikya Śaka 1682-1705 *

* Coins, ⌘ Inscriptions.

Rājmālā[51] refers to an inscription dated A.D. 1458 of Dharma Māṇikya. In this inscription Mahā Māṇikya was regarded as the father of Dharma Māṇikya and according to Tripura Vaṁśāvalī, Dharma Māṇikya ruled from A.D. 1431 A.D. to 1462 A.D. Therefore it can be presumed that Mahā Māṇikya ruled before A.D. 1431 and he was the earliest known king of Tripura having the Māṇikya title. According to some scholars it was Mahā Māṇikya who founded a kingdom during the early years of the reign of Rājā Gaṇeśa of Bengal and his newly founded kingdom was lying between Chittagong and Sylhet. They also presume that the original name of Mahā Māṇikya was Cheheong Fā.[52] It is not very unlikely that after successfully defending his newly formed kingdom against the Muslim force, Cheheong Fā assumed the title Mahā Māṇikya.

Dharma Māṇikya, the son of Mahā Māṇikya, was a powerful ruler and his reign constitutes an important land mark in the history of Tripura. Although we find no coin of Dharma Māṇikya, the Rājmālā mentions a copper plate of Dharma Māṇikya dated 1458 A.D. According to Tripura Vaṁśāśalī Dharma Māṇikya ruled from 1431 A.D. to 1462 A.D. He was a great patron of learning. It is said that he engaged the priest Durlabhendra and two Brahmins, named Sukreśvara and Bāneśvara to write a history of the dynasty. He donated lands to a large number of Brahmins in his realm and was himself a staunch and devout Hindu. Dharma Māṇikya had paternal affection for his subjects. He excavated the famous Dharma Sāgar Tank at Comilla and built temples.[53]

Ratna Māṇikya who ascended the throne of Tripura after the death of Dharma Māṇikya, may be considered the earliest of the coin issuing rulers of Tripura. These coins belonged to the period between 1464 A.D.[54] and 1467 A.D. These coins bear some common characteristics with the Muslim coins of Bengal. According to Rājmālā, he was the youngest son of king Dangar Fā. From chronological point of view, king Dangar Fā and Dharma Māṇikya were the same person. According to Rājmālā and local traditions, king Dangar Fā divided his kingdom into seventeen divisions and placed them under his seventeen princes. Ratna Fā, the youngest son of Dangar Fā, was sent to Gauḍa as hostage from Tripura. The Sultan of Gauḍa was highly pleased with the charming manners and uncommon intelligence of the prince. There the Sultan and the prince came to an unholy alliance. The prince got military help from the Sultan to capture entire Tripura for himself. With the help of the mercenary forces, he defeated his elder brothers and declared himself the king of Tripura. As a mark of gratitude Ratna Fā presented the Sultan with some elephants and a valuable ruby. In return, the Sultan recognized Ratna Fā as Ratna Māṇikya.[55] Tripura in the early part of the eighteenth century stated that Ratna Māṇikya was conferred with the Māṇikya title by the Sultan of Gauḍa.[56] It is generally believed that during his reign, a large number of Brahmins, Vaidyas and Kayasthas came from various parts of Bengal and settled in Tripura. It is said that he introduced some administrative reforms which were modelled on the pattern prevalent in Bengal. His capital as mentioned in the coins was known as Ratnapur. Sultan Ruknuddin Barbak Shah, 1455 A.D. to 1476 A.D., of Bengal was the contemporary of Ratna Māṇikya and it was probably from him that Ratna Māṇikya secured assistance to usurp the kingdom. During his time, Tripura came into cultural contract with Bengal. It was probably largely through the patronage of Ratna, Brahmanism made a significant dent into the tribal society of Tripura which was wiped out from this land after the downfall of Samataṭa and other south eastern Bengal Hindu and Buddhist kingdoms.[57] He was the pioneer in the field of cultural synthesis between the Aryan and pre-Aryan cultures in the land. His coins describe him as a devout worshipper of Pārvatī, Parameśvara and Nārāyaṇa. He was the worshipper of Chaturdaśa Devatā (fourteen Gods), which is recorded in one of his coins.[58] Chaturdaśa Devatā are cult deities that sprang out of peculiar synthesis and harmonious blending of Brahmanism and primitive religions. He introduced lion device on the reverse of his coins which became a tradition till the end of the dynasty.

After the death of Ratna Māṇikya, his son Pratāp Māṇikya became the ruler of Tripura. According to Rājmālā, he was cruel and unpopular. The leaders of the army who became very much powerful after the death of Ratna Māṇikya, murdered him.

Pratāp Māṇikya was succeeded by his brother Mukut Māṇikya. A coin of Mukut Māṇikya dated 1489 A.D. has been found.[59] His reign lasted for a very short time and appears to have come to an end before 1490 A.D. because Dhaṇya Māṇikya already issued a coin in that year. According to Rājmālā, Dhanya Māṇikya succeeded his younger brother Pratāp Māṇikya II. But we find that Mukut Māṇikya issued a coin just before the accession of Dhaṇya Māṇikya. So Pratāp Māṇikya II must be placed before Mukut Māṇikya.

It appears from a copper-plate grant dated Śaka 1410 (1488 A.D.) that Punyavati maternal aunt (wife of Daityanārāyaṇa, the army chief and defacto ruler) of Vijaya Māṇikya granted villages, situated both at hill and plain Tripura.[60] Nothing about his reign is known from any other sources. This inscription mentioned the name of one Vijaya Māṇikya who was a minor king at that time. According to D.C. Sircar, it is possible that Vijaya Māṇikya I, 1410 A.D.-1488 A.D. was Mukut's elder brother who is called Pratāp Māṇikya II in the Rājmālā and may have ruled for a very short reign. D.C. Sircar is of the opinion that Dhanya Māṇikya whose coins are dated 1490 A.D. just after Mukut Māṇikya who issued coins in 1489 A.D., could have been the son but not the great grandson of Mukut Māṇikya as stated by Rājmālā.[61] He introduced Garuḍa device on his coin, which is never found in any type of Tripura coinage. This type of Garuḍa figure on teracotta plaques are found in plenty in Udaipur, the old capital of Tripura.

Dhaṇya Māṇikya (1490-1514/15 A.D.) was perhaps the greatest of Tripura rulers. He was contemporary of Ala-ud-Din Hussain Shah of Bengal, and the latter achieved very little success, though he made strenuous efforts to conquer this hill kingdom. Dhaṇya Māṇikya started his career of conquest by subjugating a number of principalities around his kingdom. He annexed to his kingdom Khandal (Noakhali), Meherkul, Paṭṭikerā, Gaṅgāmaṇḍal, some portion of Śrīhaṭṭa, Chittagong and he also proceeded upto Arākān and Lungley (in modern Mizoram State).[62] He used the epithet Vijayindra on his coin dated Śaka 1428 (1506 A.D.) to commemorate his victories. The Rājmālā has all the praise for him. But the Muslim records gave contradictory picture of these events.

Sonārgaon inscription of 1513 A.D. refers to Khawas-Khan as Sar-i-Laskar of the country of Tripura which indicates that at least a portion of Tripura was conquered by Hussain Shah.[63] Works of Parameśvara Das and Śrīkara Nandi (poets patronised by the commanders of Hussain Shah) described that Hussain Shah had conquered a portion of Tripura.[64]

The epithets used in his coins viz. Tripurendra, Vijayindra, Chatigram Vijayi[65] certainly are the evidences of his conquest. However, during his rule, Tripura came into contact with Muslims more than once and the cultural influence of the political affairs was submerged in the art and architecture of Tripura. It is said in the Rājmālā that the rock-cut sculptures in Devatâmuḍa were carved during the reign of Dhaṇya by the soldiers of Hussain Shah.[66] Stylistically, these sculptures may be assignable to this period.

The Rājmālā praised Dhaṇya as great patron of art and architecture.[67] According to epigraphic evidence at least two temples at Udaipur were built by Dhaṇya for Ambikā and Śaṅkara respectively. A large number of images stylistically datable to the same period have been found in Udaipur. Perhaps these were fashioned in the same period in any well accomplished workshop of Tripura, patronized by the rulers. It is generally believed that Dhaṇya died sometimes after Śaka 1436 (1514-15 A.D.) as no coin was issued in the name of Dhaṇya after that period. But according to an inscription, quoted in the Rājmālā,[68] that a temple for Ambikā was built by Dhaṇya in Śaka 1442 (1520 A.D.). If Deva-Māṇikya, son of Dhaṇya is considered as the next ruler in the line, there may not be much objection to accept the view that Dhaṇya died in Śaka 1442 (1520 A.D.) and at the same year Deva became the king.[69] Kaliprasanna Sen, in his commentary on the Rājmālā gave an account of the rule of Dhvaja Māṇikya intervening between Dhaṇya and Deva.[70] Neither the Rājmālā enlists this king in its genealogy, nor any other source material is available to substantiate the above view.

The earliest available coin of Deva Māṇikya, the brother of Dhvaja Māṇikya, dated 1520 A.D. proves the fact that Deva Māṇikya became the ruler of Tripura in the year 1520 A.D. He was contemporary of Nusrat Shah (1519-32 A.D.) of Bengal. The Rājmālā accounts the victory of Deva Māṇikya over Chittagong.[71] On the other hand Mukt-ul-Hussain describes that the ruler of Tripura was defeated by Hamza Khan, the Governor of Chittagong during the reign of Nusrat Shah.[72]

Suvarṇagrāma (Sonārgaon) was conquered by Deva Māṇikya. Perhaps it was recovered by the Sultan but again Deva Māṇikya was able to capture it. This is evidenced by his coins dated Śaka 1450 (1528 A.D.) and Śaka 1452 (1530 A.D.) describing him as

Suvarṇagrāma Vijayi. He was a devout Śākta and was put to death by a tantrik Brahmin.[73] The lion insignia on the reverse side of his coins, shows that he introduced a new form which differs to some extent from that depicted on the species of his predecessors. He introduced a half moon and sun (?) symbols on the head of the lion and the slim but solid figure of animal depicted on his coins served as models to his successors.[74]

Next important ruler of Tripura was Vijaya Māṇikya who ascended the throne in 1532 A.D., after a short reign of his brother Indra Māṇikya. There is no doubt that Vijaya was one of the most powerful rulers in eastern India in the middle of sixteenth century A.D. as evidenced by his coins. He was contemporary of great Mughul ruler Akbar,[75] Naranārāyaṇa of Cooch Behar and Mukundadeva of Orissa. Some coins of Vijaya Māṇikya which are available belonged to the period between 1532 A.D. 1553 A.D.[76] The existence of these coins indicates that Vijay Māṇikya reigned for more than thirty years. He made some administrative reforms, reorganised army and recruited some Afghan cavalry in his army. Like Dhaṇya Māṇikya, Vijaya Māṇikya was also a great conqueror. He conquered Sylhet and recovered Chittagong from the Afghans. Taking advantage of the Mughal-Afghan contest, Vijaya Māṇikya invaded Sonārgaon and plundered it. That his army advanced upto the river Padmā during 1557 A.D. to 1563 A.D. is proved by some contemporary coins issued by Vijaya Māṇikya. That his kingdom was bounded by the sea is corroborated by the legend Pratisindhusimā on his coin dated Śaka 1479 (1557 A.D.). That Chittagong remained under alternate control of Vijaya Māṇikya and the ruler of Arākān is evident from the account of Ralph Fitch, who travelled through the territory during Vijaya's reign.[77] Abul Fazal in the Ain-i-Akbari mentioned 'Vijaya Māṇikya' as a ruler of an extensive area.[78]

Vijaya was not only a brave conqueror but also a great patron of religion and art. In his time Śaiva and Śākta cults were perhaps united which is evidenced by a unique Ardhanāriśvara figure, a syncretistic icon of Śiva and Durgā, on his coin.[79] He was also a patron of Vaiṣṇavism and a figure of Viṣṇu depicted on one of his coins is a beautiful example of Viṣṇu - worship. An arch shaped stone gateway having an inscription of atleast seventy six lines has been found in Mahārāni village (in between Udaipur and Amarapur).[80] The inscription depicts the construction of a temple of Viṣṇu with his consorts Śrī and Vānī in Śaka 1470 (1548 A.D.). The inscription describes the existence of a massive gate way, a big temple and metal images of Viṣṇu, Lakshmī and Sarasvatī.

Unfortunately, nothing has come to our notice yet, except the above mentioned inscription. His coins with icons on the reverse, are miniature models of plastic art practised in those days. There is no doubt, in the days of Vijaya Māṇikya, the people of Tripura came into a cultural contact with the territories other than the hilly land of Tripura, which helped a lot in the growth of art and architecture of the area. A masterful man, Vijaya Māṇikya died in Śaka 1485 or 1486 (1563 A.D. or 1564 A.D.) as evidenced by his coin dated Śaka 1485 (1563 A.D.) (which is the last coin issued by him) and a coin dated Śaka 1487 (1565 A.D.) of Ananta Māṇikya, Vijaya's son.

Ananta Māṇikya, the son of Vijaya Māṇikya was not an efficient ruler. He was completely under the control of his father in-law Gopī Prasād who had humble origin but rose to the height of position and power.[81] He usurped the throne of Tripura in the year 1567 A.D. and took the title Udai Māṇikya and issued coins in the same year. He changed the name of his capital from Raṅgamati to Udaipur, excavated a tank known as Chandra Sāgar and built a temple of Chandra Gopīnātha. According to Rājmālā he ruled for five years. Amara Māṇikya, son of Deva Māṇikya, resorted the old dynasty to its proper place after ousting Jayā Māṇikya, the son of Udai Māṇikya in 1577 A.D. He was an energetic ruler. He defeated the ruler of Tarāp, Bhulua and Sylhet and issued a coin in 1581 A.D. named 'Śrīhaṭṭa Vijayi' to commemorate his victory over Sylhet. He constructed a big tank known as Amara Sāgar and made his residence in a place which came to be known as Amarpur. It is generally believed that the second part of the Rājmāla was compiled during his reign. According to Rājmāla, Amara Māṇikya conquered Chittagong and invaded Aràkān with the help of some Portuguese adventurers. But Sikandar Shah, the king of Arākān, defeated him and occupied Chittagong.[82] The Arākani force plundered Udaipur and massacred the citizens. Amara Māṇikya left Udaipur and took shelter in the forest on the bank of the river Manu. There he was harassed by the Kukis. Being mentally depressed, Amara Māṇikya committed suicide by taking poison.[83]

Rājadharā and Yaso — Māṇikya son and grand son of Amara Māṇikya, were devout Vaiṣṇavas and at their instance Vaiṣṇavism spread over Tripura successfully. Rājadharā reoccupied the capital Udaipur from the Arārākanese. But both of them totally were indifferent in administration and warfare which resulted in the process of decline of ruling power and also of the morality of the people and the army. After the death of Rājadharā, there was a chaos in the kingdom and perhaps disputes arose among the members of the royal house for power. A careful scrutiny of the Rājmālā suggests that Yaso Māṇikya was not declared 'king' soon after the death of his father,[84] which was a local tradition since the earliest time. Probably, with the help of such chaotic condition in the royal family, an unwanted person came to power and struck coins in the name of Īśvara Māṇikya along with his queen Īśvaridevī.[85] The Rājmālā is quite silent about this man and only one coin of the said king has so far been found. Nothing conclusive can be said with such a single evidence. But it is tempting to suggest that with the opportunity of chaotic condition after Rājadharā's death, Īśvara ascended the throne and he was an unwanted person whom patrons of the Rājmālā did not allow the authors to include him in the official genealogy of the Māṇikyas. Perhaps he ruled for a very short period and in the same year (1600 A.D.) Yaso Māṇikya ascended the throne as is evidenced by coins of the same date. The image of Kṛṣṇa with a flute inscribed on his coins indicates that he was a Vaiṣṇava. In order to secure a suitable base for a military operation against the king of Arākān, Ibrahim Khan Fatehjang, the governor of Bengal under Jahangir's order launched an expedition against Tripura in 1618 A.D.[86] The king was defeated and Udaipur was captured by the Mughals and sent to Delhi. Probably he was confinded within Mughal territory and died in 1623 A.D.[87] During their stay at Udaipur, Mughals started the construction of a mosque. It remained incomplete due to their sudden departure. Situated on the north bank of the Gomati it is locally known as Masjid.

According to Rājmālā, the plains of Tripura remained under Mughal occupation for more than two years and occupied places were named as 'Sarkar Udaipur'.[88] The Mughals, however, had to quit the area and eventually Kalyāṇa Māṇikya, a descendant of Mahā Māṇikya the earlist Māṇikya ruler, was selected king by the people.[89] He remodelled his army and recovered at least some portion of the lost territory.[90]

Another Muslim account *Noubahari Murshid Quli Khani* noted:

> "Tripura is a country extremely strong by reason of abundance of its trees, the loftiness of its forts, and the difficulty of its roads. The Rājā is proud of his strength and the practices of conch blowing and idol worship prevail there. Sultan Shuja during his governorship of Bengal, left his eldest son Zainuddin Muhammad as his deputy in Rajmahal, came to Dacca, and sent his chief minister Jan Bag Khan towards Tripura, but the Khan's men failed to take any of the forts of that country even after labouring for one year. At last he had to content himself with annexing the district of Mirzapur, and making it the frontier of the imperial dominions. Many of his soldiers died from the badness of the air".[91]

The conquered portion of Tripura was enlisted as Sarkar Udaipur in the Revenue Records of Bengal Subā prepared in 1658 A.D. Nakshatra Roy, the second son of Kalyāṇa Māṇikya, was sent to the court of Shuja as hostage.

It is stated in the Rājmālā that Kalyāṇa ascended the throne in Śaka 1545 (1623 A.D.) but his earliest coins were struck in Śaka 1548 (1626 A.D.). He built Gopīnātha temple at Udaipur in Śaka 1573 (1651 A.D.) as evidenced from the votive tablet. He also renovated the Kāli temple (built by Dhaṇya Māṇikya). Kalyāṇa Māṇikya introduced half and quarter coins with a 'Śivaliṅga' inscribed on the obverse, reverse device being the same as those of his predecessors.

After the death of Kalyāṇa Māṇikya, his eldest son Govinda Māṇikya ascended the throne in 1660 A.D. But Nakshatra Roy, the step-brother of Govinda Māṇikya, secured the help of the Mughals and occupied Udaipur. Govinda Māṇikya was forced to leave Tripura. Nakshatra Roy took the title Chhatra Māṇikya and issued a coin in 1661 A.D. Chhatra Māṇikya ruled probably six years. With the help of the king of Arākān, Govinda Māṇikya became the ruler of Tripura for the second time after the death of Chhatra Māṇikya. But the Assamese envoys who visited the court of Ratna Māṇikya II recorded a speech of king Mahendra Māṇikya which stated that Chhatra Māṇikya was assassinated by Govinda Māṇikya.[92] Govinda Māṇikya made peace with the Mughals by agreeing to give them five elephants as tribute annually. The name of Govinda Māṇikya became immortal through Tagore's famous play *Visarjana* and novel *Rājarṣi*. It is generally believed that the third part of Rājmālā was compiled during his reign. The Bṛihannārada-purāṇa was translated into Bengali under his patronage. He built temples at Udaypur and Chandranātha (Chittagong). His queen Guṇavatī also built a group of temples at Udaipur. Travernier visited India at this time and he mentioned Tripura's trade relation with China.[93]

He recorded :

"His son Rāmadeva Māṇikya was also a patron of art and Brahmanical religion. It is evidenced from dedicatory inscriptions that he built at least three temples at Udaipur".

After the death of Ramadeva, the history of Tripura in the 17th century A.D. was one of gradual decay, although Tripura never became a part of Subā Bangla, never the less major portion of the kingdom, acquired by great rulers like Dhaṇya and Vijaya Māṇikya was lost to it. The rulers took less interest in the affairs of Bengal, and were spending time in religious activities.[94]

Rāmadeva was succeeded by his son Ratna Māṇikya II and his copper plate and coins dated Śaka 1607 (1685 A.D.) have been found. It was at the time of Ratna, a diplomatic relation was set up with Ahom kingdom. Rudra Sinha of Ahom line sent Ratnā Kāndalī and Arjundas Vairagi to the court of Ratna who left a vivid account of Tripura in *'Tripurā deshara kathar lekha'*.[95] They saw many temples in the capital, dedicated to Viṣṇu, Śiva and other Gods and Goddesses, and the Rājā of Tripura lived in a brick-built palace.[96]

Ratna Māṇikya II ruled Tripura for sixteen years and was murdered by his brother Mahendra Māṇikya who came to power in Śaka 1634 (1712 A.D.) as evidenced by his coin of same date.[97] A manuscript in Tripuri language having the same date contained his name.[98]

It was during the middle of the 18th century[99] the plains of Tripura which had so long been under the control of the rulers of

Tripura, had already integrated within the Mughal empire in terms of settlement and revenue, and Tripura rulers were granted zamindary rights over Chakla Rosanabad consisting of 22 Parganas. Thus the areas of Tripura which went under the Mughals consisted of one fourth of Mymensingh, half of Sylhet, one third of Noakhali and some portion of Dacca district as well.[100]

Taking advantage of the quarrel among the members of the royal family during this period, Samsher Gāzi, a Muslim clerk of a zamindar, organized an army and occupied Udaipur[101]. and Prince Kṛṣṇamani took shelter into old Agartala (six kilometres east of Agartala town) and after the fall of Samsher ascended the throne in 1766 A.D. under the name of Kṛṣṇa Māṇikya, old Agartala being the capital. Very soon Kṛṣṇa Māṇikya was involved not only with Nawab of Bengal but also the English. The English were very eager to occupy Tripura and they took the advantage of hostility between the Nawab and Tripura. Accordingly, a British troop was sent to Tripura and it found no resistance from the Rājā of Tripura who is said to have surrendered to company's army. Mr. Ralph Leak was appointed first Resident of Tripura and thus Tripura was reduced to the State of obedience to the British.[102]

Copper-plates[103] and half rupee coins of Kṛṣṇa Māṇikya have been discovered. Though the kingdom was much disturbed politically, pious activity and patronage of religion, art and architecture was in spontaneity during Kṛṣṇa Māṇikya's reign (1760-83 A.D.). He had to shift his capital from Udaipur to old Agartala. A temple for Chaturdaśadevatā and a palace were built in the locality of which the latter is in a ruinous condition while the Chaturdaśadevatā are worshipped still by the people, irrespective of all classes under the state patronage. He completed the construction of *Sateroratna* (Seventeen jewelled) temple near Comilla, the foundation of which was laid by Ratna Māṇikya II. In Śaka 1697 (1775 A.D.) he constructed a *Pañcharatna* temple for Rādhāmādhava in Kālikāganj, near Agartala. With end of Kṛṣṇa Māṇikya's reign, the land sank in chaos and disorder and never did Tripura further excel in artistic activity. Due to political turmoil and economic crisis in the land, all religious and cultural activities had come down to a very low ebb and ultimately sank into stagnation.

Inspite of constant warfare with the Muslims, Arākānese and other neighbouring territories and unlimited internal disputes, the Māṇikya dynasty did not neglect the cultural and religious side of life. During the Māṇikya rule of Tripura, it had been a place for the coexistence of several religious sects and denominations such as, Vaiṣṇavism, Śaivism, Śaktism, Buddhism along with their respective cults of animatism, animism, magic, fertility, etc.

References

1. Sarma, Ramanimohan, *Sources of the Social, Economic and Administrative History of Tripura* (Ed N.R. Roy), Calcutta 1982, p.475.
2. *IHQ* VI, pp.45-60;cf. Mukherjee, Ramarajan and Maity, Sachindra Kumar, *Corpus of Bengal Inscription*, Cal, 1967, p.65. In a seal discovered at Nalanda, Vainya Gupta has been given the title Mahārājādhirāja, which undoubtedly indicates his independent status. For this seal see, *ASI, AR,* 1930-34, p-30; also *IHQ,* XIX, p.275, For Vainya Gupta's gold coin with epithet Dvadaśāditya; see *IHQ,* IX, p.784.
3. Basak, R.G., *History of North Eastern India,* Calcutta, 1967, p.231
4. Majumdar, R.C., *History of Ancient Bengal,* Calcutta, 1971, p.8.
5. *EI,* XV, p.311;cf. Basak, R.G., *op.cit,* p.238; *IHQ*, XXIII, p.232.
6. Deb Barma, S.C., *Tripurā Smriti (in Bengali)*, Calcutta, 1927, p.149
7. Das, Ratna, *Art and Architecture of Tripura*, Agartala, 1997, p.8
8. *MASB*, I, No.6, pp.85-95;cf. *JASB, XIX,* 1923, p.375.
9. *EI, XVII,* p.357, ef.; Majumder, R.C., (ed), *History of Bengal,* Vol. I, Dacca, 1963, p.87; Basak, R.G., *op.cit,* p.202; Dani, A.H., *Indian Palaeography,* Oxford, 1963, p.134.
10. Sen, Benoy Chandra, *Some Historical Aspects of Inscriptions of Bengal*, p.280; cf; *EI,* XVII, p.357. One of the plates discovered in the ruins of the Sālban Vihāra in the Maināmati hills gives us the name of a king Balabhaṭṭa who may be regarded as a successor of Rājābhata. See, B.M. Morrison, *Political Centres and Cultural Regions in Early Bengal*, Arizona, USA, 1970, p.21
11. Basask, R.G., *op.cit*, p.228, cf; Khan, F.A., *Maināmati, A Preliminary Report on the Recent Archaeological Excavations in East Pakistan,* Karachi, 1964, p.2.
12. Roy Choudhari, N.R., *The History Past* (ed Ganchoudhpuri, J), N. Delhi, 1980, p.15.

13. Bhattasali, N.K., *Iconography of Buddhist and Brahmanical Sculptures in the Dacca Museum,* 1974, New Delhi, p.6.
14. *IHQ*, XXIII, pp.221-41, cf.; Shamsul Alam, A.K.M., *Mainâmati,* Dacca, 1982, p.8.
15. Majumdar, R.C., *op.cit*, p.81.
16. Basak, R.G., *op.cit*, p.244.
17. The exact find spot of the copper plate which is now in collection of the Asiatic Society, is unknown, it has been edited by D.C. Sircar in *JAS*, Letters, XVII, 1951, pp.83-94. Two more inscriptions of this family have been reportedly recovered from the excavation at Sālbanvihāra, near the Lālmai Mainämati hills. One of them belongs to Bhavadeva, the other to his father Ānandadeva, See; Chowdhury, Abdul Monin, *Dynastic History of Bengal,* p.149.
18. *EI*, XXVI, pp.313-18.
19. Mukherjee, B.N., *The Coin Legend Harikela,* Monthly Bulletin of Asiatic Society, January, 1976, p.10.
20. Allan, J, *Catalogue of Coins of Gupta Dynasty,* p.CVII.
21. Mukherjee, B N, *op.cit,* p.9.
22. *Ibid.*
23. Mukherjee, Ramaranjan and Maity, Sachindra Kumar, *Corpus of Bengal Inscriptions,* Calcutta, 1967, p.24.
24. *EI*, XVII, 349
25. *EI,* XII, 136-42
26. *EI*, XVII, 188-92
27. Majumdar, N G, *Inscriptions of Bengal,* Vol. III, Rajshahi, Varendra Research Society, 1922, pp.165-66; cf. *EI,* XXXIII, Part III, pp.134-40.
28. *EI*, XVII, pp.189-90.
29. Majumdar, R.C., *op.cit*, 1943, Dacca, pp.192-7.
30. *Ibid.*
31. Shamsul Alam, A K M, *op.cit.,* p.12.
32. Khan, F.A., *Mainâmati,* Dacca, 1964, p.21.
33. Roy Choudhuri, Nalini Ranjan, *op.cit,* Delhi, 1980, p.16.
34. Mukherjee, Ramaranjan & Maity, Sachindra Kumar, *op.cit*, p.22.
35. *EI,* IX, pp.232-33.
36. *Ibid*, pp.232-33.
37. *EI*, XVII, pp.353-55.

38. *Indian Culture,* Vol.IX, pp.121-24, cf.; Roy Choudhuri, N.R., *op.cit,* p.17
39. *Chattal Inscription of Damodaradeva,* Vide, Majumdar, N.G., *Inscriptions of Bengal,* III, p.158
40. Khandal was conquered by Dhaṇya Māṇikya (Śaka 1412-36) and was under zamindary of Tripura upto the independence of India.
41. Debbarma, S C, *op.cit,* pp.43-44
42. Paṭṭikerā is identified with modern Patkara near Comilla.
43. Ahom kings were also using the word pha at their names end. In Tripura language phā literally means 'father' and it also means a 'leader' and a 'respectable person'. However, the title phā used by the Ahom and Tripura rulers might have had the same origin.
44. According to the Śrī Kailas Chandra Sinha, one branch of the Shan dynasty of Burma set up as independent kingdom on the eastern side of Kamrup. The members of this family were outsed by another tribe of that area and migrated to Tripura and formed the kingdom (Rājmālā p.8).
45. Das, Ranta, *op.cit,* Agartala, 1997, p.10
46. Rājmālā, p.8.
47. It is said in the Rājmālā that Ratna Māṇikya (15th century) strengthened his kingdom with the help of the Sultans of Bengal, pp.68-69.
48. Majumdar, R.C. (ed), *History and Culture of Indian People* (Delhi Sultanate), VI, p.209. The earliest coin of the Māṇikyas of Tripura is that of Ratna Māṇikya dated A.D. 1464. So it is useless to presume that coins with lion device on their reverse were prevalent in the earlier part of 15th century until and unless we get some more data on this point.
49. *Rājmālā,* Education Directorate, Govt. of Tripura, 1967, Agartala, p.17
50. Majumdar, R.C., Bāṅgladeśer Itihāsa, II, p.484. No coin or copper-plate of Mahā Māṇikya has so far been found. Madhava Kandali, an Assamese poet, who translated the *Rāmāyana* in Assamese, mentions one Varāharājā Mahā Māṇikya as his patron. Kalirama Medhi identifies this Mahā Māṇikya with the Tripura king of the same name. Medhi, Kalirama, *Assamese Grammar and Origin of Assamese Language,* Preface, Nothing definite can be said, however, at present state of our knowledge.
51. *Rājmālā,* Education Directorate, p.27. Inscription has not yet been recovered.

52. Majumdar, R.C., *op.cit*, p.486.
53. Except on account in the Rājmālā no archaeological or any other evidence for the period reigned by Mahā Māṇikya and Dharma Māṇikya has yet been recovered. The Rājmālā mentioned them as great patrons of art and literature, though nothing is survived to prove the real factors.
54. Coins of Śaka 1964 A.D. are the earliest dated coins of Ratna. But some undated coins have been recovered having legends on both obverse and reverse as on Muslim coinage. These coins may be placed on an earlier period. Besides, the lion device on the undated coins of Ratna are in experimental stage.
55. It is stated in the Rājmālā that Ratna defeated his seventeen brothers and recovered the whole territory of Tripura of which those people were chiefs. *Rājmālā*, Education Directorate, pp.18-19.
56. Bhuiya, S.K. (ed) *Tripura Burunji*, Gauhati, 1962, pp.34-35.
57. Ahom ruler Suhungmung (1497-1539 A.D.) assumed the Hindu name, Savarganārāyaṇa which is an index of the gradually increasing hold of Brahmanical Hinduism upon this Shan royal family and the people. Royal family of Tripura might be a branch of same Shan people. Hinduisation of Tripura started earlier than Ahom, might be due to rich past tradition and as an effect of geographical situation.
58. Chowdhury, V. and Roy, P., *'Representation of Chaturdaśadevatās on a coin of Ratna Māṇikya deva', JNSI, XXXVI*, Parts I-II, pp.111-113; worship of Chaturdaśa devatā is still prevalent in Tripuras, one of the presiding festivals. The above mentioned coin is the only numismatic evidence to prove at least one king as a patron of said worship.
59. Lahiri, Bela *"Coins of Tripura: Their Essential Features"* in Rajendra Kirtishala, Silver Jubilee commemorative volume, Agartala, 1995, p.32.
60. Dutta, Joytish Chandra, *Bhumi Lekhyapattrer Aloke Tripurar Bhumi Byabastha*, Directorate of Higher Education, Govt. of Tripura, 1987, p.1.
61. Roy Choudhuri, N R, *Tripura Through the Ages*, 1977, p.IV.
62. Singha, K C, *op.cit*, pp.75-77.
63. *JASB*, old series, XLI, 1872, pp.333-34.
64. Mukhopadhyaya, Sukhamay, *Banglar Itihaser Duso Bachar*, Cal, 1996, pp.327-28.

65. Sarma, Dr. Ramanimohan, *Coinage of Tripura, Numismatic Notes and Monographs,* No.17, Part I, The Numismatic Society of India, 1980, pp.3-4.
66. *Rājmālā*, p.30.
67. *Ibid.*
68. Dev Sarma, Chandradaya, *Silalipi Saṅgraha,* Govt of Tripura, Agartala, 1968, p.1 cf.; *Rājmālā,* p.30.
69. A coin of Deva Māṇikya date Śaka 1442 (1520 A.D.) has been found and preserved in Government Museum Agartala. See Das, Ratna, *op.cit*, p.22.
70. Sen, K.P., *Śrī Rājmālā*, II, p.178.
71. *Rājmālā*, p.33.
72. Mukhopadhaya, Sukhamay, *op.cit*, pp.321-24.
73. *Rājmālā,* p.33.
74. Das, Ratna, *"Itihas prasanga Tripura Mudrā",* Gomati (special issue), Govt of Tripura, Agartala, December, 1974, p.35.
75. *Tripura District Gazetteers*, pp.81-82.
76. Lahiri, Bela, *op.cit*, p.34.
77. Singha, K C, *Rājmālā*, p.90.
78. Fazal, Abul, *Ain-I-Akbari,* Vol. II, translated by Jarret & Sarkar, Calcutta 1942, p.130. The *Ain-I-Akbari,* refers to Vijaya Māṇikya's reign in the following words. "Adjoining Bhati is an extensive tract of territory inhabited by the Tipperah tribe. The name of the ruler is Vijaya Māṇikya. Whoever obtains the chieftainship bears the title Māṇikya after his name and the nobles that of Nārāyan. He has a force of two hundred thousand footmen and a thousand elephants. Horses are scarce".
79. He introduced for the first time a trident symbol on the back of the lion insignia of Tripura which means again union of Śaiva and Śākta cult, if we consider trident as the symbol of Śiva and lion for Durgā.
80. The inscription was edited by Dr. D.C. Sircar in *IHQ*, XXXIII, 2, 1957, pp.99-196.
81. Singha, K.C., *op.cit,* p.88.
82. Sarkar, J.N., *History of Bengal*, II, Dacca, 1972, 2nd edition, p.243.
83. *Rājmālā*, p.63.
84. *Ibid.*
85. Das, Ratna, *'Itihas Prasanga Tripura Mudrā',* p.38.

86. According to Baharistani-Ghayabi, the king of Tripura resisted the Mughals with an army of "one thousand cavalry, sixty thousand infantry and two hundred elephants" in *"Baharistani-Ghayabi"*, Vol. II, translated by M.I. Bora, Gauhati, 1936, p.537.
87. *Rājmālā*, p.67, The *Rājmālā*, corroborated the statement of Mirza Nathan in the Baharistani-Ghayabi where a detailed account of the battle between Mughals and the Tripura was narrated.; cf. *Baharistani-Ghayabi* of Mirza Nathan (tr. Borah), II, p.537.
88. *Ibid.*
89. *Rājmālā*, p.76.
90. Petter Heleys, a European visitor, mentioned in 1652 that the ruler of Tripura had frequent fights with the Mughals. See, Roychaudhuri, N.R., *op.cit*, p.25.
91. Another Muslim account Naubahari Murshid Qulikhani, quoted in Roychoudhuri, N.R., *op.cit*, pp.25-26.
92. Bhuviya, S.K., *op.cit*, p.85.
93. Travernier, *Travels in India*, tr. John Phrlip, Bangbasi office ed, 1905.
94. Chatterjee, S.K., *op.cit*, p.135.
95. Bhuviya, S.K., *op.cit*, p.IX.
96. *Ibid.*
97. Majumder, R.C., *op.cit*, p.497.
98. An unpublished *M.S.S.*, now, presented in Government Museum, Agartala.
99. It happened during the time of Jagat Māṇikya the Rājmālā did not mention him in its genealogy.
100. Stewart, C., *History of Bengal*, pp.266-67.
101. The *Gazināmā*, by Seikh Manchar, gives a detailed account of his activities.
102. Guha Thakurta, S.M., *Tripura*, National Book Trust, Govt. of India, Delhi, p.16.
103. Dutta, Joytish Chandra, *op.cit*, pp.9-10.

3

DIFFERENT RELIGIOUS SECTS IN TRIPURA

The religious history of ancient Tripura is, in fact, the religious history of the *Prāchya deśa* or the eastern India.[1] Of course, regional variances are there, still its overall history and development prior to the twelfth century A.D. is inextricably mixed up with the religious history of ancient Sylhet, Samatata, Noakhali and Chittagong.[2]

Paucity of archaeological evidence from Tripura, makes it difficult to ascertain the introduction to the Brahmanical religious pattern in Tripura. It is also not known exactly when the Aryans penetrated to the domain of religion in Tripura. The fact that Buddhism flourished in different parts of Tripura from the early times has been attested by the discovery of various archaeological materials. A copper-plate inscription from Gunaighar proves and Buddhism flourished here sometimes before 507-508 A.D.[3] Similarly, different forms of Brahmanical religion, viz., Vaiṣṇavism, Śaivism and Śaktism were prevalent as early as seventh century A.D. A good number of Sūrya images, some of which measure about eleven feet high, have been recovered from the Pilāk Jolaibāḍi area of south Tripura and these objects belonged to a considerably early period. Such colossal figures of Sūrya from eastern India has not come to our notice yet.[4] Gaṇeśa was also a popular deity among the people of southern Tripura. Śaiva faith was also popular and ordinary phallic representation of the god, was more frequently worshipped. Only one image of Śiva an anthropomorphic form has been recovered from

Pilāk-Jolāibāḍi region. Perhaps north Tripura was the seat of Śaivism and orthodox Brahmanical preachers selected Unakoti hills of the region which was largely populated by the tribal people. Different types of Śiva images are found scattered over the Unakoti hills. Perhaps it was a Śaiva place of pilgrimage of north eastern India during tenth-eleventh centuries A.D.[5] In the pre-Māṇikya period, different religious sects of Buddhism and Brahmanism received royal patronage, as a result of which sculpting of such colossal images and the shrines could be installed. In Bengal the Khaḍga, the Chandras and the Pālas rulers were followers of Buddhism, while Vaiṇya Gupta, Śaśānka and early Sena rulers were Śaivas. The Varmans, the later Sena kings and Deva family were Vaiṣṇavas. Viśvarupa-sena and Keśava-sena were Parama-Sauras.[6] They have the equal zeal and veneration for other creeds. It may tentatively be assumed that in Tripura, the contiguous territory of Bengal, the same religious climate was prevalent and spread of sculptures in this area was a sure index of it. The same spirit of religious toleration was present in the Māṇikya period also. Moreover, in this period, the old religious faith and cults of the autochthonous people seems to have been given a new form and content through contact with the Indo-Aryan world of Brahmanism through Sanskrit and Bengali. Brahmanical spirit was also at work. But the old rites which have been harmonized with Brahmanical ones began to carry on with pomp and grandeur (e.g., worship of Chaturdaśadevatā). Buddhism perhaps lost the royal patronage of Tripura since fifteenth century A.D. because no royal record on this matter has yet been found. Rulers were devout worshippers of Śiva, Śakti, Viṣṇu and Chaturdaśadevatā which is evidenced by their coins and inscriptions. Temples were dedicated to Ambikā, Girijā, Viṣṇu, Śiva and Chaturdaśadevatā. In addition to these better known religious practices, there were groups who continued animistic and non-idolatic rituals. A hybrid type of religion, perhaps resulting from the admixture of Aryan and non-Aryan cults, flourished in late medieval period. A number of images belong to this period with peculiar iconography uncommon in Indian art history.

The sources of the religious history of Tripura show that while Tripura formed a part of the mainstream of the Indian religions, it also exhibited some distinctive features. In fact, believers of these atheistic systems were also to a great extent responsible for the introduction of various religious systems and practices prevalent in the region.

Buddhism

The north eastern region of the Indian sub-continent was closely associated with the life and career of Buddha. Tripura and its adjoining regions seemed to be an important centre of Buddhism since the period of Aśoka[7] and continued to be so for several centuries thereafter. In an inscription of the Maurya period found at Mahāsthān[8] mention is made of Puṇḍranagara and also of the *Chhavaggiyas*[9] who according to some scholars, belonged to a Buddhist sect. According to B.M. Barua[10], Buddhist sect had a centre in Puṇḍranagara as early as the Maurya period. No definite evidence has so far been produced about the prevalence of this faith on such an early period. The first archaeological record of Buddhism in Tripura is found in the form of an epigraph during the first decade of the sixth century A.D.

It is stated in an epigraph of the Gupta king, Vaiṇya Gupta that the king made donations in favour of Buddhist and Buddhist institutions in that region. His Gunaighar (Tippera district) inscription dated in the Gupta year 188 (508 A.D.)[11] records the gift of some land to a congregation of Buddhist monks (Śākyabhikṣu) residing in a monastery built by Mahārājā Rudradatta on whose request the grant was made. It consisted of 11 pāṭakas of khila land in 5 plots, in the village Kānteudaka in *Uttar-Maṇḍala,* as follows:

(1) 7 pāṭaka and 9 droṇavāpas (2) 8 droṇavāpas (3) 3 droṇavāpas (4) 30 droṇavāpas and (5) 1¾ pāṭakas. The gift was made to meet the cost of maintenance of the worship of the Buddha in the Āśrama Vihāra of Avalokiteśvara, its future repair, also expenses for the purchase of perfumes, flowers, lamps, incense etc. as well as to provide food, clothing, medicines and other necessaries for the resident monks. That Buddhism was quite active in the locality is shown by the reference to another monastery, called Rājā-Vihāra. Āchārya Jitasena, who was the head of the Vihāra (Vaihārika) had his residence close to the monastery.

The financial position of the monastery was thus sought to be made secure and stable through a proper utilization of the resources provided by the gift aiming, in fact, at the creation of a self-sufficient economy for the establishment concerned. It is probable that the monastery was assured of a regular supply of food and similar requirements out of the products of its estate. For other articles, perhaps part of the estate was distributed on suitable terms and conditions to artisans and manufactures to meet the requirements of the monastic establishments mentioned in the inscription. Local labour and skill were available in and near Gunaighar as indicated by the presence of carpenters and physicians referred to in the inscription wherever such grants were made in the area, with similar conditions attached to them, it was the resident Buddhist communities who had to look after the necessary economic arrangement for their maintenance. It further demonstrates that despite his own Śaiva persuasion as evidenced by the full-seal attached to his charter, the Gupta monarch, in keeping with his family tradition of religious toleration not only allowed the propagation of Buddhism in his kingdom but his royal patronage always helped the spread and growth of Buddhism in region.

The sixth century A.D., the Mahāyāna form of Buddhism, had found its way all over Tripura.[12] This is possibly due to the influence of Tantricism. It is known that with the introduction of Tantricism, the religion developed into highly esoteric tantric form. The two main branches of this Tantric Buddhism in the area were — Kālachakrayāna and Vajrayāna. A large number of sculptural representations — like Tārā, Heruka, Mañjusri, etc. have been discovered from this region. Hiuen Tsang who visited India in the first half of the seventh century A.D. referred to the kingdom of Samataṭa which included the major part of Vaṅga proper. According to his account, it had included within its political boundaries a part of the central Bengal in addition to the region of the Tippera district. During his visit of Bengal, he found in Samataṭa thirty Buddhist monasteries with 2000 brethren of the Sthavira School as well as a stūpa, the construction of which was traditionally attributed to Aśokarājā. Not far from it was a Saṅghārāma with an image of Buddha in it.[13] Hiuen Tsang further tells us that a line of Brāhamaṇa kings ruled in Samataṭa in the first half of the seventh century A.D. and that Śīlabhadra, the abbot of the Nālandā monastery belonged to this dynasty. He is said to have built a monastery about 20 li monastery south west of Guṇmati monastery.[14] The Brāhmaṇa family to which Śilabhadra belonged may have later adopted Buddhism. R.C. Majumdar holds that, "this Brahmanical royal dynasty seems to have been over thrown by a line of Buddhist kings whose names contained the word 'Khaḍga' as an essential element."[15]

The Buddhist Khaḍga rulers have left two copper-plates found at Āshrafpur,[16] 30 miles north east of Dacca, beside an inscription engraved on an image of Śarvānī at Deulbāḍi[17], 14 miles south of Comilla. The Āshrafpur plates were issued from the victorious head quarters at Karmānta identified by some with the modern village of Baḍkamta, 12 miles west of the town of Comilla.[18] I-tsing in his memories refers to Seng-chi who came to India by the southern sea-route and reached Samataṭa where he found Rājabhaṭṭa ruling over Samataṭa, he was Buddhist *upāsaka* who used to make every day a hundred thousand statues of the Buddha with earth and read hundred thousand *ślokes* of the *Mahāprajñāpāramitā-sūtra.* He also used to take out procession in honour of the Buddha, with an image of Avalokiteśvara at the front and make pious gifts. In his time, there were 4000 monks and nuns in the capital. "The Buddhist prince Rājarājabhaṭṭa, the son of Devakhaḍga of eastern Bengal, may be held to be identical with this Rājabhaṭa, who was ruling Samataṭa sometime before A.D. 671". The copper-plates referred to above give the genealogy of the khaḍgas mentioning khaḍgodyama, Jātakhaḍga, Devakhaḍga and Rājarāja or Rājarājabhaṭṭa. From one of the Āshrafpur plates we learn that king Devakhaḍga granted a piece of land measuring nine pāṭakas and ten drones to Ācharya Saṅghamitra, head of several Buddhist monastic establishments. Another Āshrafpur plate records a gift by prince Rājarāja comprising six pāṭakas and ten droṇas of land in favour of the monastery of Saṅghamitra. Both the charters begin with verses in praise of the Buddha on the Buddhist religion. Both the plates were written by the same clerk Puradāsa, a devout Buddhist. The messenger is also a Buddhist. The mound in which the plates were found marked the site of the monastery in whose favour the grant was made. There is sufficient evidence to show that all the kings of the Khaḍga dynasty were Buddhist.[19] Discovery of a number of Buddhist images from the villages around Baḍakamatā mound in the last quarter of the nineteenth century and a recent find of a beautiful image of Mārichī from a village only four miles south east of Baḍakamatā, prove undoubtedly its Buddhist character.

Another Buddhist dynasty connected with the some region was that of the Rātas, known from a copper-plate discovered at Kailan[20], near Comilla. The charter was issued in the 8th regnal year of Śridhāranarāta, called Samataṭeśvara i.e. lord of Samataṭa. It is recorded that the Mahāsāndhivigrahika Jayanātha approached the king for a grant of 4½ pāṭaka of land which he desired to dedicate to the *Bhagavat Tathāgataratna* (Buddha) or the *Ratna-traya* for the worship of the Buddha, the reading and writing of Buddhist religious texts and for provision for food, clothing and other necessaries for the *Ārya-Saṅgha* (Buddhist monks). The land donated was situated in Rankupottaka in the Nidhānikhabobbā subdivision of the Guptīnāṭana district, within the jurisdiction of the Kumārāmātya of Devaparvata, the Rāta capital, encircled by the river Kṣīrodā which is the modern Khira or Khirnai.[21]

The same region, more or less marked by Buddhist influences, is noted in a copper-plate grant issued from Devaparvata[22] on the southern end of the Maināmati hills by king Bhavadeva, son of Ānandadeva. The seal used in the charter resembles the Pāla and Chandra seals. Probably the pattern became popular after its use by the Deva kings. The upper part of the seal contains the emblem of the sacred wheel (*dharma-chakra*) with eight spokes, flanked by two deer. Below the wheel is the legend which reads : Śrī-Abhinava-(mṛgāṅka.)[23] King Bhavadeva is described in the charter as a *parmasaugata* i.e. a devout worshipper of the Buddha. It is recorded in the grant that Vibhūtidāsa approached Mahāsāmanta Nandadhara with a request to submit his prayer to the king. King Bhavadeva subsequently made a grant of 7½ pāṭaka of land in favour of the Ratnatraya of the Veṇḍamatī-Vihārikā which was the local Buddhist monastery of Veṇḍamati. Veṇḍamatī may be the name of the place or the monastery. The 7½ pāṭaka of land with udranga granted by in four different plots in the Peranāṭanaviṣaya, which are as follows — (1) 2½ pāṭaka in Vahaka-khaṇḍa in Veṇḍamatī; (2) I pāṭakas in Ekkarakoṭṭa (3) 2 pāṭaka in Mañjikkakoraka and (4) 2 pāṭakas in Koḍḍāvāra.

Two more grants of this dynasty have been discovered from the Śālvan Vihāra in the Lālmāi Maināmati ridge near Comilla.[24] One was issued by Ānandadeva, son of Viradeva and another bore the endorsement of Bhavadeva, son of Ānandadeva.[25] Not long after the regin of Bhavadeva, the dynasty came to an end, and the Samataṭa country passed to the Pālas.[26] From the evidence produced above it will appear that this region was a prominent centre of Buddhism. The available land grants were in most cases made in favour of Buddhist monasteries, which tended to strengthen the economic foundation of such organizations.

The existence of another Buddhist family in the region is revealed by a single copper-plate inscription discovered from the Bara-akhara temple in Chittagong.[27] Palaeographically it is datable to the ninth century. It is an incomplete land grant. The grant was made by a certain Kāntideva, the king of Harikelā from the city of Vardhamanāpura[28] in Harikela (Sylhet-Comilla Chittagong region). The record has disclosed the names of three successive generations: Bhadradatta, Dhanadatta and Kāntideva. The religious inclination of these rulers is mentioned as such : Bhadradatta, a devotee of Jina (Buddha), his son, Dhanadatta, versed in the Purāṇas and the *Rāmāyaṇa* and his wife, a princess named Vindurati, a devotee of Śiva, and their son, Kāntideva is a Buddhist. It is only Kāntideva who is given the title *Paramasaugata Parameśvara* and *Mahārājādhirāja*. Kāntideva's mother is described as mahābhūbhṛt Sutā.[29] The seal attached to the plate is of unique interest. The figure of the lion enshrined in a temple depicted on it, is supposed to stand for Buddha[30]. Some scholars are inclined to regard it as a Jaina symbol. But the title Paramasaugata used by Kāntideva shows that he was a Buddhist. Whether or not Kāntideva was related with Bhavadeva of Samataṭa has not yet been determined and in the absence of any detailed information about Kāntideva's reign or any other person of this family it has not been possible to reconstruct the history of Buddhism during the reign periods of Kāntideva and his predecessors.

Another independent dynasty that flourished in Tripura during the period of the Pāla supremacy deserves mention. It consisted of the rulers whose names end in Chandra. In fact, politically as well as religiously the Chandras occupy an important position in the annals of early medieval Tripura. Next to the Pālas, these Chandra rulers who may be placed between C. 825 A.D. to C. 1035 A.D. were staunch supporters of Buddhism.

A graphic picture of the religious faith of this dynasty is demonstrated in the epigraphic record in Śrī Chandra and his successors. Thus the Rāmpāl (near Dacca) plate of Śrī Chandra, bearing the *Dharmachakra* seal, opens with a verse in honour of Jina (i.e. Buddha), Dharma and also indirectly of *Saṅgha* and it then says : "His (i.e. Pūrṇa Chandra, the founder of the dynasty) son Suvarṇa Chandra .... became a follower of the Buddha."[31]

The information contained in the above extract is important since it clearly indicates that it was Suvarṇa Chandra, the second member of the family, who embraced Buddhism. In other words, Suvarṇa Chandra's father (and presumably also his other predecessors) were followers of Brāhmanical religion. In fact, none of the Chandra records contains any hint whatsoever as to the Buddhist affiliation of Pūrṇa Chandra. The Rāmpāl charter says that 'his name was mentioned on the foot stools of images, on pillars of victory, copper-plates etc.' From Suvarṇa Chandra onwards all the rulers were devoted Buddhists, as attested by the epithet, *Paramasaugata,* prefixed to the names of respective kings as well as by the *Dharmachakra* seal engraved on their copper-plate grants.

The first verse of the Rāmpāl plate describes Lord Buddha as "the unique receptacle of mercy" (*Karuṇaikapātram*) and the *Dharma* as 'the unique lamp of the world (*jagadekadīpah*). It further says that in consequence of the worship of Buddha and Dharma the entire noble-minded *Saṅgha* of monks transcends the series of continuous existence.[32] In other words, the *Saṅgha* can thus attain *Nirvāṇa.* The passage is thus essentially Mahāyāna in character.

All the six inscriptions of Śrī Chandra, discovered at different places of east Bengal such as Paschimbang,[33] Madanpur[34] and Dhulla[35], record the royal benefactions to individual Brāhmaṇas or *Maṭhas* (i.e. Brāhmanical institutions). The remaining inscriptions, hailing from Kedarpur and Edilpur, are incomplete and donees are unknown. The interesting point concerning these grants is that the king donated lands to the Brāhmaṇas or Brāhmanical institutions with invocation of Buddha and dedicated the same in the name of Lord Buddhabhaṭṭārika. This again proves that Śrī Chandra and his successors followed like the Pālas the age-old religious toleration. While in Rāmpāl charter the gift of land was made in favour of Śāntivārika or 'the priest in charge of propitiatory rites' on the occasions of Kotihoma ceremony, we find in the Dhulla copper-plate that the land-grant was made in favour of a similar Śāntivārika on the performance of a certain propitiatory rite called Adbhutasanti, during the Homa Chatushtaya or the Four Homas. Thus Śrī Chandra, though a Buddhist, used to take active part in Brāhmanical observances of this nature and this fact is thus of considerable importance in the present context. As regards Śri Chandra's benefactions to his own religious faith, no record testifying to the fact has so far come to light, but it is reasonable to believe that he patronised it considerably.

Only one land-grant of the reign of Kalyāṇa Chandra,[36] the son and successor of Śri Chandra, has come to light. It records the donation of land to a Brahmin Pandita. While it shows his religious catholicity, we are in the dark about his active support of his own faith.

The excavation at Lālmāi-Maināmati hills in the Maināmati region has yielded two copper-plates of Laḍaha Chandra[37]. It is the same region where the records of Bhavadeva have been discovered. Laḍaha Chandra, son and successor of Kalyāṇa Chandra, granted lands by these copper-plates in the name of Vāsudeva (Viṣṇu). Interestingly enough, it is also known from them that the Chandra king went to Varanasi and bathed many times in the Ganges and is said to have showered the rains of gold and spread spotless fame in all directions by his erudition and poetical genius. Thus Laḍaha Chandra, though a Buddhist (his plates give him the usual epithet Parama-Saugata and they bear the *Dharmachakra* seal as well), held Brahmanism in esteem and not only supported it but also like his grandfather occasionally followed Brāhmanical rites and rituals.

The records of Govinda Chandra, the son and successor of Laḍaha Chandra and the last king of this dynasty does not throw any light on the nature of the benefection towards Buddhism during his reign. His solitary copper-plate[38] discovered from the same excavated site at Maināmati shows that the grant was made in favour of *Nateśvarabhaṭṭāraka* i.e. Śiva. In this copper-plate hope is expressed that Brahma may bestow welfare on him, Viṣṇu may sustain his body and Indra may kill his enemies. Thus though Govinda Chandra is mentioned as a Parama-Saugata in this copper-plate, it appears that like his father and other predecessors, he had a distinct predilection for Brāhmanical religion.

The Buddhist Chandras were succeeded by the Varmans in this region who were Brāhmanical in their creed. In the Belava copper-plate of Bhojavarman[39] of this dynasty issued from Vikramapura, he is given the epithet Parama-Viṣṇava, containing a reference to the Viṣṇu Chakra-mudrā. Though the Varmans were Brāhmanical with the Vajrayogini inscription, the reign of Sāmalavarman records a gift of land in favour of a Buddhist temple of Prajñāpāramitā built by Bhīmadeva, noticed at Somapura in the village Vajrayogini which, according to some were situated in the district of Dacca.[40] It was the birth place of Dīpaṁkara, the great Buddhist scholar and saint.

After the fall of Deva dynasty the Tripuri tribe became powerful in hill Tripura and they gradually extended their hold in the plain lands of Tripura. Inscriptions and other archaeological evidences prove that Buddhism was the dominating religion in the plain lands of Tripura from the sixth century A.D. onwards. In the hill Tripura, it existed along with the Chākmās and Maghs tribes. Both tribes are strong followers of Buddhism. But Māṇikya royal family was a devotee of Brāhmanical religion. They had devotion to Brāhmanical Gods and Goddesses in their creed. They did not issue any land grant for Buddhism. The Rājmālā, a chonicle of the royal family hardly makes any notable description about Buddhism.[41]

The Buddhist Vihāra became an important religious and cultural centre in plain land of Tripura from the sixth century A.D. onwards. Vihāras have been a symbol of religious architecture in Buddhism. All the monasteries were centres of education and religion. But before the rise of Buddhism, Indian ascetics used to lead the wandering life of a Parivrājaka. Probably Brāhmanical ascetics sometimes lived at one place (*ekatra*) or at a fixed residence (*dhruvaśalā*) during the rainy season when it was difficult to move from place to place. In early Jaina literature there are references of fixed abodes for ascetics. Buddha realized that some arrangement for the residence of the monks was required specially during the rainy season and he advised his followers to live 'each according to the place where his friends acquaintances and intimate ones might like. This gave rise to 'Vassāvāsa' i.e. rain-retreat.' In course of time two types of Buddhist settlements came into existence — (1) the *āvāsa* in the country side and (2) the *ārāma* in or near a town. Both providing accommodation for congregations of fellow monks. The earliest avāsa was of a nature of a colony where the monks lived together, as described in the *Mahāvagga*. The *ārāma* literally means 'a pleasure ground'. When an *ārāma* was given to Buddhist monks permanently it was called a *Saṅghārāma* i.e. an *ārāma* belonging to a Sangha. Such residence (i.e. *Saṅghārāmas*) must have been meant for the accommodation of monks whose number was comparatively large and therefore different from a simple *ārāma*. Early Buddhist literature furnishes us with names of *Saṅghārāmas* (i.e. Vihāras) at Rājagriha, Vaiśāli etc.

The monastery at Gunaighar was a great centre of Buddhist learning around 507-508. A.D.[42] Gunaighar is a place near Comilla (Tippera district) where there was evidently an ancient Vihāra named Āśrama-Vihāra where an assembly of Buddhist monks (*Śākya-bhikṣu*) lived. The deity installed in this Vihāra was Avalokiteśvara.[43] In the neighbourhood there was another monastery known as the Rājā Vihāra. The names of these two Vihāras appear to be significant. The word '*āśrama*' means a hermitage, the abode of an ascetic or sometimes *bhikṣus*. It may not be proper to presume that the name 'Rājā' or king may have built as in case of it and so it was thus named. The inscription records the grant of several plots of land in favour of the Āśrama-Vihāra which was situated in populous locality of the Rājā Vihāra in the Tippera district. The boundaries with details and measurements of all the plots were given. From this Dr. B.C. Sen comes to the conclusion, that the localities indicated were inhabited by a thriving population, endowed with advantages of transport and communication and with Buddhist and Brāhmanical institutions flourishing side by side.[44]

One of the Āshrafpur plates refer to the monastery of Saṅghamitra and in another plate Saṅghamitra is described as the head of several Buddhist monastic establishments. In both the plates gift of land are recorded. We may presume that there were many monastic establishments near the victorious head quarter (*jaya-karmanta-viskat*) at Karmānta identified with the modern village of Baḍkamta, 12 smiles west of the town of Comilla (Tippera district)[45]. From Baḍkamta and its neighbouring villages a large number of Buddhist images were found, which prove the site to have been a Buddhist centre.[46] Saṅghamitra was the owner of at least one of the monasteries and was appointed head of several monasteries in the neighbourhood.

The inscription of Ranavankamalla Harikālatera,[47] dated Śaka 1141 (1219 A.D.) makes mention of a Buddhist monastery in the city of Paṭṭikera dedicated to the Goddess Durgoṭṭārā, a form of Tārā described in the *Sādhanamālā,* in whose honour the king made a grant of 20 dronas of land situated in the village named Bejakhaṇda in the city of Paṭṭikera, Tippera district. Paṭṭikera was a well known seat of Buddhism in earlier times. Its name occurs in a Cambridge Manuscript of the *Aṣṭasāhasrikā Prajñāpāramitā* dated 1015 A.D.[48] containing the picture of a sixteen armed goddess with the label Paṭṭikera Cundā-varabhavaue Cundā. She seems to have been a popular goddess in the region early in the 11th century A.D. The Burmese and Arākānese Chronicles, belonging to 11th and 12th centuries A.D. contain many references to the kingdom.[49] This kingdom lasted at least till the 13th century A.D. as proved from the above inscription of Harikeladeva. He may have made a grant of land in favour of this monastery, provided this identification is proved.

Cordier's catalogue refers to a Vihāra named Kanaka stūpa Vihāra which it located in Paṭṭikeraga (Paṭṭikeraka).[50] This Paṭṭikeraga had been identified by some scholars with the well known Paṭṭikerā in Tippera district.[51] Vinyaśrīmitra was a *bhikṣu* attached to this monastery.[52] In the same passage Cordier also refers to Yaśobhadra of Kashmir and the region of Vaṇgabhūmipati Śrīmad Haribrahmadeva. This name resembles that of Harikeladeva. It is interesting to note the similarities in respect of some important personal names and places such as Haribrahmadeva and Harikeladeva; Paṭṭikeraka and Paṭṭikerā etc. It may be possible that the unnamed monastery in Paṭṭikerā to which Harikeladeva made a gift of land may be identical with the Kanaka-stūpa Vihāra mentioned by Cordier.

One of the largest centres of Buddhistic culture of early mediaval Tripura remained under the mounds Lālmāi-Maināmati hill range of the Tippera district, five or six miles to the west of Comilla town lies the Maināmati-Lālmāi ridge.[53] The range was a prominent centre of Buddhism. The prevalence of the Buddhist Monastic establishment is known from the discovery of various archaeological objects — viz., ancient structures of bricks, richly decorated with Terracotta Plaques and ornamented bricks, images of Buddhist Gods and Goddesses etc.[54] Recent excavations and explorations have thrown light on the spread and prevalence of Buddhism in various parts of the area.

Śālban Vihāra — Śālbanpur mound have revealed remains of a 550 feet square Buddhist monastery, which was renamed Śālban Vihāra due to its proximity to the sal forest in the west.[55]

The big monastery, consisting of 115 monastic cells, was built around a spacious courtyard with a cruciform shrine in the centre. The monastery was approached from the mouth by 174 feet long and 3½ feet wide brick-paved path and entered through a 74 feet wide gate way. There is an entrance hall (measuring 32' x 23') from where a flight of steps lead to the inside of the monastery courtyard. The entrance hall is flanked on the both sides by two guard rooms followed by the monastic cells.

The boundary wall of the monastery which also serve as the back wall of the monastic cells is still six feet high and 16½ feet thick. The cells, separated from each other by 5½ feet thick walls, were provided with 3½ feet wide door passages which opened to a 8½ feet wide verandah. The door passages were provided with wooden doors secured on iron hinges. The cells are almost uniform in size, each measuring 12' x 12' on an average with the exception of a few rectangular cells, the largest of which measures 16½ feet by 10 feet (cell no. 29). The central shrine is also square in shape, the sides measure 80 feet and stands 12 feet above the ground level. There are a few steps which led to its sanctuary. The original structure of the central shrine was built on a large scale, resembling in plan a great cross with chapels built in the projecting arms, each containing a bronze image of the Buddha. The shrine has a circumambulatory passage. This chapel, according to tradition was meant for the worship of Haḍi-Pa, the guru of Gopī Chandra and his mother.' The cells had fire places and most of the cells contained niches where they kept images and oil-lamps. Besides, brick alters were discovered in some cells for images.[56] In one of the cells, a bronze image of seated Padmapani on a lotus throne was found. The image is 3½ inches high. Household objects and other antiquities were found in all cells.[57] At the north-west side of the Śālban Vihāra, a small shrine has been unearthed. The purpose of this construction is unknown. In addition to the structural remains, the most important and significant discoveries are the inscribed copper-plates, coins, caskets, seals, pottery, terra-cotta pieces, gold ornaments, silver ingots and other utensils etc.

There is no specific evidence about the authority of this Vihāra, although a copper-plate bearing the name of Bhavadeva and belonging to the first phase of occupation makes us to believe Bhavadeva's authority over this monastery.

Ānandarājā's Palace

A big mound was excavated in the Maināmati-Lālmāi region, which represented a monastery, each of its sides having the length of a furlong. It was located about one and half mile south of Kuṭila Mura and four miles to the south-west of Comilla.[58] This mound stands at the eastern side of the cantonment road and is hardly a mile north from Koṭbari, Comilla.[59] The local people knew it by the name of Ānandarājā's palace. B.C. Sen suggests that Ānandadeva, possibly the founder of the monastery, may be identified with king Ānandadeva, father of Bhavadeva of Devaparvata.[60] Two hundred yards east of the palace was a big pond known as Ānandarājā's *dighī*. Many antiquities were discovered at this excavated site including images of Buddha, Padmapani etc. Ramachandran concludes : 'Ānandarājā's palace mound in Maināmati was definitely a monastery, probably the renowned Paṭṭikeraka monastery itself and the coin in question was a symbolic issue of this.' But it appears that the two were not identical, as they have different names by which they were distinguished from each other.

Bhojarāja's palace — Bhojarāja's palace is situated half a mile south of Ānandarājā's palace. The ruin represents a large monastic site. Its area is about 400 square feet and it is 15 feet high. In appearance it resembles the Ānandarājā's palace with a small mound in the centre. It is thirty feet high. There is a square temple with massive walls and with 'its basement profusely decorated with carved plaques and ornamental bricks.' The approach to the monastery was from the north where there is a gate.[61] The discovery of six feet square chambers in the centre suggests that the 'central structure may have been composed of box-like chamber as at Medh'. The ruins are made of bricks of various sizes,[62] terra-cotta plaques with interesting carving, pottery etc.

Kutila Mura

Kutila Mura site is located about three miles north of Śālban Vihāra. The entire area is enclosed by recessed panels. On top of the hillock, within the enclosure, three stūpas are found side by side on a common plinth. These stūpas are surrounded by other stūpas and structures spread over an area, measuring about 280 feet from north to south and about 225 feet from east to west. The main stūpas are approached from the east by a wide staircase that ascends in three stages across the massive boundary wall and leads to three rectangular entrance halls. The dimension of northern hall could not be accurately measured due to its highly dilapidated condition. The southern hall measures 37'-9" x 51'-6" and the central one 45'-7" x 55'-5". Behind the halls are the three stūpas in north south alignment. The square base of the stūpas are on a common plinth and each measures 39'-9", 36'-10" and 47'-7" from north to south. The square bases support circular drums and hemispherical domes. The central stūpa is still 10 feet high from the plinth. The three stūpas possibly represent the Buddhist Trinity or the Three jewels i.e., the Buddha, Dharma, and Saṅgha and thus form an unique group of monuments rarely met elsewhere in the sub-continent.

The ground plan of the central stūpa is in the shape of a *Dharmachakra* or the Wheel of the Law. The hub is represented by a deep central shaft and the spokes by brick wall which have formed eight cells or box-chambers. From these cells a number of broken pieces of stone sculptures of soft grey stone have been salvaged. These depict, in high relief, figures of the Buddha and Bodhisattvas stead on lotus throne and attended by lay worshippers. Hundreds of miniature clay votive stūpas containing minute terracotta seals, inscribed with the Buddha and the Saṅgha are made of solid brick masonry, each with a deep central shaft which also contained a large number of clay miniature stūpas and terracotta jealings. The outer face of the drums of these stūpas are relieved with a number of small corbelled niches, intended perhaps as receptacles for oil lamps.[63]

On the west of the Triratna stūpas, remains of nine brick stūpas have been exposed. Of these nine, seven smaller stūpas are built on a common platform and aligned in north-east to south-west direction, on both ends of this group of stūpas there are the remains of two slightly bigger stūpas. Remains of another stūpa was also found near the south-east corner of the southern most stūpa of the Tri-ratna group. Superstuctures of these stūpas are completely missing. In plan they are round with square bases ranging in size from 27 square feet to approximately 15 square feet.[64] From inside the deep shaft in the centre of these stūpas a number of miniature clay stūpas were also recovered.

Two of the stone sculptures found inside the stūpa-shaft, representing the *Dharmachakra,* bear some inscriptions on their pedestals. Palaeographically they may be dated around seventh century A.D. and as such the Tri-ratna stūpas may also be tentatively dated to that period. It should, however, be noted that the shrines of Kutila Mura show three distinct phases of repairs and rebuildings. In the first phase, there were probably two entrances, almost in the middle of the eastern wal! and the other near the northern end of the same wall was pushed backwards and the only entrance was provided in the middle of the eastern wall and the other near the northern end of the same wall. In the second phase the eastern boundary wall was pushed backwards and the only entrance was provided in the middle. The three oblong halls in front of the stūpas were also extended in the second period. These are enclosed within circumbulatory passages. There is also an antechamber at the back of the southern most hall which indicate that the halls also served the purpose of shrines and images of Buddha or Bodhisattvas were once installed therein for worship. Remains of the third period of the shrines are visible only in the oblong hall infront of the middle stūpa and in the eastern boundary wall. A number of fireplaces discovered at the back of the main stūpas probably belonged to the latest phase of the shrines.[65] Functions of these fire places could not be explained satisfactorily. Perhaps those were built later for cooking food for large gathering. From the remains of different periods we may conclude that the shrines at Kutila Mura were in active use for a long period, beginning from seventh century to at least thirteenth century A.D.

Rup Ban Mura

The mound is located south of Ānandarājā's palace. Northern fringe of the mound meets the Comilla - Kālir Bazar Road in a gentle slope but the other three sides are steep. The mound is about 60 feet high from the metalled road. Though bricks were robbed from this site during the second world war a square monastery measuring 400x400 feet enclosing a 47x41 feet cruciform central shrine with re-entrant angles and recessed corners, richly decorated with terracotta plaques and mouldings could be detected.[66]

During the war, the military contractors disturbed two structures here, but a couple of others escaped spoilation. Probably, a number of ancient structures are now lying hidden under. During the preliminary survey by Ramachandran a large number of terracotta plaques were recovered in lose condition and many more were seen *insitu* in the basement of the exposed structures. The plaques were found depicted with scenes drawn from the life of the people, nature and many other subjects from popular folk tales and Jataka stories. In addition to the terracotta plaques, an excellent group of terracotta corner brackets and ornamental bricks were also gathered from here. Unfortunately these are now lost. It is also reported that seven pots, containing hundreds of bronze votive images of Buddha, were discovered from the site by the brick robbers. Only 13 of these image could be recovered from them. These tiny images, only about 2 inches high represent Buddha in earth-touching attitude. "The iconographic details and workmanship of these images" to quote Late Ramachandran, "are similar to those of the inscribed votive bronzes" recovered from the Jhewary in Chittagong District, to the ninth eleventh centuries A.D. The underlying structures are seen to be coeval in date with the antiquities recovered so far.[67]

Koṭbāri Mura

This mound is located about a few furlong west of the Rupban Mura. In c. 1803, the site was first detected during the construction of the Comilla-Kālirbazar Road and erroneously identified as the remains of a fort.[68] It appears to be a large monastic site. After digging, ruins of a Pyramidal temple 'with re-entrant corners of walls and surrounded by rows of cells' is visible. The outer area appears to be 100 square yards square and the presence of a central shrine in the centre, is about 33⅓ square feet. The entrance was through the northern wall. From here were discovered large sized bricks, plaques, pottery etc.[69]

Rupban Kanya Vihāra

Rupban Kanya's palace mound is located south of Ānandarājā's palace.[70] It contains traces of an extensive brick structure and enclosing walls, also 'a stone cubical pillar base showing the design of a *caitya* window on each side was found in the centre of the mound suggesting the existence of a stone *maṇḍapa* or shrine'. The mound measured

400 x 400 square feet and 15 feet high. The ruin probably represented a monastery and may have been named after a princess of the royal family. The first part of the name may be that of a beautiful princes Rupban while Kanya in Bengali means a daughter.[71]

Charpatra Mura and other sites

Some scholars regard the Maināmati National cemetery and the Army bungalow as remains of monastic sites.[72] Reference may also be made to the Vaiṣṇav Mura mounds. Although the name is purely Hindu it is regarded as a Buddhist site. In this ruin a large tank is noticed, it measures approximately 2000' x 1000'. On the northern side of this tank are the remains of a large monastery which still awaits exploration[73]. Besides these, there were many other mounds and shrines, which are not Buddhist in nature. Among them mention may be made of Charpatra Mura. At the top there is a shrine, dedicated to Laḍaha-Mādhavadeva. From this site four inscribed copper-plates were recovered, three belonged to the Chandras and one to Viradharadeva[74]. All these plates transfer land to God Śri Laḍaha-Mādhava. This name is not heard of before but it may be inferred that it is not a Buddhist God.

Caṇḍi Mura

An important site is Caṇḍi Mura named after goddess Caṇḍi. It is located two miles south east of Rupban Mura and this is also a very high and extensive mound 60 feet high and about 500 x 200 yards in extent. Two brick temples stand on the top, one for the worship of Caṇḍi[75] and the other for Śiva. At the eastern foot of this mound lies a tank.[76] Two images of black basalt were recovered from the tank and are worshipped in the temple of Caṇḍi. One of the images represents Mañjuvara (a Mahāyānist pantheon) and the other was Sūrya, a Hindu deity. Both the deities belonged to the later Pāla period. It is interesting to find the worship of a Buddhist deity in a Hindu temple originally built for a Hindu Goddess, Caṇḍi. Not only that, but both the deities, Mañjuvara and Sūrya were worshipped in the same temple. From this it appears that the site was originally dominated by the Hindus but subsequently Buddhism became predominant. Such instances are not rare in our history. Secondly, in course of time, the difference between the two religions waned away and ultimately people of both the religions began to worship all gods as one.

A large number of sculptures are collected from the adjacent villages of Maināmati-Lālmāi hills. The image of Heruka, Tārā, Mañjuvara, and Mārichī, are the most important sculptures of tantrika Buddhism. These sculptures reveal a gradual change in form of Mahāyāna Buddhism in Tripura in 7th - 8th centuries A.D.

Image of Heruka

This black stone image of Heruka, measuring 3'-4" x 2'-0" was collected from the village Lajair under police station Kachua, District Comilla. He is depicted dancing with his left leg upon a corpse, while the right raised on the left thigh. He wears a necklace of 22 human skulls joined by entrails. His face with fierce looking eyes and bared teeth is terrible to look at and the right hand of the image is missing. In his left hand he holds a human skull containing wine.[77] On his left shoulder he bears a *Khatvaṅga* with a fluttering banner attached to it and placed against his breast like a sacred thread. His headgear is decorated with five skulls and the hair arranged upwards in the form of a crown containing a Dhyani Buddha Aksobhya. As mentioned earlier the right hand of the image including some portions of the slab is broken and missing. Hence, it is not possible to know what he was holding in his right hand and how many figures are lost. However, in its present condition the god is surrounded by six female attendants. The uppermost female figure is in *Ardhaparayanka mudrā* with raised sword in her right hand and a stūpa in the left hand. The lower one, standing in the same pose, holds a *Vajra* and a *Khatvaṅga* in her right and left hands respectively. Opposite to this figure on the right side of Heruka, is depicted a female figure in *Tri-Vikarama* pose with *Aṅkusha* in her right and a skull and *Khatvaṅga* in her left hand. The pedestal is also decorated with three female figures, the middle one being an archer shooting an arrow.

Heruka is one of the most popular gods of the tantric Buddhists. He is regarded as protector against all worldly evils. In *Sādhanāmālā,* Heruka is described in various forms in different names and a regular tantra is devoted to his worship. In our country Heruka image is very rare. So far we know there are only two images found both in Comilla district, and one is preserved in the Mainămati Museum while the other in the Dacca Museum.

Image of Tārā

This two handed 5'-6" inches high (breadth of the panel 1'-9" inches) Tārā in sand stone was collected from Lajair of Kachua P.S. in Comilla district. Though greatly affected by weather, the image is still remarkable for its graceful, tall and slim figure. The Tārā, standing in *tribhaṅga* pose, holds a half-blown lotus in her left hand and keeps the right hand slightly raised in *Varada Mudrā.*[78]

Mañjuvara

The image of Mañjuvara in black stone (2'-1" x 1'-4") was collected from the old zaminder house of Sacha, P.S. Matlab, district Comilla. It is in a good state of preservation, except that the back slab is broken and missing from above the arms of the seated deity. The nose, point of the chin, top of the crown and fingers of the hands are also damaged.

The image of the god has two hands and is seated in *lalitasana* on the back of a roaring lion with upturned face. He keeps his two hands infront of the chest but the mudrā can not be properly identified due to the damaged condition of the hands and figures. According to the *Sādhanāmālā,* he would be in the *Dharmachakra mudrā.* Position of the hands in this mutilated image also suggests that mudrā. The other identifiable attribute of the god, a book on a lotus is also missing with the missing parts of the stela, but the stalk of the lotus is partially visible near the left arm of the god.

The god wears rich ornaments such as anklets, bracelets, armbands, kuṇḍalas and necklace of three chains. A three pointed crown, the top of which goes up in the shape of *karanda mukuta,* is partially broken. Upper body of the god is completely bare. The lower garment, a short dhuti which reaches only up to the knee, is kept in position on the waist by the waist band.

The folds of the dhuti are shown by incised lines of the thighs. The navel and the eyes are treated summarily. There is no attempt to show the naturalistic movement of the lion below. The pedestal below the lion is simple, semi-circular with only one projection in the centre.

On this projection appear three devotees, one with a *pattabasha* and the other two with folded hands. On either side of this projected portion, the pedestal is decorated with small incised flower. The backslab also shows simple decoration.

This interesting sculpture was executed in the period when Buddhists in Bengal, particularly the tantrika Buddhists, introduced many new gods and goddesses and is rarely met in the flourishing age of Buddhism. These new imports into the folds of divinities have a great similarities with the gods and goddesses of Nepal and Tibet. The image of Mañjuvara[79] is not common in Tripura and Bengal.

Image of Mārichi

It is regarded as the Śakti or counterpart of the *Dhyānī Buddhya Vairochana*. This eight handed blackstone image, measuring 2'-4" x 1'-1", has three faces and six eyes. Her left face is a hideous pig-face. The four right hands hold the thunderbolt, the elephant goad, the arrow and the needle, while the left three hands hold Aśoka leaf ending in a bunch of flower, a bow, a noose and the fourth raised in *tarjani mundrā*[80]. *Dhyānī Buddhya Vairochana* is crowned with a tiara. Inside a *Caitya,* the goddess sits on chariot with the right leg bent and the left stretched. The chariot is drawn by seven pigs and driven by *Rāhu,* the fabulous deveuner of the sun and the moon at the time of eclipses. The spire of a Caitya is depicted at the top of the stela from the two ends of which sprout forth two luxuriant branch of Aśoka. The image was collected from village pior of Comilla district.

Pilāk Vihāra

There is yet enough scope of study as regads the Pilāk Vihāra which was situated at Belonia in South Tripura, locally it is known as Pilāk Pāthar. The ancient mounds of this region, situated in a low-lying area, are now being largely converted into agricultural fields and homestead lands. In course of these operations, many antiquities including stone and metal sculptures, terracotta plaques and sealings have come to light. They may be ascribed to the seventh to twelfth centuries A.D. and have got a close stylistic affinity with those recovered from Maināmati culture complex and Chittagong. Pilāk yields monumental sculptures in stone and statuettes in metal affiliated to Brahmanism and Buddhism. On the evidence of the mounds still found at Pilāk we know that this holy place was a Mahāyāna Buddhist centre during the eighth and ninth centuries. This Vihāra is infested with various mounds, icons of Buddhist and Hindu deities and ruins of temples. A number of gold coins, terracotta temples, plaques and sealings with the depiction of the stūpa and the Buddhist creed have been found here.[81] Not only that, a large number sculptures mainly statues of Buddha, Avalokiteśvaras, Chundā were discovered from the area.

In bronze, the most notable example is the image of Avalokiteśvara, about 14 cm in height and badly corroded, was found from Pilāk Jolaibāḍi region of south Tripura.[82] Bedecked in valayas armlets a short *hāra* ear-ornaments and high *jaṭā-mukuṭa*, the Bodhisattvā with a broad face, is standing with a slight flexion on the pericarp of a lotus resting above a plain pedestal. While his right palm displays *Vara-mudrā,* the slightly raised left holds the stalk of a lotus. With a beaded border edged by tongues of flames at intervals, the long halo with a semicircular top is crowned by an ornate triangular motif. The image is ascribable to about the ninth century A.D.[83]

One important stone image was found from Jolaibāḍi area and is woshipped in a modern temple called Vāsudev-bāḍi. The image is three headed, six armed and standing in *ālīḍha* posture, with the left leg bent at the knee and right leg stretched. The upper left hand holds a bow, the corresponding right bearing an arrow. The natural left palm is against the chest, presumably displaying *tarjani,* it holds a noose. Attributes in other hands are defaced beyond recognition. The top of the back-slab is semicircular. The height of the visible portion of the image is 43 cm. the width being 29 cm., while the nose of the image is inlaid with gold and the eyes in silver in recent years, a protruding tongue is a modern addition. The body of image is abraded and practically defies correct identification, though one feels tempted to identify it with Mārīchī. The *Dharmokosha Saṁgraha* of Amṛitānanda describes a six-armed variety of the images of Mārīchī, in which the three headed goddess is stated to have in her right hands an arrow, a thunder bolt and an elephant goad and in the left hands a bow, a bell and noose.[84] Numerous standing and seated images of Buddha of the medieval period have been discovered at different places in south Tripura. These icons indicate great popularity of image worship.

On the eastern slope of Pilāk lies, partly buried, is a large sandstone image of a two-armed *Bodhisattva.* The tall and slim figure is standing with a slight flexion on a *Viśva-padma* above a plain pedestal. The damaged right palm was presumably in *vara-mudrā,* while the left palm (broken) holds the stalk of a flower which, in its damaged state, is unlike a conventional lotus. The features of the face are lost. Against the stupi-shaped coiffure is possibly the figure of a *Dhyani* Buddha. Standing on *Viśva-padmas* rising above the pedestal are Tārā on the dexter and Hayagrīva on the sinister, both having their individual halo with a semicircular top carved out to the back-slab. Displaying *vara-mudrā* with her right palm, the two armed Tārā carries in her left hand the stalk of an *utpalā* while the principle pair of hands of the four armed pot bellied Hayagrīva is foloed in *añjalī,* the upper right is *Vandanābhinayī,* the object in the corresponding left being uncertain. The presence of these two attending deities would indicate the identification of the Boddhisattva with Avalokiteśvara. On either side of the head is a stūpa with a cylindrical drum, a somewhat shouldered dome, a squarish harmikā and a chhatra crowned by a conical finial. Above each of these two stūpas is vidyādhara flying through clouds. Over the head of the Bodhisttva is an umbrella. The top of the back slab, is 2m. 88cm., the maximum and minimum widths being 1m 37 cm. and 1m 16 cm respectively. Of fairly good workmanship, the image is ascribable to above the ninth century A.D.

Another image of Avalokiteśvara of about the same age, is collected from the same slope of the Pilāk mound[85]. The stone cut of which this image was fashioned appears to have been of two layers, superimposed one above the other. The weathered upper layer (Coarse-grained), about 3 cm. thick, has mostly disappeared exposing the smooth comparatively fine grained, greyish core. Originally, the image appears to have been a good one with tall physignomical frame. The features of the face have completely been lost. With right hand in *Vara-mudra,* the Bodhisattva, standing in *samapada,* holds with his left hand (forearm missing) the stalk of a full blown lotus (details lost). On the dexter of the Bodhisattva, near his right leg, is possibly Tārā (bust exfoliated) standing with an inconspicuous flexion on a *Viśva-padma* and holding the stalk of an *utpala* with the left hand, the right palm being on the waist. The corresponding figure by the side of the left leg of the Bodhisattva represents the pot-bellied dwarfish Hayagriva standing also with a flexion. The right hand is *vandanābhinayī,* the left being on the waist; there appear to be two more arms. On either side of the head of the Bodhisattva is a stūpa with a moulded base, a cylindrical drum, an elongated hemispherical dome, a necak-like member and a *chhatra* crowned by a thick finial. Above each stūpa is a flying *vidyādhara* with a garland in hand. The back-slab is shaped like an elongated horseshoe and gradually narrows down at the base. The height is 1 m 76 cm., the maximum width being 95 cm.

Another large sand stone image of Buddha was found from Syamsundara Āśrama Tilla of Pilāk. It is standing in *sama-pada*[86] on a lotus above a plain pedestal. The image is badly mutilated and the head is missing. While the shoulders and chest are disproportionately broad, the long legs are rather slim. The left hand of Buddha is pendant by his left side. That the right hand (fore-arm missing) did not hang is apparent from the fact that the portion of the back-slab immediately below the broken end of the arm is finished and the broken end is thicker suggesting a bend. It appears thus the right palm displayed *abhaya mudrā.* The halo, relieved against the back-slab is slightly pointed at the crown. From the top of the halo rise four shoots and the stick ending in an umbrella. On either side of the halo is a *Vidyādhra* with a garland flying through clouds. Below the *Vidyādhara* on the sinister is a stūpa with a cylindrical drum, a hemispherical dome, a squarish *harmikā,* a *chhatra* and a finial with curved corners, the back-slab, broad near the top and narrow near the bottom, is blunt but pointed at the crown. It is 2 m 61 cm high (excluding the inconspicuous tenon), the maximum available width being 1 m 14 cm.

Two more images of Buddha are collected from this Pilāk region. Of them, one[87] is made of coarse grained sandstone and it is finer of the two. While the modelling of the body is proportionate and sensuous, the face, somewhat rubbed, shows the clam and contemplative expression. Bearing the imprint of the later Gupta artidiom, the image does not appear to be later than the ninth century A.D. The entire right arm along with the adjoining part of the back-slab is missing. In the left palm is the hem of garment. By the side of the left leg of

Buddha is the two-armed dwarfish Hayagriva standing with his left leg bent and the right stretched. His hair is arranged in a large bun on the crown of the head. While his right palm holds a staff, the left rests on the left thigh. Behind him is a halo with a semi-circular top. By the left side of the head of Buddha is a miniature stūpa with a moulded base, a drum with a top moulding, an elongated hemispherical dome, a low *harmikā* and a thick *Yaṣhti*. The height of the back-slab with an arched top is 1 m 18 cm, the width being 46 cm.

The other image, is shown standing in *sama-pada* Buddha, holds with his left hand the hem of the *sanghāti,* the right palm possibly displaying *abhaya-mudrā.* On either side of the broken head is a stūpa with a moulded base, a cylindrical drum, a doine and a finial. Above each stūpa is a flying *vidyādhara.* The backslab, with curved corners, is broader near the top. It is 1 m. 11 cm high, the maximum width being 72 cm.

An image of the goddess Chundā made of sand-stone was found at Pilāk and is now worshipped in the Rājeśvari Āsram at Muhuripur. It is interesting not only for its imposing size but for representing Chundā in her eighteen-armed form. The height of the visible portion is 1m. 55cm., the width at the visible part of the base is 79 cm. The lowest part along with the tenon is covered by masonry. Unfortunately the image is highly abraded and suffered badly from peeling. Being worshipped it is being daily smeared with oil and vermilion and covered with ornaments made of glazed metal foils. It is also affected by soot arising out of kerosene-lamp. Some parts of the limbs and the face have been crudely restored by the Sevaits. All these have affected the image to such an extent that hardly anything is left of its original grandeur. The goddess is seated in *Vajra-Paryankāsana* on a *Viśva-Padma.* The principal pair of hands is near the chest, the mudrā being somewhat resembling *dharma chakra mudrā* or *chundā-mudrā.* One of the right hands is in *Varamudrā* on the right knee, the corresponding left one, on the left knee, possible fearing a flask, these two palms are partly renovated. Another right hand holds along a sword or a spear and one of the left hands carries the stalk of a lotus. Other attributes are beyond recognition. In the upper part of the back-slab which with curved top corners is inconspicuously pointed at the crown, are defaced figures, possibly of five *Dhyānī*-Buddhas. The accretions and the darkness prevailing in the room where the image has been enshrined stood in the way of our proper study of the image.

The occurrence of a multiarmed image of Chundā in a Pilāk area is quite natural in view of the great celebrity of the sixteen armed image of Chundā of (Paṭṭikera area around Maināmati Lālmāi range in district Comilla of Bāṅglādesh) which is not at a great distance from Pilāk area and the kingdom of which in its hey day might have extended its sphere in the adjoining parts of the present Tripura including Sonāmurā and Belonia subdivisions. As is well-known the latter image was illustrated in one of the miniatures of Cambridge University Library Manuscript of the Ashṭasāhaśrikā Prajñāpāramitā (no. Add 1643), dated in the year 1015 A.D., under the caption '*Paṭṭkera chundāvarabhavane Chundā*'. The Pilāk image is the only one, so far noticed, found in the area near the Maināmati-Lālmāi range. The miniature is sixteen armed, while the Pilāk image has eighteen arms as in the stone image of Chundā from Niyamatpur (District-Rajshahi)[88].

Avalokiteśvara, the god of love and compassion, was a favourite god of Tripura and in it the traces of the grace and attributes of Viṣṇu and Śiva of Hinduism are discernible.[89] Avolokiteśvara was popular in Mahāyāna and Vajrayāna sects of Buddhism. Made of sandstone of poor quality, the image is body corroded and the stone is coming out in flakes. The Bodhisttva with a slim figure is standing with an inconspicuous flexion on a small *Viśva-padma* above a pedestal. His right arm is entirely missing, while the left held a lotus-stalk, most of which has disappeared. From the pedestal have issued two small lotuses, each supporting a standing figure. The one of the sinister is the pot-bellied Hayagriva with straight hairs. With his left palm resting on the thigh, he holds in his right hand a staff. The height of the extent part of the image (possibly of the ninth century A.D.) is 1 m 18 cm. and the maximum width is 54.6 cm.

Another stone slab found in Pilāk area, is square at the base and circular at the top. On the top surface are two depressions, marking the soles of the feet. The side of the circular part is relieved with a row of rising petals, while at its base and carved on the flat surface of the square part is another row of petals, the two rows present the appearance of a *Viśva-padma,* the soles being on the pericarp. Bored in the soles are tow sockets in a straight line. The front side of the square part bears in the centre an eight petalled flower within a squarish compartment, while at the two corners is a squatting lion with a single head (at the extreme corners) and two bodies (one on the front side and the other on the adjoining side). These two sides beyond the body of the lions also contain an eight-petalled flower within a squarish compartment. The back side is left unfinished. The slab is 24 cm. high and 48 cm square at the base.

A badly defaced image (perhaps Buddhist)[90] was found at the Pilāk area[91]. The image, possibly four armed, is seated in *lalitāsana* on a *Viśva-padma.* Both the lower palms rest on knees, the right one displaying *vara mudrā.* The top corners of the back-slab, which gradually narrows down towards the bottom are curved. The height of the image is 43 cm, the maximum width being 21.6 cm.

Another Avalokiteśvara image, with tall and slim body, standing on a lotus resting on a pedestal (buried), was found in same area (Pilāk region). With the stalk of a lotus in his left hand, the Boddhisattva[92] wearing the *jaṭā-mukuṭa,* displays *varada mudrā* with his right hand. Over the elongated halo is an umbrella, while on a either side of the head is a stupa possibly resting on a lotus, the stalks of which descend down. By the sides of the legs of the Bodhisattva are Tārā (on the sinister) and Hayagriva are in *añjalī* pose and the upper left *Vandanābhinayī,* the object in the upper right being indistinct. The back-slab is semicircular at the top. While the face is retouched, the eyes and nose of the figure are coated with silver. The height of the visible portion of the image (of about the ninth century A.D.) is 1 m 70 cm., the width being 70 cm.

The terrific god Vajrahumkara is a deity of the *Akshobhyakulā.* A stone image of Vajrahumkara[93] was found somewhere in Tripura and is now housed in the Royal Palace at Agartala. He stands in *Pratyāliḍa* pose on a double petalled lotus. He is three faced and six-armed. His two hands hold *ghaṇṭa* and a *vajra* and are locked in *Vajrahumkara Mudrā.* The top most right hand holds a sword and other hands are not clear. It is datable to the early medieval period.[94]

Another terrific god Hevajra is associated with *Akshobhya* and in him one finds resemblance with the terrific aspect of Śiva. A fine image of Hevajra, Saktibirahita, found at Dharmanagar in north Tripura is of great inconographic interest.[95] The image has a thin coating of gold. The god is shown standing in *Ardha-paryaṅka-Nṛtyāsana* pose. On left, the plams of the five hands are missing. He has eight heads and sixteen hands, which carry skull-caps containing various animals and a deity. Miniature dancing figures of eight goddesses are placed in eight directions round the god. This image belongs to the eleventh century A.D.

The monasteries of the Maināmati Lālmāi range, were close to one another, forming a connected group in the neighbourhood of the Śālban Vihāra which seems to have enjoyed a status of central importance from the historical stand point as one of the earlier Buddhist institutions in ancient Tripura. The historical importance of this region is shown by the discovery of some valuable antiquities including copper-plates, coins, terracotta, seals etc. in the different mounds. As early as the sixth century A.D. Vaiṇyagupta of the Imperial Gupta dynasty, was the first to have made a grant in favour of a Buddhist monastery in this part of Bengal. His grant to a congregation of Buddhist monks recorded in a copper-plate discovered from Guniaghar, a village in the district of Tippera in the neighbourhood of the Śālban Vihāra and his association with this region as indicated by a newly discovered plate of the same king is significant, the establishment of the Āśram-Vihāra referred to in the Guniaghar grant shows the important part he played in the course of Buddhism in the locality. He may have imported the idea of building big monastic establishments from Nālandā and it was he who may have been the first to select the site and put the idea into effect. In course of time other monasteries were constructed with the help of royal patronage in the neighbourhood (namely the Rājā Vihāra, monastery of Saṅghamitra, Vendmati Vihārikā etc.). Side by side, big monasteries were also constructed as mentioned in connection with our account of Maināmati Lālmāi region. The Buddhist monarchs of the Maināmati Lālmāi region were convenient and suitable for the purpose of creating impressive centre of religious culture and tradition which became dominant during the reigns of Vaiṇyagupta and some of the rulers belonging to the Khaḍga, the Rāta, the Deva and the

Chandra dynasties who are known as builders of temples and monasteries here. In this connection it may be noted that among these rulers the Devas were specially active in their patronage of Buddhist institutions. Their inscriptions and seal suggest that Bhavadeva, the most powerful of them, may have built both the monasteries viz. the Ānandarājā's palace named after his father and the Śālban Vihāra. No Chandra plates have been discovered from the Śāblan Vihāra.

The appearance of the Chandras may have led to the shifting of importance to another area and the session of monastic activities in the Śālban Vihāra area. Three plates[96] belonging to the Chandra kings were found in Charpatra Mura together with another plate belonging to Viradharadeva. Laḍaha Chandra of the Chandra dynasty, installed a Hindu deity and named it after himself, Śrī-Laḍaha Mādhava and also granted land in its favour. Probably the shrine in Charpatra Mura became important during his region after the deity was installed by him. Viradharadeva in the 13th century A.D. donated land in favour of Laḍhava Mādhavadeva. The Charpatra Mura and the shrine of Laḍhava-Mādhava thus remained popular till the 13th century A.D. The rulers of the Chandra dynasty changed their religious habits, although they remained Buddhist, as known from their inscriptions where they called themselves — *Paramasaugata.* This practice went on till the reign of king Govinda Chandra. Thus the new mound (Charpatra Mura) at the neighbourhood of the older Buddhist mounds may be regarded as testifying to the transformation of an originally Buddhist centre into one of Brāhmanical influence and culture. It may be noted that none of the Chandra kings built big monasteries like the Devas and the Pālas, neither of them are known to have made gifts to Buddhist monasteries or institutions. Some of the Chandras may have been militarily powerful but not great builders. Although they claimed to be Buddhist, their connection with the cause of Buddhism was rather formal. In fact, they were more Hindu than Buddhist. Their policy was sympathetic to the cause of Brahmanism like some of the Pāla kings who at any rate built large monasteries at some places and to have maintained and supported them. But there is no such evidence of patronage of Buddhist institutions by the Chandras. It was only the Devas in the region who were strong supporters of Buddhism and the Buddhist religion. The political attainments of the Devas were not great like those of the Pālas or even the Chandras. They were an independent dynasty devoted to cultural activities rather than political. They were builders of large monasteries and as such may have set an example followed by some later dynasties in Bengal. The idea was taken from them by the Pālas. The glory of Maināmati was substantially due to them. The result of excavations at the site leaves no room for doubt that it was a centre of Buddhist culture. The ruins may have been those of a flourishing capital of a Deva line of kings generally assigned to the first half of the 8th century A.D. The Devas contributed much towards raising the Maināmati-Lālmāi range to the position of a celebrated Buddhist centre. It was from them that the Chandras got it and enhanced its glory still further.[97]

The monasteries as centres of Buddhism must have influenced the life and faith of the people of the neighbourhood and thus paved the way for the acceptance of Tantricism that bridged the gulf between Mahāyāna and Hinduism. The Chaṇḍī Murā mound referred above, in the Maināmati Lālmāi range is a monument providing relics of the worship of Chaṇḍī at the same palace with Mañjuvara and Sūrya, thus testifying to the religious transformation in one of its prominent phases. In this context reference may be made to some other inscriptions found in the neighbourhood of Maināmati-Lālmāi range. Of the four inscriptions discovered later, mention has already been made of two (i.e. the plate of Harikeladeva, in which land is donated to a Buddhist monastery at Paṭṭikera and the plate of Viradharadeva who made a gift of land to Śri Laḍaha-Mādhava mentioned above). Of the remaining two inscriptions the first is the Mehar in the Chandpur sub-division of the Comilla district,[98] 'eighteen miles south, to south-west of Maināmati Mandir.'[99] It is dated in the Śaka year 1156 (A.D. 1234). The gift was made in favour of twenty Brāhmaṇas by a royal officer named Ghantiṣa. The second is the Sobharampur plate of Damodaradeva discovered from Sobharampur, Burichang thana[100], 'six miles north, north-east of Maināmati Mandir.'[101] The gift was made by the king himself to two Brāhmaṇas. These instances point to the steps taken to Brahmanise the region which had for some centuries been dominated by Buddhism. But Buddhism could not be wiped out altogether and there are still traces of its survival.

Harikela was centre of Buddhist learning in the seventh Century A.D., I-tsing speaks of Harikela (O-li-Ki-lo) as the eastern most country of eastern India[102]. He refers to Wu-hing, whom he met at a place six Yojanas east of Nālandā. Wu-hing stayed at Harikela for a year and then went to Mahabodhi, Nālandā and Tilodha. Wu-hing was a Chinese priest and a 'Dhyāna Master' of Nālandā, his Sanskrit name Prajñādeva. Another monk named Tan-Kwang who came to India, settled and died in Harikela. He won the respect and affection of the king and was happy to build a temple in Harikela. He also collected books and images from here. The name of the monastery or the centre where these foreign priests stayed and studied in Harikela is not available. So great was the influence of Buddhism in this part of Tripura that king Kāntideva was deeply impressed and adopted it as his personal faith though his father professed a different religion.[103]

No inscriptions have been noticed so far in Jolaibāḍi-Pilāk of south Tripura, it is difficult to reconstruct its religious history. It is, however, almost certain that the area, being contiguous to the ancient kingdom of Samataṭa (Noakhali and Comilla districts) had close contacts, religiously, culturally and sometime politically with that kingdom, the prolonged history of which is more or less known. The Gunaighar copper-plate mentions one Āśrama Vihāra dedicated to *Ārya*-Avalokiteśvara. A mound in Pilāk containing a colossal image of Avalokiteśvara is still known as Āśrama tilla, and whether this place can be identified with Āśrama-Vihāra will be in a state of assumption until we get some more definite record. So it is assumed that, Buddhism, was able to influence the extreme southern part of the land and it is tempting to suggest that a monastery was established at Pilāk which was contemporary of Maināmati Vihāra and it was dedicated to Avalokiteśvara. It seems likely in view of the colossal stone images of Avalokiteśvara which have been unearthed from this site, but *dearth of definite inscriptional evidences makes it hard to identify this place with any known Vihāra of ancient times*. But there is no denying the fact that the region played a vital role for spreading Buddhism in the neighbouring countries. N.K. Bhattasali is of opinion that Buddhism spread from Bengal to Arakan and Burma en route Tripura[104] and the fact is evidenced by a bulk of art pieces recovered from the southern part of Tripura.[105]

Śaivism

The essence of the Śiva cult as traced in the epics and the *Purāṇas* displays a complex character owing to its origin reflected in some elements of pre-Vedic time. The cult god Śiva is recognized as the god of destruction in Brahmanical triad. In early and medieval literature he is known as the god of gods and is responsible for revelation of all the Āgamas. He is known to hold the power of concentration of mind and confers skill in accomplishment of arts like music and dancing. Abundance of myths centering round the god in later scriptures, discloses two opposite characteristics of the god, viz. the Vedic and the non-Vedic; and the claim of the latter seems to be more valuable proving his existence felt by the people living outside the Vedic society.[106]

The physical phenomena of violent storms, thunder bolt, flood, epidemic, death and disease formed the background conception of the Vedic Rudra, the counterpart of Rudra Śiva. That is why in his anthropomorphic aspect he predominated the power of malevolence and drew fearful respect from the Vedic seers who propitiated him with prayer and sacrifice. This trend of mischief making and its propitiation are uniformly present in his character throughout the Vedic literature and attained a developed form with absorption of various ideas and elements from different sources.

The hundred designations of Rudra in the *Śatarudrīya* section of the *Yajur Veda*[107] display a well developed and distinct trait of Rudra on the basis of his two main opposite characters viz. the benign and the malign. In the *Atharva Veda*[108] Rudra gets other designations like Bhava, Śarva, Mahādeva, Paśupati, Ugra, and Īśāna to which one more Aśani is added in the *Śatapatha-Brāhmaṇa.* Reference to these names of Rudra is also found in *Sānkhyāyaṇa, Kaushitaki* and other *Brāhmaṇas.*[109] The conception of Rudra having two opposite traits viz. Śiva and Ghora, is very clearly depicted in the *Mahābhārata.*[110] This *Mahābhārata* is possibly the main source for the growth of Śaiva legends in the *Purāṇas* as well as the later development of Śiva images representing his pacific and terrific aspects.

Some outlandish characteristics of Śiva as found in the Purāṇic myths, rather, strongly support the view of Śiva's popularity among the people who used to live outside the Vedic society. It is worthy of referring to one Vrātya-kāṇḍa[111] of the *Atharva Veda* in this connection. The Vrātyas, in the Brahmanical scriptures, are uninitiated roaming vagrants without having any Vedic sacraments. But in the above hymn of the *Atharva Veda,* they appear to be different from the current belief. Here they are men of great knowledge and their god is Ekavrātya having other synonyms, viz Rudra, Paśupati, Ugra, Mahādeva and Īśāna. They attained so great position that a Vrātya guest is found capable of banning even the performance of Agnihotras. The passage seems to be highly suggestive in regard to Rudra's association with people who revolted against all kind of sacrifices. In the second *anuvāk* of the said hymn we find Ekavrātya being reddened with anger, producing Rājanyas. The passage is greatly significant from the point of view that although the Rājanyas, according to the *Varṇāśramadharma* of the Aryan society were identified with the Kshatriyas, they were not much before their recognized incorporation in the Aryan society. Before attaining such status of the Kshatriyas, they were nomadic hoards living side by side with the Dāsas or the Dasyus. This we can infer also from *purusha sūkta* of the *Rig-Veda.* Rājanyas in the said hymn were identified with the two arms of the *purusha.* Careful consideration of the passage implies the significant distinction between the Rājanyas and Kshatriyas. The former were uninitiated people but attained the status of the second *Varṇa* i.e. the Kshatriyas after their acceptance to the Vedic society. It seems to us that both the Rājanyas and Vrātyas of the above Vrātya hymn were people of some rank. So, whatever position might have been attained by Ekavrātya, it is almost certain that he was regarded to be different from all other Vedic gods.

In the *Aṣṭādhyāyī* of Pāṇini, Rudra is also known as Śarva and Bhava. Besides, there are other names such as Giriśa or Giritra,[112] Kapardin[113], Śambhu, Hara, Śaṁkara, Tryamvaka, Āśutoṣa, Bholānātha, Bhaveśa. From the post-Vedic period these different designations of the deity, amalgamated with the name of Rudra-Śiva. Moreover, the inscriptions bearing Kedāreśvara, Yogasvāmī, Vindeśvara, Dhandheśvara, Amareśvara, Baṭeśvara, Bhadreśvara, Dhaneśvara, Maṇḍaleśvara, Someśvara, Jalpeśvara, Siddheśvara, Śūlpāṇī, Atulanātha, etc. also throw light on the wide and popular existence of this deity. The inclusion of these names show that orientation of the structure of social groups took place in the post-Vedic period and that many of the early tribes and groups which had been frowned upon by the Vedic society were absorbed into it owing to the powerful intellectual and social impact of these tribes during the Upaniṣadic period which was a stage of great cultural and philosophical ferment and resurgence.[114]

We need not go, in detail, regarding attributes of a Mohenjodaro god analogous with those of Śiva, because the much discussed engraving of the protogod on a roughly carved seal discovered among the ruins of the Indus Valley Civilization.[115] It manifests many points of the popular elements of the Yogic Śiva claiming the beginning of this cult in the period of the pre-historic civilization.

In fact Śaivism or the worship of the god Śiva was an important cult which claimed a large number of adherents among the people in ancient India. The magnificent temples dedicated to Śiva around every where from Amarnātha and Kedārnātha on the western Himalayas and Paśupatinātha in Nepal, through Varanasi, Avanti, Ujjayani, Kālañjara, Somnātha, Śrīśailam, Śrīkālahasti, Kāñci and Chidāmbaram besides many others to Rameśvaram situated at the gate of Laṅkā.[116] The towering spires of some of these splendid religious foundations bear testimony to the pervasive and beneficent influence of Śaivism on large sections of our people. In Tripura, Śiva is the most popular and universally adored deity.

Vedic religion did not spread over Tripura during the earliest time. The indigenous religious life of ancient Tripura centered round the worship of the fourteen gods of the tribals[117] and the aboriginal *liṅgas* and afterwards Brahmanical religion penetrated into this region. The non-Aryan god Śiva's worship might have been prevalent in Tripura even before the arrival of Brahmanical religion. *Liṅga* worship of the non-Aryans was not only popular in Tripura, but during the early historical period it had also radiated its influence on people of neighboring states.[118] The Vrātyas[119] have proceeded to Tripura from other areas and they absorbed the religious thought of *Liṅga*-worshippers in the name of Pāśupata cult.[120] Inscriptions, available from the time of the Guptas onwards, are sources of information regarding the diffusion of Śaivism[121] in Tripura. By the beginning of the sixth century A.D., the worship of Śiva also passed over to eastern

Bengal under the patronage of Mahārājā Vainya Gupta. The Gunaighar copper-plate[122] of Vainya Gupta (507-08 A.D.) records a grant of land from the victorious camp of Kripura, by the king who meditated on the feet of Mahādeva (Mahādeva Pādānudhyāta). In this record, a temple of Pradyumneśvara has been mentioned, rather incidentally, in connection with the demarcation of the boundary of the land grant.[123] Most scholars have taken Pradyūmneśvara as a combined from of Hari Hara[124] (Pradyūmna and Īśvara) i.e. Viṣṇu and Śiva. The combination of Hari and Hara in one image forms the theme of this icon.[125] In this aspect both Śiva and Viṣṇu are united in one image. The iconographic details given in *Vāmana-purāṇa* are quoted in *Śabdakalpadruma*.[126] Another important information of Śaivism, the seal of the Gunaighar inscription, bears the figure of a bull. It is the vehicle of Śiva.[127]

The Āsrafpur plates point to the special favour offered by the Buddhist kings of the Khaḍga dynasty of Samataṭa in the seventh century A.D. Each of these plates bears a royal seal which contains in relief the figure of a couchant bull along with the legend Śrīmad Devakhaḍga[128]. It evidently shows that the growing popularity of Śaivism even attached the mind of the Buddhist Khaḍga rulers. Moreover, the Śaiva leaning of this royal dynasty is known from another inscription, where Prabhāvatī, the queen consort of Devakhaḍga, is said to have covered an image of Śarvānī with gold.[129] Śarvānī is the Śakti of Śarva, one of the eight distinctive forms of Rudra mentioned in the Atharva-Veda. That Śarvānī is the Śakti of Śiva is also corroborated by a verse in the Khalimpur copper-plate of Dharmapāladeva, where Śarvānī is explicitly called the wife of Śiva.[130] The Tippera grant of Lokanātha[131] shows that the ancestors of Lokanātha were devotees of Śaṅkara. It is a parallel instance proving ardent devotion of a reigning king of Tripura towards Śiva.[132]

An inscribed record on the pedestal of Naṭeśa image, coming from Bharellā in the district Trippera, assigns the date of its installation to the 18th regnal year of the Chandra king Laḍaha Chandra[133]. The dedicatiors of the image, Bhavadava and his father Kusumadeva, may claim their royal origin, because both are endowed with the appellation "Deva" at the end of their names. The declining condition of the Sena rule gave opportunity to the Deva dynasty to establish their authority over Tippera-Noakhali region. The above local chiefs were the governors of the same locality where the Devas rose to power. It is not unlikely, that the above chiefs were the predecessors in the line of the famous Deva kings.[134]

Unakoti, an important Śaiva centre of Tripura, is situated at Kailasahar sub-division of north Tripura district and is about 180 kilometres north east from Agartala. Here, on a vertical rock cliff extending over a kilometre, number of rock cut sculptures are lying. Besides rock cut sculptures on either sides of the hill, the remains at Unakoti consist of a number of sand stone sculptures scattered here and there, stone pavements, debris of bricks and stones, and a brick basement of a temple.

Among the Unakoti sculptures are to be found two representations of Chaturmukha[135] *Liṅgas.* A Chaturmukha *Liṅga* is now worshipped at an elevation of the Unakoti hills. The three faces of Śiva are carved on the three sides of its Rudra Bhaga and the back face is damaged. The height of the image is 92 cm.[136]

Another Chaturmukha *Liṅga* of Unakoti bears four well carved figures shown up to the waist on four sides of its Pūja-Bhaga. There is uniformity in the four figures of Yogī Śiva.[137] The inscription on this sculpture, the lone example of pre-Māṇikya period, consists of a couple of words in the Proto-Bengali character of the eleventh-twelfth century A.D.[138] The double curves of the eye brows on both the Mukhaliṅgas spell out the sensitiveness of the eyes which is characteristic feature of the eleventh and twelfth centuries sculpture of Bengal. The ekamukhaliṅga[139] dated eleventh and twelfth centuries A.D. is placed on the upward slope of the Unakoti hills. The shape of this Mukhaliṅga is spherical and the face of Śiva is curved on it.

A unique colossal head image of Śiva along with two female attendants appears on either side of the head gear of the god is carved on the rock wall of the Unakoti- hills. Local name of the image is Unakotiśvara. It has a vertically set third eye marked on the forehead, half-moon on the crest and trident as well as the accompanying figure of the bull, the female figures identified with Durgā and Gaṅgā on account of their respective vehicles (simha and makara) lend support to this view. The three eyed deity holds firmly a trident in the middle of the shaft with his grip in the manner which is not found in the classical or medieval art of eastern India, though often found in the art of Burma.[140] Rest of the hands are missing. The figure is about 33' high including minutely ornamented head gear which is itself 11' in height. The sculpture is carved out of flat square plane. The divine face with three bulging eyes does not express any mental state of bliss and calmness, as is felt in the images of earlier period. An interesting feature of the rock-cut of Unakoti lies in the absence of eyebrows in most cases and the specimen under discussions in a relevant illustration. The mouth is a long narrow slit with vertical lines representing teeth, broad ears, like those of an elephant, are decorated with *dheri* type of ear ornament of the tribal people of Tripura,[141] again a noteworthy feature of the art of Unakoti. The figure has long moustache turned upwards ending in a loop. The head gear, broken on the top, is interesting, and from what remains it is clear that it is intricately ornamented and not the traditional Jaṭāmukuṭa of Śiva. This type of crowning of Śiva is absent even in other examples of Unakoti.

This colossal bust of Śiva appears to have had a significance in the religious history of Tripura as well as cultural history which has so far been missed by the scholars. We are inclined to take the above noted bust as the only surviving record of the influence of the Devarāja cult which was prevalent in medieval Combodia and adjacent countries.[142] In other words, this cult of deified kingship was a major trait of the cultural history of south-east Asia. Now as regards Tripura though no epigraphical or monumental record testifying to the existence of the said cult has been discovered at Unakoti or in any part of Tripura as yet, certain facts tend to allow us to make presumption that it had penetrated into north-Tripura, possibly through the land route of upper Burma, Manipur, Ahom state and Cachhar.[143] First Śiva is known as 'The king of Gods' among the tribes of Tripura. Secondly, the *Rājamālā* legends ascribe the foundation of the lunar dynasty of Tripura to one Trilochana (of whom the Māṇikyas were descendants), who was born by the blessing of Siva[144]. He was widely venerated by the people as a part of the God Supreme, i.e. Śiva. We are told that he has three eyes and the *triśula* emblem. Evidently this portrait is strongly reminiscent of the Devarāja cult and Trilochana was the deified king of Tripura. Thus the *Rājmālā* tradition indicates the influence of the Devarāja cult in Tripura in early medieval times and this seems to be corroborated by the above-noted bust of Śiva with an ornamented crown instead of the usual *jaṭāmukuṭa*. In this respect one may recall the colossal heads of Lokeśvara at Bayon in Combodia. It is suggested by some scholars as the portrait of the king who is an incarnation of Bodhisattva Lokeśvara.[145]

On the left of the central panel, there might have existed several figures, but at present only two heads, one of Śiva and other a Devī though very badly defaced, survive. This gigantic head bears the terrific aspects of Rudra-Śiva. The colossal head image measures 9mx8m. Iconography of the image is similar to the image of Unakotiśvara Śiva.

It has a vertically set third eye marked on the forehead. It wears an ornamented conical crown and ear-rings. The upper lip and the lower lip are indicated by the two horizontal lines only. The vertical teeth are shown in between these two horizontal lines. The face bears the double contour lines on the upper part of the eyes and the brows are absent. The nose is flat and the nostrils are flaring. The image is regretably damaged as to make its proper appreciation difficult.

On the right of the central panel, on a slightly raised plane, there is a bearded male bust with matted locks of hair spreading over his either side. The god is two handed and has a conchshell and a rosary in his two hands[146]. Iconographically, this may stand for Śiva. Though in general the image is stiff and disproportionate, some amount of animation is noticeable in the modelling, in the fluttering of the matted lock.

On the dexter of this example, a four-handed full figure is executed which is standing in *pratyālīdha* position. Clad in *dhoti,* the figure has bow and an arrow in his normal hands and a *khaḍga* in the upper right, the upper left hand being lost, he has three eyes, matted hairs arranged in a high bun and heavy ear-rings with spiral design of the *patrakuṇḍala* type, he is standing on a vehicle, which is beyond recognition. This is apparently related with above-noted figure and probably in the hybrid form of Śiva. It is influenced by Mongoloid culture. Rudra Śiva as the Lord of Dance is represented in various Nṛitya pose. Even his fondness for dance is testified by the epithets viz. Nṛtyakpriya, Nityānṛtya, Nartana and Sarvasādhaka in the Śiva-Sahasranāma. He is also designated with Nṛtyaśīla, Vādyanṛtyapriya and Nartanaśīla in the *Vāyu-purāṇa.* A number of Naṭeśa images, though, generally common in south India, have come to light from the south eastern part of Bengal.[147] A Naṭeśa image with an inscription, dated in the 18th year of Laḍaha Chandra is an exhibition of the idea presumably inconsistent with what is said earlier in regard to its popularisation in Bengal by the Sena kings. The popularity and patronisation of the Naṭeśa images in the adjoining regions of Dacca is to be traced in several Naṭeśa icons discovered from the vicinity of Ramapāla, a village still bearing the name 'Naṭeśvara' is the reminiscent of what is viewed above.[148]

These Naṭeśvara images are of two types having ten or twelve hands and dancing on back of his mount. The ten handed variety closely follow the description found in *Matsya purāṇa*[149] where the emblems of the god held in right hands are *khaḍga, śakti, daṇḍa, triśūla,* and in the left ones are *kheṭaka, kapāla, nāga, khaṭṭvāṅga.* On the two other remaining hands, right shows varada and the left holds rosary. South Indian Bronze Naṭarāja figures, dancing on the Apasmārapuruśa, are four handed.[150] Naṭarāja images found in Dacca and Tippera districts[151] hold a vīṇā across the brest by the first pair of hands, the second pair, a serpent as canopy and the remaining pair is seen over the clotted hair marking time. A unique image of a twelve handed Naṭarāja of the eleventh the twelfth centuries A.D. was found at Khowai north Tripura district. It now belongs to a north private collection and is under worship. The relief under study portrays Śiva Naṭarāja as dancing on the back, of his bull mount Nandi in the chatura mode of dance in which the left leg is raised, although the toes touch the base, here the back of animal. The divine dancer is endowed with twelve hands and the usual *ūrdhvaliṅga* ithyphallic trait.[152] He holds up a snake by his uppermost pair of hands, exhibits a *mudrā*-handpose, marking us the time above his head by the next pair of hands and playing on a Vinā lyre by the normal right and left hands, but it is not clear whether he uses any metal bar for setting the pitch. The remaining right hands of the god shows from the above kettledrum, a *pāśa* -(noose) and *akṣhasutra* (rosary) and the left ones, also from above a *kapāla* (skull-cup), a *triśūla* (trident) and a *kamaṇḍalu* (water vessel). Śiva is probably flanked by Gaṅgā and Yamunā, who are standing respectively on their mounts, the dolphin and the tortoise. If so, the absence of Gaurī, the consort of the god, will be a noticeable feature of the composition. The back slab seems to be remarkably plain except for the *kirtimukha,* the lower portion of which is a bit indistinctly visible and a raised border enframing the sculpture. The workmanship of this piece is indifferent and there is an emphasis on the verticality in the composition. Stylistically it can be dated to the eleventh-twelfth century A.D.

So far four twelve armed specimens of Śiva Naṭarāja of the Khowai type have been found and all of them are in stone. There find spots are all now located in Bāṅglādesh and their names are Outshahi, (Dhākā district), Uttar Raikhal (Dhākā), Maniari (Rajshahi) and Durgāpur (Chittagong)[153]. The first two are kept in the Bāṅglādesh National Museum at Dhaka, the third at the Varendra Research Museum at Rajshahi while the fourth is in the Indian Museum in Calcutta. The Asutosh Museum of the Calcutta University has in its collection a sculptural specimen of the twelve handed image, but its upper part having been lost it is not possible to say any thing about the position of the upper hands, that is whether these hands hold the snake and displayed in the time beating *mudrā.* Further, in this image the divine dancer is accompanied by Nandi and Bhringi instead of Gaurī and Gaṅgā or Gaṅgā and Yamunā as seen elsewhere. The twelve handed specimens of Śiva Naṭarāja of the Bengal school are thus five,[154] including the present image, now under worship at a private residence at Khowai.

Images of Śiva as cosmic dancer discovered within the geographical limits of undivided Bengal spell out a distinctive iconoplastic diction. They admit of different varieties in respect of the number of hands, which vary from eight to twelve and other iconographic features but in each instance Śiva is seen as invariably dancing on the back of his mount, Nandi. In general the bull is depicted as standing, either facing right or left, and rarely seated. The Śiva on the bull type of Naṭarāja images originated most probably in West Bengal in the early part of the tenth century A.D., shortly it went to East Bengal and gained popularity and later travelled not only to the neighbouring regions of Assam and Orissa but also to the extra Indian territories of Nepal and Vietnam.[155]

Typologically the Khowai image shares the features of the examples of the Bengal School. It has its own distinctive character and is not exactly identical with the other four icons of the twelve handed type. The Khowai image differs from the rest in the position of the bull, while the animal faces right in the other three, it faces left in the present image. In the Uttar Raikhal specimen the bull is seated, while in the Khowai it is standing and is seemingly about to dance on seeing the dance of his master. In this respect the present icon is similar to cognate specimens. In the present relief the god as in the Outshahi, Uttar Raikhal and Durgāpur examples is dancing in the *chatura* mode but it differs from the Maniari piece where Śiva is dancing with his legs crossed the left going over the right. While the Khowai piece depicts the god with *Vinā,* as seen in the four icons, it differs from the Durgāpur sculpture, where Śiva is seen as engaged in showing the *gajahastra*-elephant-trunk pose by his right hand and throwing the other hand in a similar pose. The backslab of the others, particularly the Maniari piece, is sumptuously decorated, but the present image has a plain backslab. Besides the pedestal of the Khowai relief has very few figures on its pedestal, but the pedestals of other are enriched by a number of figures. Plastically too the image under discussion exudes a feeling of difference from others. The Śiva-Naṭrāja image of Khowai town of Tripura is a significant example of the repertoire of the Naṭarāja figures of the Bengal School and it was either imported from the Comilla region of the present day Bāṅgaḷdesh or was fashioned by a local artist who was once a member of Comilla group or was earlier conversant with the iconoplastic diction expressed by the Śiva-Naṭarāja[156] images of the Bengal School.

Another important figure, both stylistically and iconographically, is the five faced[157] and ten handed (of which the bull set of right hands is missing) feature perhaps an image of Śiva, because a snake clings to his body like a sacred thread. All the faces are arranged in a single tier of which the relatively well-preserved central face is prominent. The facial treatment bears an impress of a stamp of South-East Asian idiom and looks like a Javanese sculpture delineating an Indian theme. The god stands with slight flexion and the body is little bulky and heavy. Hands and legs are bold and heavy, but less pliable. The garment is tied with a broad waist band. Among the *āyudhas,* a bow can only be recognised which is clasped in middle with all the five fingers, a mode met within Burmese sculptures.[158]

Umā-Maheśvara is another composite form that prevailed through out India in the early medieval period. It has been discovered from different parts of Tripura. The Āgamic literatures[159] and the iconographic texts[160] referred to this type of image by the name of Umā-Aliṅgana, Umāsahita Chandraśekhara, Somāskaṇda etc. In such images we find Umā or Pāravatī with her right hand placed on the right shoulder of her consort and seated in the Āliṅgana or Sukhāsana pose on the left thigh of the deity. The *Viṣṇudharmoṭṭara* and *Śiva-tāṇdava Stotra* mention this form of Śiva[161]. This conception of the deity was also known to the author of the *Bṛhat Saṁhitā.*[162] According to Varāhamihira, Śiva in his human form was generally sculpture with a third eye in the front, a crescent moon in his head, a trident in his right arm and Gaurī or Umā, his consort, on the left. The invocatory verse of the Sanskrit drama *Mṛccha-kaṭikā* refers to this particlar form of Śiva. It describes that the lightening like arm of Gaurī was placed against the blue neck of Śiva. Exhaustive directions regarding the composition of this type of image is to be found in the *Matsya purāṇa.*[163] The popularity of this composite icons of Śiva are not unknown to the people of Tripura. A finely executed image of Umā-Maheśvara made of black stone was found at Udaipur, south Tripura district, in which Śiva is shown in Sukhāsana with his consort Umā. The god and goddess are represented as embracing each other. He has the Utpala in his upper right hand, while the normal right hand is placed on the right breast of Umā. The left normal hand embraces the goddess's waist below her left breast. The other left hand holds the trident. The right hand of the goddess embraces the neck of the god and the left hand holds a mirror. This image of the twelfth century A.D. was found at top of Unakoti hill. Though much of the details have been lost now, it has two hands and is elaborately dressed and ornamented and seated on a high *āsana*. His left hand on the opposite side passes round the body of the goddess and supports her left breast while the remaining parts are hidden.

The cosmic couple is popularly known as Kalyāṇasundara. This type image of Śiva-Pārvatī belong to the *saumya* or śānta group. This composite view is representing the marriage ceremony of Śiva-Pārvatī hence it is also designated as Vaivāhika or Pāṇigrahana form of Śiva-mūrti. The *Varāha Purāṇa* and *Matsya Purāṇa* mention this form of Śiva. Vaivāhika or Kalyāṇasundara types composite Śiva icons indicate the story of Śiva's marriage with Umā. It is to be noted that these above mentioned *Purāṇas* describe the story of Śiva's marriage. A broken Kalyāṇasundara murti of Śiva made of sand stone was found at Unakoti, north Tripura district. The image is badly mutilated and the lower portion of the god along with the figure of goddess is damaged. The god stands on *padmapīṭha* in the middle of a stele. The goddess stands in front of Śiva, her feet partly rest on the two feet of the god. Near the waist of the god and on its left side stand the figure of a male and a female, representing probably Himavat and Menakā pouring water from Kusha, this illustrates the Abhiṣekasriya. This image is also attributed to the eleventh-twelfth centuries A.D.

A group of five figures carved inside a multifoiled arch are so arranged as to assume a cruciform pattern in Devatāmuḍā, south Tripura district. The topmost figure in the panel represents Śiva as a dancer with a *ḍamaru* and a *singā* in his hand. The middle lier represents Śiva in his *Vaṭuka* Bhairava form. He is flanked by Kārtika and Gaṇeśa who are seated. Incidentally, dogs are depicted near the pedestal. A considerably damaged figure of a female is found seated in the lower panel.

The composition consists of five registers of uneven shape and size which are schematically arranged and each of them has been carved individually almost in the same plane and in low-relief with the result that there is hardly any scope of display of light and shade. In comparison to other relief (Durgā relief, Viṣṇu relief etc), the present panel is technically more advanced and the relief is comparatively bolder than the earlier one. Though much exfoliated, the relief gives an impression of rounded modelling, not seen in the previous one. Further, the interplay of light and shade has been effected here to some extent through the deep cuts of the panels and the parallel lines, and rhythm and animation have been created by the flexions of the body, fluttering of the matted hair, and the carve of the horns of the deities. The style of carving of this panel closely resembles to that of the figures executed on a hill at Lungley in Mizoram which is not very far away from Devatāmuḍā. All the above evidences both epigraphic and literary, are too fragmentary to give any graphic picture of the prevailing Śaiva sects in Tripura. But it can be said with some amount of certainty that Śaivism, like other parts of India, was popular and prevalent in this region from the early medieval period.

Vaiṣṇavism

The word "Vaiṣṇavism" is to denote the cult of Viṣṇu the Vedic solar god. But Viṣṇu in the epic and the purāṇic age was but the composite form of three divine entities, namely, the Vedic god Viṣṇu, the cosmic god Nārāyaṇa and the human god Vāsudeva-Kṛṣṇa.[164]

Cycles of legends about some Kṛṣṇas are found in the Vedic literature. An upshot of all these Kṛṣṇas may be enumerated in following way:

(a) Rishi Kṛṣṇa—father of Viśvakāya[165]

(b) Certain Asura Kṛṣṇa living on the bank of the river Aṁśumati.[166]

(c) Kṛṣṇa of Āṅgirasagotra.[167]

(d) Two Kṛṣṇas belonging to Hārita gotra.[168]

It is apparent that these Kṛṣṇas were different entities distinguished from the Kṛṣṇa of the *Mahābhārata*.

In the *Chhāndogya Upaṇishad,* certain Kṛṣṇa, son of Devakī, is found to have been the disciple of Ghora Āṅgirasa.[169] A shadow of this Upaṇishadic Kṛṣṇa might have fallen of the Kṛṣṇa of the great epic, because in this epic we find him both as the son of Devakī and disciple of Ghora Āṅgirasa. In this connection, partial influence of Āṅgirasa Kṛṣṇa and a projection of Viśvakāya-Kṛṣṇa upon Vāsudeva-Kṛṣṇa aṣ found in the *Śrīmad Bhagavat*[170] cannot entirely be set aside. The name Vāsudeva occurs in the Pariśishṭas of some Vedic literature where conceptions of Vedic Viṣṇu, cosmic Nārāyaṇa and historic Vāsudeva are mingled to form the cult god of later Vaiṣṇavism. The idea would be clear from the following Viṣṇu-gāyatrī.[171] Vāsudeva declares himself in the *Gītā* as Viṣṇu among the twelve Ādityas. Thus, the religious idea about the solar god Viṣṇu, cosmic god Nārāyana had been blended with the idea of Vāsudeva Kṛṣṇa when their pre-eminent power gave them highest place among other gods.

As regards the Gopal aspect of Kṛṣṇa, stream of legends came into being in the late *Pūrāṇas* and in the *Harivaṁśa* and a spirit of eclecticism in the conception of the composite god of the Vaiṣṇava cult, took a new shape even before the advent of the Christian era.

The development of the cult god Viṣṇu depends on the blending of the above divine entities, but the term 'Vaiṣṇava' to denote the followers of Viṣṇu had its origin in still later ages. In the *Padma Tantra,* the word *Vaiṣṇava* to denote a follower of Viṣṇu is remarkably absent. The synonyms to denote the followers of Viṣṇu are to be found in the above Tantra in a verse which may be quoted below:

"Sūris-Suhṛit-bhāgavatassāt-Vataḥ Pañchkalāvit /
Ekāntikścha tanmoyaścha-Pañcharātrika ityapi //"[172]

Among these synonymous terms Bhāgavata, Sātvata, Ekāntika and Pañcharātrika were regularly used by the followers of Viṣṇu. From the epigraphical standpoint we may corroborate the above view on the basis of instance found in the record of the Greek ambassador Heliodorous who erected a pillar with an image of Garuḍa in honour of Vāsudeva[173]. In the inscription (C. second century B.C.) Heliodorus designated himself as a Paramabhāgavata. The expression Vaiṣṇava is found for the first time in an interpolated passage of the great epic,[174] but historically appears in some of the records of Traikūṭaka kings (fifth century A.D.). But this term found in the Traikūṭaka epigraphs has less value as even the imperial Gupta sovereigns in their coins and epigraphs are found to bear the title Paramabhāgavata.

Early trace of Bhāgavatism in India can be had from Pāṇini and Patañjali.[175] This is also proved by the identification of Vāsudeva with 'Herakles' supported by the Greek itineraries.[176] Bhāgavatism originated in Mathurā and the adjoining regions, becomes conclusive from the *Mahābhārata* and the *Purāṇas.* Words like 'Saurasenai' 'Herakles', Methara and the river Jobares quoted here and there by the Greeks from Megasthenes' account, evince the existence of a special class of Vāsudeva worshippers who used to live in the city of Mathurā and Kṛṣṇapura (Cleisobore) on the bank of the river Yamunā.[177] Epigraphic data from third century B.C. to the first century A.D. are the early documents of the history of the Vaiṣṇava faith. Besides the Besnagar pillar inscription of Heliodorous, another important record of C. second century B.C. from Nāgari (Madhyadeśa) gives in detail the commemoration of a shrine in the Nārāyaṇa vāṭaka by Sarvatāta Gajāyana where the images of the gods Vāsudeva and Saṅkarshaṇa were installed.[178] Broken pillars, namely Tāladhvaja and Makaradhvaja discovered in Besnagar throw some new light on the worship of Balarāma and Pradyūmna (Kāmadeva).

That the five hero gods of the Vṛishṇīs, viz. Saṅkarshaṇa, Vāsudeva, Pradyūmna, Aniruddha and Śāmba were the objects of veneration, has been epigraphically proved by an inscription recovered from the village Morā near Mathurā. The record was dedicated by Ṣoḍāsa, son of Mahākshatrapa Rajubulā (first century A.D.). These epigraphic details testify the prevalence of Vaiṣṇava faith in the form of hero worship and all these heroes were close relatives of Vāsudeva Kṛṣṇa. The doctrine behind the worship of this group of gods was recognised to be the '*Vyūhavāda*', which was the central theme of the Pañcharātrikas. Among the above five gods the worship of Śāmba, became obsolete in course of time and the rests were known as four '*Vyūhas*' among the Pāñcharātrikas. According to the doctrine underlying the four '*Vyūhas*' Vāsudeva stands as the supreme god. Saṅkarshaṇa, Pradyumna, and Aniruddha are his emanatory forms. It is, however, laid down in the texts each '*Vyūha*' is Viṣṇu himself and from the four original '*Vyūhas*' emanation of three *Vyūhas (Vyuhantara, Murtyantara)* follows:

1. From Vāsudeva emanates Keśava, Nārāyaṇa and Mādhava.
2. From Saṅkarshaṇa, Govinda, Viṣṇu and Madhusūdana.
3. From Pradyumna, Trivikrama, Vāmana and Śrīdhara and
4. From Aniruddha, Hṛishikeśha, Padmanābha and Dāmodara.

Another group of twelve Vidyeśvaras (so designated in the *Mahāsanatkumāra-Saṁhitā*[179]) come into being further from the four principal *Vyūhas* as given in the *Padma-Tantra.*[180] From the *Vyūha* Vāsudeva sprang another Vāsudeva who emanated Purushottama who again emanated Janārddana. By similar process, from Saṅkarshaṇa sprang another Saṅkarshaṇa, from him Adhokshaja and from Adhokshaja, Upendra emanated. A Pradyumna being emerged out from Pradyumna created Nṛisiṁha and from Nṛisiṁha came out Hari. The process of emanation from Aniruddha was similar creating further Achyuta and Kṛṣṇa. Thus, the total number of twenty four varieties of Viṣṇu (*Chatur-Viṁsati-Murtti*) was formed by twelve sub-*Vyūhas* as well as by twelve Vidyeśvaras. The development of twenty-four varieties of Viṣṇu was completed during the end of Gupta period.[181]

Vaiṣṇavism was the most widely prevalent and popular religion of Tripura region from the sixth century A.D.[182] It comes to light from the epigraphic record from the village of Gunaighar in the district of Tippera.[183] In this record, issued in Gupta year 188 (i.e. 508 A.D.) during the reign of king Vaiṇyagupta, a temple of Pradyumneśvara has been mentioned, rather incidentally, in connection with the demarcation of the boundary of the land grant. Most scholars have taken Pradyumneśvara as a combined form of Hari and Hara. In the opinion of Dr. P.C. Bagchi, though Pradyumneśvara represented Viṣṇu, it also stood for a different composite icon of Harihara.[184] It will not be out of place here to mention that there is a small mound called as 'cūdārpād' probably connecting a Gupta temple, at Gunaighar (ancient Guneka grahara, distict Tippera), where from at least two beautiful carved stone images of Viṣṇu, probably belonging to the late Gupta or early Pāla period, have been discovered. They are still being worshipped there. It is to be considered where, 'cūdārpād' is identical with 'Cūḍāmaṇi-nagar', mentioned in line 28 of Gunaighar Copper-plate inscription of Vaiṇya-Gupta.[185]

The Tippera copper-plate[186] inscription of Lokanāthā, belonging to the seventh century A.D. refers to the worship of Bhagavān Ananta-Nārāyaṇa (a form of Viṣṇu-Anantaśayin on Śeṣaśayin) in Tripura region. King Lokanāthā issued this document through his Sāndhivigrahika, Praśanta deva and it records a grant of land to his own Brāhmaṇa mahāsāmanta Prodōshaśarman who made an application to his chief through the king's son, prince Lakshmīnātha as *dūtaka,* granting him a plot of land in the forest region (*aṭavi-bhūkaṇḍa*). In the granted piece of land the *mahāsāmanta* desired to erect a temple, wherein he wished to found an image of Ananta-Nārāyanaṇa Pradōshaśarman[187] prayed for land for the maintenance of the daily worship of this god with *bali, charu, sattra* ect. and for the dwelling of Brahmanas versed in the four Vedas (Chaturveda), whose number exceeds a hundred. The amount of land allotted individually and in some cases jointly, is also clearly mentioned in the document. In the first verse the god Śaṅkara is invoked. Ananta-Nārāyaṇa is said to have been adored by even some chief gods, the Asuras, the Sun, the Moon, the Kubera, the Kinnaras, the Vidyādharas, the chief Serpents, the Gandharavas, the Varuna, the Yaksas and others.[188]

The inscriptional evidences of the Gupta and post Gupta periods show that god Ananta-Nārāyaṇa or Nārāyaṇa reclining on Anantanāga was popular in different parts of India.

The seal, attached to the Tippera grant, bears in relief, a figure of the goddess Lakṣmī or Śrī, standing on a lotus pedestal being sprinkled by two elephants from two sides with water. This is the 'Gaja Lakṣmī' motif, so characteristic of the indigenous Indian Coins.[189]

Another significant fact that may be brought to notice here is that in this plate, which we take to have belonged to the age of anarchy (*Mātsya-nuyāya*) in Bengal. From the accounts of the Chinese pilgrim Hiuen Tsang we learn that during this time he could find no sign of Buddhism in Kāmarupa, We cannot possibly connect this plate with any of the Kāmarupa kings of that time. We have seen that the ancestors of Lokanātha were devotees of Śaṅkara and that his own Brāhmaṇa, wished to set up an image of Ananta-Nārāyaṇa. The prevalence of Brahmanic religious influence in eastern India at the time can be rightly inferred also from the mention of the sacred fires, paurāṇic deities, Brāhmaṇas versed in the four Vedas etc.[190]

The next Vaiṣnavite record comes from Kāilān.[191] It was issued by the *Paramavaiṣṇava* king Śrīdharaṇa Rāta. In this record the king has been shown as a devout worshipper of the god Puruṣottama (Jagannātha?), a form of Viṣṇu. Other qualities pertaining to this Vaiṣṇava king consisted of 'Karuṇā', 'anabhimataprāṇa-nigrahe', and 'anekapraṇī-koṭī-sahasra-jāvitasya pradāyaka.' He was indeed a Parama-Kāruṇika. King Śrīdhāraṇa Rāta was very liberal in administering his religious policy. Himself a *parama*-Vaiṣṇava, he did not interfere with the religion of others, and appointed one Jayanāga, a Buddhist, to a high ministerial post. He went so far as to grant some *pāṭakas* of land to the aforesaid minister for erecting a Buddhist vihāra in the capital city. After the fall of the Buddhist dynasty of the Chandras, the orthodox Brāhmaṇical dynasty of the Varmans became powerful in east Bengal and they were undoubtedly staunch Vaiṣṇava.[192] The Viṣṇu-Chakra seal on the Sāmantasār (a village in Faridpur district), copper-plate grant of the reign of Hari Varman, a Paramavaiṣṇava, has undoubtedly proved his attachment with the Vaiṣṇava faith.[193] The Belava copper-plate of Bhoja Varman issued in the fifth year of his reign from his capital city Vikramapura, records a land grant made by the devout worshipper of Viṣṇu, the *Parameśvara, Paramabaṭṭāraka Mahārājādhirājā,* king Bhoja Varman who meditated upon the feet of the Mahārājā-dhirāja Sāmala Varman, to Ramadeva Śarman, incharge of the kings' holy shrine (*śāntyāgāra,* line, 45), son of Viśvarūpadeva Śarman, grandson of Jagannāthadeva Śarman, great grand son of Pitāmbaradeva Śarman, who was an inhabitant of the village of Siddhala in north Rāḍha, and who hailed from Madhyadeśa.[194] It is interesting to note that the kings and queens of the Varman dynasty have been compared with divinities like Viṣṇu-Kṛṣṇa and Laksmī. Lines 5 and 6 of the grant seem to indicate that Viṣṇu and Laksmī re-incarnated themselves as Kṛṣṇa and Rādhā.[195] Manifestations of Viṣṇu have also been described in the next few lines. In line sixth 'descent' of Hari to this world as Kṛṣṇa, 'who though a partial incarnation of Viṣṇu,[196] sported with one-hundred milk maids as the stage-manager of the *Mahābhārata'.* Indeed the Varamans have been described here as the relatives of Kṛṣṇa. King Hari Varman of the Yādava dynasty has been compared with Kṛṣṇa of the Sātvata (Hari is also a name of Viṣṇu-Kṛṣṇa). It is apparent from a study of the grant in question that both the epic and paurāṇic stories relating to the Kṛṣṇa saga were mingled or synthesized in this region in the early medieval times. It is also clear from this epigraphic record that the royal panegyrists of the medieval times had a peculiar fancy in comparing the royal personages with Viṣṇu and his incarnations, when the kings were Śaivas or Buddhists, similar associations of them with Śiva or Buddha were suggested by their *praśastikāras.* Apart from naming Viṣṇu or Kṛṣṇa, the Varāha and Dāśarathī-Rāma incarnations have also been referred. King Bhoja Varman, as the grant shows, was a Parama-vaiṣṇava. So, it was but natural that land was given by means of a charter, affixed to a seal of Viṣṇu *Chakra,* in the name of god Vāsudeva.[197] After an exhaustive study on the plate, it is clear that the record is very significant from various points of view. First, the name of preceptors of the Varman kings are the different appellations of Viṣṇu. This shows a great influence of the Vaiṣṇava faith among the general mass of the society.[198] Secondly, Ramadeva Śarman, the preceptor of Bhoja Varman, was resident of Belava, a village in the Narayanaganj subdivision of the district of Dacca, and great grand father, Pitāmbaradeva Śarman was an inhabitant of Siddhala in north Rāḍha.[199] The importance of Siddhala in north Rāḍha as a centre of Vaiṣṇavism is also recorded in the Bhuvaneśvara stone inscription of Bhaṭṭabhavadeva (11), which mentioned to the temple of Nārāyaṇa or Ananta-Nārāyaṇa.[200] The inscription opens with a *namaskāra* to Vāsudeva and invocations to Hari and Vāgdevatā (i.e. the goddess of speech, Sarasvatī). Thirdly, Pitāmbaradeva Śarman, as recorded in our epigraph migrated from Madyadeśa, the original home land of this faith of the Vaiṣṇavas.[201]

Though the Chandra kings were staunch followers of the Buddhist faith, yet the Maināmati (near Comilla in the Tippera district of Bāṅglādeśa) plates[202] of Laḍaha Chandra (c. 1000-20 A.D.) and Govinda Chandra (c. 1020-45 A.D.) disclose that the latest members of this family repudiated the Buddhist faith of their predecessors and they made grants of land in favour of a Vaiṣṇavite or Śaivite deity in the name of Vāsudeva-bhaṭṭāraka or Śiva-bhaṭṭāraka. Although these two kings are also conventionally called Paramasaugata, these documents make it clear that they adopted paurāṇic Hinduism. Laḍaha Chandra being specially devoted to the god Viṣṇu and Govinda Chandra to Śiva.[203] The two records of Laḍaha Chandra open with the Vaiṣṇavite *maṅgala:*

Om namo Bhāgavate Nārāyaṇāya[204]

It is interesting to note further that Laḍaha Chandra's gifts were made in favour of the Vaiṣṇavite god Laḍahamādhava-bhaṭṭāraka, installed by and named after himself. Laḍahamādhava, really means Mādhava installed by or named after Laḍaha and Mādhava is a well-known name of the god Viṣṇu-Kṛṣṇa.[205] Another copper-plate from the same place issued by Vīradhara deva (eleventh-twelfth century A.D.) bears on both sides of its seal the wheel of Viṣṇu.[206] King Vīradharadeva who is regarded as an ancestor of Harikāladeva of the kingdom of Paṭṭikera[207] was a worshipper of Viṣṇu. Besides the representation of the Viṣṇu Chakra or the Sudarśana-Chakra, the grant was made in favour of god Vāsudeva under the name Laḍahamādhava (Śrī Laḍahamādha vabhidhāna Śrī Vāsudeva Bhaṭṭārakāya)[208].

The Paikpāḍā image inscription of the reign of Chandra king Govinda Chandra[209] records the installation of an image of Vāsudeva at Paikpāḍā, (a village in Vikramapur, Dacca district), by Gaṅgādāsa, son of Paradāsa. The record bears a testimony to the fact that Vaiṣṇavism was popular among the merchant class of the contemporary society. The next epigraph, important for our purpose, comes from Bāghāurā village near Brāhmaṇbāḍia, district Tippera.[210] This image inscription was issued during the 3rd regnal year of king Mahipāla-I, the son and successor of king Vigrahapāla II[211]. King Mahipāla-I, brought a new epoch in the annals of the Pāla dynasty in as much as he revived the Pāla empire from a moribund state. The inscription shows that the kindom of Mahipāla-I also included the Samataṭa region. The inscription, engraved under the lotus feet of a standing image of god Nārāyaṇa (Vāsudeva) of about three feet in height, records that a Vaiṣṇava merchant, Lokadatta, son of Vasudatta and an inhabitant of village Vilakindaka installed an image of the god in Samataṭa in the 3rd regnal year of king Mahipāla-I. In lines 2 and 3 of the inscription, it is stated that the said merchant caused the consecration of an image of the god in question for the religious merit of himself as well as of his parents. It is apparent that the family of Lokadatta had Vaiṣṇavite leanings. It also appears from a study of the inscription that the said image was possibly consecrated in a temple in village Vilakindaka[212] (of the Samataṭa region). This inscription also proves that a certain portion of Samataṭa was a strong hold of Vaiṣṇavism. It may not be out of place here to mention that a discrepancy has crept in naming the deity as Nārāyaṇa, for it has been rightly shown by J.N. Banerjea[213] that the mode of placing the attributes in the four hands of the deity would indicate that this image was one of Trivikrama-Viṣṇu of the order of the 'Caturvimiśati mūrtis'.

All the evidences at our disposal tend us to believe that by the closing point of the first millennium A.D. the geographical orbit of Vaiṣṇavism had extended remarkably on almost all the parts of the region. It may, however be mentioned in this connection that the grant of land in the name of Vāsudeva or Nārāyaṇa is a common practice among the rulers of the area, no matter whether they were Buddhist or Vaiṣṇavites. From the eighth century A.D. onwards, the development of Vaiṣṇavism may be proved by a number of Viṣṇu images of the Pāla and Sena period, discovered in different parts of Tripura. The earliest Viṣṇu image[214] made of stone found at Pilāk is an interesting variety of Trivikrama. It is four-armed figure, its back, right and back left hands are placed on the heads of the Gadādevī and Chakrapuruṣa respectively, the right front seems to have been the abhaya pose, the left one probably holding a conch shell. This image is assigned to the eight century A.D.[215] In this connection we may mention some of the Brahmanical images associated with the Vaiṣṇava faith belonging to the eight to fifteenth century A.D. Before that we have to note a brief account of Varāhamihira about the description of Viṣṇu's iconography. According to him,[216] the breast of Viṣṇu should be marked with the sign *Śrīvatsa* and adorned with the *Kaustubha* gem. Viṣṇu should be yellowish green in complexion like a lin flower and clad in yellow garments, his face being placid, he wears *kuṇḍalas* and a *kiriṭa,* his neck, breast, shoulders and arms being full and fleshy. He may be represented eight, four or two armed. In the case of an eight armed image, three of his right hands hold a sword, a mace and an arrow, the fourth being in the *śāntida* pose.[217] The hands of the left should carry a bow, shield (*Kheṭaka*), discuss and conch. If he is intended to be four armed, his right hands show a mace and *śāntida mudrā,* while the left ones carry a conch and a discuss of the two armed image, the right hand should be shown in *śantida mudrā,* the left one holding a conch shell. The four armed images of the deity which are commonly met with generally depict one or other of the four *vyūhas* or some of the *vibhavas* (i.e. incarnatory forms). The human incarnation of Viṣṇu are usually endowed with two hands while the Viśvarūpa variety multi-handed. The twenty four forms[218] of the four-armed Viṣṇu images can hardly be distinguished from one another. G.N. Rao thus points out, "all these twenty-four images are very alike, they are standing figures, with no beads in the body possessing four arms and adorned with *karīṭamukuṭa* and other usual ornaments each of them stand upon a *Padmāsana.* The difference in the any two of these images are to be made out by the way in which the śaṅka, the chakra, the gadā and the padma are found distributed among their four hands.[219] Trivikrama category of icon was the most popular and commonest form in ancient Bengal and Tripura. The attributes in its lower and upper left hands are śaṅka and chakra and lower and upper right hands are gadā and padma respectively. The commonest form of Viṣṇu image of the eleventh and twelfth centuries discovered at Baddarghat near Agartala, is a specimen of black stone sculpture, and the arrangement of attributes in its four hands follows the order of Trivikrama. The gadā and chakra are held by the right upper and left upper hands, and padma and śaṅka by the lower right and left hands.

The growing variety of iconographic forms in the later period denotes the corresponding growth and complexity in Vaiṣṇavite mythology, which is projected in these figures. Among the three categories of Viṣṇu images, viz., *śayaṇa, āsana* and *sthānaka,* the entire region seems to have a special liking for the last one.[220]

Śayaṇa or fully recumbent images belonging to any of the Brahmanical cults are extremely rare.[221] This type of extant Viṣṇu images has not yet been discovered in Tripura. The only recumbent image associated with the Brahmanical pantheon is the Śeṣa-Śayaṇa or Ananta Śayaṇa image of Viṣṇu.[222] Although this type of representation of Viṣṇu is very common is south India, but not a single image of this type except the image in the temple of Aśvakrānatā, north Gauhati, (Assam), has so far been discovered from this part of India during the period of our review. The worship of Bhagavāna Ananta-Nārāyaṇa, referred to in the Trippera copper-plate of the seventh century A.D. may, however, represent a form of Anantaśayaṇa Viṣṇu, though it is quite difficult to say anything definitely in this regard.[223]

Āsana type of images of Viṣṇu are also comparatively rare in this part. The figure of a seated Viṣṇu image is represented on a terra-cotta plaque of the main shrine at Paharpur in Bāṅglādesha.[224]

As a seated figure, the deity is depicted as holding the usual attributes, viz., śaṅka in the lower right hand, chakra in the upper right, padma in the lower left and gadā in the upper left hand. Geographically Paharpur does not belong to a area of Tippera but it is hopefully believed that like Paharpur, Mainămati, Mahasthana and Pilāk, a rich religious complex will be exposed one day in the area by the spade of archaeologists.

Among the *sthānaka* variety of Viṣṇu images, mention may be made of the black basalt image of Viṣṇu of the eleventh-twelfth centuries A.D. hailing from Unakoti in the north Tripura district. It belongs to the Acyuta[225] variety. The god stands in this pose. The padma and chakra are held by the right upper and left upper hands and gadā by the lower right hand, while the rest is missing.[226] The contemporary image of ten-armed Viṣṇu[227] standing in *sthānaka* pose, accompanied by Lakṣmī and Sarasvatī, is of great iconographic importance. This image was found at Noagaon.[228] The god carries in his eight hands chakra, hala, dhanuk, śaṅka, gadā, khaḍga, sara and padma. Its back right and back left hand are placed on the head of Lakṣmī and Sarasvatī respectively. Next we may mention the Bāghāurā (Tippera, Bāṅglādesha) image belonging to the reign of Mahipāla-I. A standing image of Nārāyaṇa in black slab stone has been discovered in the Pilāk in Belonia subdivision of south Tripura District. It is still at the site, in an inclined position, mostly burned below ground near the western edge of the Thākurani baḍi mound. The back-slab is 3m. 20 cm high and 1 m. 66 cm wide.[229] The major part of the front side being buried, the details could not be recorded.[230] The stone image of Viṣṇu of the eleventh-twelfth centuries A.D. was found from Udaipur in south Tripura district. The image lies in the combination of its wealth and exuberance of decorative designs. The facial treatment in each case is oval with pointed chin and the lips, the lower one of which is slightly modelled in a rounded curve, are drawn downwards, bearing with the simple of bliss and contentment.[231] A not very sharp nose, which merges into two curves of eye brows to the pointed chin, there is a downward trend which is relieved only by the round cut of the face. The lively modelling of the torso is suggestive of warm flesh.

Another stone image of Viṣṇu was found from Udaipur in south Tripura district. It stands in the *sthānaka* pose, accompanied by Lakṣmī and Sarasvatī. The gadā and chakra are held by the right upper hands and padma and śaṅka by the lower right and left hands.[232]

A little down the valley in Unakoti, in north Tripura, from the stream bed rises a block of perpendicular rock measuring about 35'x90' approximately. The whole wall has been utilized for a single panel, which consists of a seated Gaṇeśa, two elephant-headed standing human figures and Viṣṇu in the proper righted end. The Viṣṇu has high *kirīṭa-mukuṭa,*[233] heavy earrings and a necklace and he is clad in a short *dhoti* reaching the thighs. The figure of god is stout and heavy but some of the limbs, particularly the hands, are apparently weak.

An important feature of Vaiṣṇavism was the worship of Viṣṇu's incarnatory forms *(avatāra)*. The name of the standard list of ten *avatāras* are *Mīna matsya* (Fiṣh), *Kurma* (Tortoise), *Varāha* (Boar), *Narasiṁha* (Man-lion), *Vāmana* (Dwarf), Paraśurāma, Rāma (Dasarathi) Balarāma, Buddha and Kalki.[234] Of them, Narasiṁiha form of Viṣṇu images were found in Tripura. The earliest literary reference to this form is to be found in a later passage of the *Taittirīya-āranyaka*[235] where he is described as having claws and sharp teeth. A similar reference is also found in the *Mahānārayaṇa Upaniṣad.*[236] The *Mahābhārata*[237] speaks of the incarnatory form of Viṣṇu. But the myth of the Nṛsiṁihavatara is found in an amplified form in the *Harivaṁśa.*[238] The *Bhāgavata Purāṇa,*[239] *Matsyapurāṇa*[240], *Agni Purāṇa*[241] describe the image of Nṛsiṁha. A large number of iconographical representations of this form of Viṣṇu, found from different parts of Tripura, is itself a testimony of the prevalence of this incarnatory form of Viṣṇu in this region. This early images of Nṛsiṁiha are of two handed but with the expansion of popularity of this form, iconography became complex and varied, growing into multiple hands like four, six, eight, twelve, sixteen and thirty two.[242] In Tripuira, we have got, two images of Nṛsiṁha, one is four handed and other's six handed.

The first image of Nṛsiṁha[243] was found in the Thākurāni baḍi mound of Pilāk. It is now housed in the Tripura Government Museum, Agartala (museum Acc.No-s/51). Made of coarse grained sandstone of dark-gray colour, the image is badly weathered and its lower portion is missing. The four-armed figure is standing with its left leg bent and the right stretched. The two natural hands are in the attitude of piercing the belly of Hiraṇyakaśipu placed on the left thigh and left bent knee. The upper left hand holds a śaṅka, the object in the corresponding right hand being broken.[244] The manes are shown on the chest in a manner resembling V-shaped necklaces. Stylistically this may be assigned to the late 8th century A.D., when a trial of Gupta idiom was still in view.[245] This specimen bears no sign of disagreement in the composition of the main theme with the directions given in the *Matsya Purāṇa,* except that the deity is of four armed. With two hands he is rending upon the entrails of Hiraṇyakaśipu[246]. The scene of Hiraṇyakaśiupu expostulating with Prahlāda is depicted on the left and emergence of the man-lion from the pillar kicked by Hiraṇyakaśipu is shown on the right. In this connection, we may mention, a four handed image of Nṛasiṁha procured from Rāmapāla, is now preserved in the Dacca Museum collection.[247]

Another independent carving of Nṛsiṁha[248] in a well preserved condition has been found at Unokati. The god has a visible face of a lion and six hands. The god stands in the *aliḍha* pose on a half round plain pedestal, has an ornamental crown over hand and the usual ornaments necklace with a hanging locket, *vanamālā,* sacred thread, etc. are displayed. His upper pair of hands hold chakra and śaṅka. With two hands he is ripping open the entrails of Hiraṇyakaśipu. The middle left hand holds the head of the demon, while the right is in the *abhaya mudrā.* This image may be assigned to the eleventh and twelfth centuries. A.D.[249] A similar image with an elaborate execution of the entire episode has been found at Pāikore in the district of Birbhum.[250]

The peak of gods or Devatā-muḍā as it is called, is an extensive hill range (a bifurcation of Badamuda hills) is situated between Udaipur and Amarapur on the both banks of riger Gomati. This has become a place of interest owing to the panels of rockcut sculptures carved out of high rocky walls facing the river Gomati. The antiquity of these objects hardly goes back beyond the fifteenth century A.D. when these Indo-Mongoloid rulers came within the fold of Hinduism and the temple building and coin-minting activities began under the Māṇikya patronage. In this aspect, Pañcha Deva-Devi panel is the most important edifices of religion in Tripura. In the middle of the panel, is carved a *dhyānī* four handed Viṣṇu image, the height of which is I meter 50 cm. The gadā is held by the right upper hand.

Another interesting characteristic of Vaiṣṇvaism is the worship of Gopala-Kṛṣṇa in the form of Gopala's various activities in the boyhood. By the beginning of the sixth century A.D. Bengal had become one of the strongholds of such form and some sculptural representations depicting various incidents centering round the activities of boy Kṛṣṇa and Balarāma legends have been discovered through out Paharpur in the district of Rajashahi, Bāṅglādesh. The popularity of this cult which led to the employment of the local artists for decorating the feats and legends of boy Kṛṣṇa seem to have formed an essential element of Vaiṣṇavism. A Venugopāla image is found in Udaipur, south Tripura. Another six handed Kṛṣṇa was recovered from the Rādhāmādhava temple. It is now housed in Government Museum, Agartala. It is a stone plaque[251] and a measurement of 2'6"x1'x8". His upper two hands hold a flute, and other two hands hold a Dhanu. The lower right hand holds a *Kamaṇḍalu* and other hand is not clear.

Śaktism

The universal energy personified in the mother goddess delivers the concept of Śakti. The beliefs and ideals of the Nomadic people like proto-Austroloid, Mediterranean, Mongoloid and Alpine mingled with those of the heterogenous people helped to develop a new civilization.[252] Added to such waves to racial elements Aryanisation of the socio-religious practices formulated a cultural complementary to the religious set up of Tripura. The contents of Śakti worship though scanty and fragmentary are to be viewed on this historical background.

The position of the deities conceived as the female energy was in a negligible state in the period of the *Rig Veda*. Of course, certain hymns of the *Rig Veda* carry the notion of the duality, in the creations of the universe.[253] Terms like, *Janitṛi, Pitarā*[254] are highly suggestive in sustaining the faccied union of the heaven and earth who were conceived to be the progenitors of all the deities and the universe. Another important female deity Ushā (dawn) at the time of *Rig Veda* is poetically imagined as the mistress of the sun.[255] But above all, the place of Aditi is unique in the Vedic literature being fancied as the personification of sky or of the universal nature. Sometimes, she is the sister of Vasus and in a later cosmogonic hymn, she plays the role of both the mother and the daughter aspects of *Daksha-Prajāpati.*[256] In one passage of the *Atharva-Veda*[257] she is worshipped with her brothers and sons for protection. Mutual relation of both the mother and the daughter aspect in the same person is to be viewed in daughter of Ṛishi Ambhrina, the seer Vāk of the *Devī, - Sūkta*[258] of the *Rig-Veda*. Having realized herself as the living soul (*chiṇmayi*) of the universe (*Sarvabhūteśvarī*) she mentions herself as the progenitor of father Dyau. Not only so, this very *Sūkta* in the *Rig-Veda* bears the prolific germ of the philosophical speculation of Śakti worship. An interesting point to be noticed in the conception of the supreme function of the Devī is her mother, daughter and sister aspects uniformly present in the mother cult.

Incidental evidences relating to the position of the supreme goddess can be gleaned from the earlier literature where mere appearance of some designations of the mother can hardly be recognised as having the role of Śakti worshipped by the Śāktas of the later age. *Śrī* and Bhadrakālī in the *Sāṅkhyāyana-grihya-Sūtra* of the *Rig Veda,*[259] Bhavānī as the wife of Bhava in the *Hiraṇyakeśī Gṛhya sūtra,*[260] Kālī and Karālī mentioned in the *Muṇḍakopanishad*[261], Haimavatī and Umā as personified Brahmavidyā in *Kenopaṇishad*[262], Ambikā, the sister of Rudra in the *Vājasaneyi-Saṁhitā* are all designations of the mother but bearing no concrete evidence of the development of her cult. It is the *Taittariya Āraṇyaka* of the black *Yajurveda*[263] where Ambikā is described not only as the spouse of Paśupati Rudra, but is identified with Devī[264]. Two more designations viz. Kātyāyanī and Kanyākumārī in the Durgā-gāyatrī of the same text[265] furnish a point of significance in the later history of Śaktism. The philosophical idea to be noted behind her make Vairochanī (Knower of Brahma)[266] began to exercise its influence over the cult goddess Durgā.

Fragmentary evidences regarding assimilation of some tribal goddesses showing growth of a accretions in the development of Śakti cult are to the found in two *Durgā-stavas* of the great epic[267] as well as in the *Āryāstava* of the Khila *Hari-vāṁśa.*[268] Siddhasenānī (general of the *Siddhas*), the dweller on Mandara, Kaumārī, Kālī, Bhadrakālī, Chaṇḍi, Tāriṇī, Vijayā, Jayā, Vasudeva bhaginī, Slayer of Mahiṣāsura, Kauśikī, Umā, Śākambharī, destroyer of Kaiṭabha, Svāhā, Svadhā, Saravatī, Sāvitri, Mahādevi, Jambhanī, Mohinī, Māyā, Hṛī, *Śrī* and Sandhyā are names of the goddess found in one of the two *staves*. In the other the prayer of Yudhishthira incorporated a graphic picture of Devī's iconographic features. She being born in the womb of Yaśodā and belonging to the race of Nandagopa was endowed with four arms with emblems of sword and shield. Her perpetual abode was on the mount Vindhya and her thirst was quenched only with spiritual liquor, flesh and sacrificial victims.

Further source of tribal elements of the Mother in a stanza of the *Harivaṁśa* where the supreme goddess is described as being worshipped by the Śabaras, Barbaras and Pulinḍas;

"Vasasi Tvaṁ Mahādevī vaneshūpavateshu cha/

Śabaraivva rvaraiśchaiva pulindaiścha supujitā//[269]

Her residence on Himalayas and Vindhya, her love for sacrificial victims, flesh and wine represent her close association with the cult of fertility brought to India by the early invaders like the Mediterranean or the Armenoid race. Scattered evidence in regard to worship of such proto-goddesses in the Indus Valley region come to be known from the archaeological remains of Harappa and Mohenjodaro.[270] Śākambharī and Aparṇā, two designations of Mother found in the orthodox literature seem to be relics of aboriginal conception of the Earth Mother so vividly represented on the well known seal from Harappa.[271]

The *Devī-Mahatmya* of the *Mārkaṇḍeya Purāṇa* displays a spirit of eclecticism providing scope for tracing deeper sense of assimilation in the concept of the Mother from both the Āryan and tribal strata. But the trait of the Mother, as universal energy personified, preoccupies an idea of her supreme position as the creator, preserver and the destructor of the universe in the Tantras, which are distinguished from other scriptures by their "immense array of female personality."[272]

During the post Gupta period, *Jayadratha Yāmala* composed perhaps in mid-India issuing conception of Īśāna Kālī, Rakshā Kālī, Vīrya-Kālī, Prajñā-Kālī, Ghora-Tārā, Yoginī-chakra and Chakreśvarī[273] indicates an idea of the practice of Śāktism in northern India. The wave of Śāktism in Bengal during the 7th-8th centuries A.D. is derived from the evidence of *Devī Purāṇa* where practice of Śakti worship in the mode of left-hand-path (*Vāmāmargī*) is frequently met with. According to the account of the *Purāṇa,* Devī was worshipped in different forms after the manners of the *Vāmācara Śāktas* in different places in Rāḍha, Varendra, Kāmākhyā and Bhoṭadeśa.[274] Apart from the above information, the contents of the *Purāṇa* ensure apprehension regarding early existence of a *Devī Śāstra,* the material of which were handled by Purāṇakāra himself, pushing back further the prevalence of Śakti worship in Bengal.[275] Literary evidence may be corroborated by archaeological remain in the Pāhārpur panel depicting a man holding his tuft of hair in the right. Some scholars are of the opinion that the scene is likely to represent a symbol of devotion to the mother goddess by voluntary self sacrifice of a Śākta votary.[276] In the 7th patala of the Kubjikā tantra[277] we find the reference of Tripura as a great Śākta centre :

Śrūyatām Sāvadhanena siddha pīṭham pativrate,

Yasmin Sādhanamātreṇa Sarvasiddhiśvaro bhavet

Māyāvatī Madhupurī Kāsī Gorakṣakāriṇī

Hingulā ca Mahāpīṭham tathā jālandharampunaḥ

Jvālāmukhī Mahāpiṭham pīṭham Nagarasambhavam

Rāmagirirmahāpiṭham tathā Goddavarīpriye

Nepālam Karṇa Stūrañce Mahākarṇam tathā priye

Ayodhyā ca Kurukṣetram Siṁhanādam manoramam

Maṇipuram Hṛṣikeśam Prayāgañca tapovanam

Badari ca Mahāpiṭham Ambikā ardhanālakam

Triveṇī ca mahāpiṭham Gaṅgāsagarasaṅgaman

Nārikelañca Virajā Uḍḍiyanam Māheśvarī

Kamala Vinalā Caiva tathā Mahiṣmatī Purī

Vārāhi Tripurā caiva Vāgmatī Nilavāhinī

Govardhanam Vindhyagirih Kāmarūpam kalauyuga

Ghaṇṭakarṇo hayagrivo mādhavaśca Śuresvarī

Kṣiragrāmam Vaidyanātham Jāniyādyāmalocane

The wide development of Śakti worship in Tripura caused the productions a large variety of such Devī images. The worship of the female deities is even today a common feature in Tripura. Śakti worship prevailed originally among the Indo-Mongoloid[278] race of Tripura as Matai Katarmā. Śāktism is the blend of Āryan and non-Āryan streams of thought. It is a federation of cults where the main principle is the Tantric way to reach the goal. Tantricism was practiced in Trīpura and this tantric worship gradually developed in iconography. Tantricism was the predominant religion of Tripura from the eight to the fifteenth centuries A.D. The god and goddess of the Śaiva form of Hinduism became the deities of the Śākta-Tantra. P.C Bagchi advocates that, "the basis of Śāktism was a well established system as philosophy like the *Sāṁkhya* in which *prakriti* and *purusha* play the same role as that of the Śakti and Śiva. Once this philosophy was accepted, the affiliation of various local or tribal goddesses to *prakritis* became a matter of course."[279]

Irrespective of their creeds almost all the people of the Hindu society pay homage to mother goddesses inspite of their traditional family-deities, like Śiva, Viṣṇu etc. In Tripura, Śaktivāda is generally recognised as an integral part of the religion, not so much as a separate cult. Not only among the Śāktas, but in almost all other religious sects-the Śaivas, the Vaiṣṇavas, the Sauras, the Gāṇapatyas, an important place is occupied by Śakti.[280] Epigraphical evidences of the existence of Śakti cult in Tripura, though meagre, have also been found. The first that attracts our attention is the Deulbāḍi[281] (about 14 miles south of Comilla, Bāṅglādesh) image inscription, now in the Dacca Museum, of the middle of the seventh century A.D. It records that Prabhāvatī, the queen consort of the king Devakhaḍga, out of reverence of for Śarvāṇī, covered image of the deity with gold.

The Tripurasundarī Temple inscription of Dhaṇya Māṇikya bearing the date *Śaka* 1423 (1501 A.D.) is an important source of information regarding the Śakti religion in Tripura. This inscription is of two parts, first one is engraved on the east side of temple, and second on the south side of the temple. It is recorded that in ancient times there lived an accompanished king named Dhaṇya-Māṇikya. It is said that his charity was comparable with that of Karṇa of the *Mahābhārata.* Being pleased by his worship Indra descended to the Earth from the Heaven. In 1423 *Śaka* (1501 A.D.) he constructed a sky scraper temple in the name of the goddess "Ambikā."[282] After him Mahārājā Kalyāṇadeva, ruler of Tripura brought the Earth oppressed by enemies under his control. His son Govindadeva, a warrior was prominent among the kings. He endowed gold to Brahmin women. The dedicatory inscription gives the name of the founder of temple, Dhaṇya Māṇikya the foundation year of temple in 1423 *Śaka* or 1501 A.D. and other two devotee kings Kalyāṇa Māṇikya (1626 A.D. to 1656 A.D.) and his son Govinda Māṇikya (1656-1660 A.D. to 1667-1674 A.D.) Another inscription tells us that the Rāma Māṇikya (1673-1685 A.D.), son of king Govinda Māṇikya, renovated and repaired this temple. A devoted worshipper of Ambikā, the king Rāma Māṇikya took up this project of beautification of the temple in 1603 *Śaka* era (1681 A.D.) Tripurasundarī is the presiding deity of this revered temple.

The copper-plate inscription, at the throne of the Caturdaśa Devatā temple of Kalyāṇa Māṇikya (1626-1656 A.D.) furnished us with some interesting information for the study of Śaktism in Tripura.

It is written in Sanskrit language but in Bengali script. It records the successor of Kalyāṇa Māṇikya, prince Govinda-Māṇikya's greatness and bravery etc., who gave the throne to Girijā Devi for the blessing of her in 1571 *Śaka* (1649 A.D.)[283]. But it is true that Girijā Devi and Caturdaśa Devatā is not same deity. However, we do not find any deity name Girijā Devi in *Rājamalā,* a chronicle of Māṇikya dynasty.

Girijā Devi is most probably Devi Durgā, the daughter of Girirāj or Himalayas. There is a slight hint in the verse of this inscription (*Śrī Śrī Govinda Deva Himgiritanayayai hi Sinhāsanagryaṁ*) to the Devī Durgā or Devi Girijā legend. It is clear from the inscription that both the Māṇikya rulers were devotees of goddess Girijā. However a possible misplacing resulted the throne being used for Caturdaśa Devatā.

Full swing of Śakti worship in Tripura during seventh to sixteenth century A.D. may be ascertained from a large scale discovery of the images of the Mother Goddess. Two and four handed standing images of the goddess with variant attributes, symbols and attendant figures were generally worshipped in Tripura though six and ten handed varieties were not unknown. According to different iconographic features, the Śakti images recovered from the different parts of Tripura are Śarvāni, Durgā, Mahishāsuramardini, Kālī, and others.

Śarvānī, one of the sixteen aspects of Durgā in the *Brahmavaivartta Purāṇa,* is to be recognised from a specimen from Deulbāḍi. The figure of the goddess is endowed with eight hands carrying weapons like arrow, sword, discuss, conch-shell, trident, bell shield and bow. The description of the goddess shows affinity with that of Bhadra Durgā, Bhadrakāli, Āmbikā, Kshemaṅkarī found in the *Sāradātilaka Tantra.*[284] Tracing of its identification should not be given much weight as no literary evidence of later date can be admitted for recognition of this present image of so early date. Śarvānī is the Śakti of Śarva, one of the eight forms of Rudra in the *Atharva-Veda.* In the *Brahmavaivartta-Purāṇa* the goddess is involved for salvation of every living being.[285] Another an exceedingly charming bronze image of Śarvānī is recovered at Hrishya-mukha,[286] near Pilāk, south Tripura district. It is now in the government museum of Tripura. The eight handed goddess stands in *Sthānaka* pose on the central *padmapītha.* The front surface of the pedestal below the lotus seat is fully covered by flora and vegetal devices and a figure of lion with one of its paws raised in the right corner. On the left, all arms are missing excepting the lower one which holds a Ghaṇṭā. On right four hands are partly extant and the first, third and fourth hands hold a conch, a discuss and sword respectively, while the rest is missing. This image is assignable to nineth-tenth century A.D.

The important aspect of the mother is Durgā, who is widely popular in Tripura. Countless images of this aspects of the Devī come sharp from various parts of this country. It is believed by some scholars that the concept of Durgā as a ten armed Goddess has its sources in the *Rig Veda* where the wonderous Goddess Ushā advances with ten arms.[287] Purānakāras ascribe the name Durgā to Umā or Pārvatī because of her exploit of a delivery from the confinement of hell, re-birth, fear, disease and punishment of Yama.[288] In the *Mārkaṇḍeya Chaṇḍi*, the Mother has been called Durgā following her heroic achievement as a subduer of the demon Durgā[289]. In another place, she comes to be known as a vessel for crossing the ocean of the world[290]. Above all, Durgā was originally the presiding deity of fort (Durgā) and is repeatedly mentioned in the *Purāṇas* like Devī and Devī Bhāgavataṁ.[291] A fine specimen of two armed Durgā[292] (*Saumya*) found at Unakoti is shown standing on the back of a lion. She wears a short necklace and a Śari fastened with an ornamental belt at the waist. This image is attributed to eleventh and twelfth centuries A.D. The figure is standing with slight flexion bedecked with simple jewellery pronged headgear a characteristic feature of Māṇikya and Ahom sculptures and also common in earlier Burmese specimens.[293]

Another fourteenth-fifteenth century A.D. female head found at Unakoti, may be identified as Durgā and it though very badly defaced, survives. The head of the deity with her spreading matted locks, third eye and soft neck lines is one of the best specimens of Unakoti. Swirling matted hair animates the sculpture. Long ears with Kuṇḍalas, carved on the same plane, are not as disproportionate, as noticed in other examples. Soft fleshliness of the ears and the neck attest to a sure hand of chiselling. The figure is bedecked with a pearl necklace, minutely designed earrings and a beaded tiars on the forehead used to tuck and swinging hair (equally an out landish feature) as it were. On the right side of Devī is another male head, probably of Śiva. Locally those are popularly known as Śiva Durgā.

The most important icon is the Mahishāsuramardinī type whose independent worship is still popular through out Tripura. Many images of Durgā in her Ugra form have been discovered in Tripura.

The *Mārkaṇḍeya-Chaṇḍi* introduces the principal career of the mother in the attitude of slaying the demon Mahishāsura. The idea of the onslaught of the goddess over the Asuras arose from that the subduing the demon Mahisha. The word 'Mahisha' in the *Rig Veda* in the sense of beast occurs many times except once, which, according to Sāyaṇa signifies "great''[294]. It may be presumed that the episode of Mahishāsuramardinī indicating slaying of an Asura by the goddess, undergoes changes with the plight of the Devī subduing a buffalo demon. The pre-historic sources of Mahishāsuramardinī gives apprehension in regard to her identity with Virgo of the Mediterranean people because this tribal goddess is very close to Durgā the goddess of fort.

Victorious campaigns over the Mon khmers (who were of mixed origin from the Caspian, Austroloid and Alpine) by the Mediterraneans seem to be in the background of the episode of Mahishāsuramardinī. Like the cows to the Vedic Āryans, the buffalos to the people of Mon khmer were the most pious animals. The auspicious symbol of the invaded took the form of Mahishāsura subdued by the goddess Virgo of the invaders. Archaeological remains of three faced statue with buffalo horned heads from Mohenjodaro and Harappa denoting Mon khmer deity also corroborate the historic information to be true.[295] Ths historic evidence of Mahishāsuramardinī is to be attested by the discovery of image of the goddess belonging to the reign of Chandra Gupta II. A circular clay seal from Nālandā is occupied in the main area by a standing Mahishāsuramardinī figure with four arms holding sword, trident, shield and bell.

The goddess is almost invariably represented with ten arms but in the early medieval sculptures found in Tripura, she is very often found having only eight arms. A unique image of eight armed Mahishāsuramardinī[296] in stone was found at Pilāk and is now housed in the temple of the Rajesvari Āśram at Muhuripur. The goddess stands *ālīḍha* pose. The right leg of the image is firmly placed on the head of the buffalo demon and the left one rests on a plain pedestal. In the four hands on the right, the goddess carries the asi, chakra, sarā, and trisūla thrust into the body of the buffalo and the four hands on the lefts holds the dhunu, taṇka, sṛpa and tail of the buffalo demon. This image may be dated to the eighth century A.D.

Similar image of Mahishāsuramardinī suffered partial damage during its transport to the Āsrama at Muhuripur. The damaged face has been crudely re-done and the semi circular top of the back slab restored by the sevaits. With one foot on the head of the buffalo demon (depicted in the animal form), the goddess is in the attitude of piercing the neck of the buffalo with a trisūla held in one of her right hand. The three remaining right hands bear an arrow, a wheel and a sword (in the uppermost hand). The lower left hand holds the tail of the buffalo, the next a bow, the third a shield and the fourth (uppermost) a snake (tail alone preserved). Stylistically, the image may be dated to the eighth century A.D.

Similar image of the deity is also discovered from Thākurāni tilla mound, Pilāk. The upper part from the chest is missing. The tenon would suggest that the image was enshrined as the principal deity within a shrine. The available height above the tenon is 1m 16cm, the maximum width being 77 cm.[297] The state of the preservation of available part is extremely unsatisfactory. The goddess is standing with her right leg stretched and left leg bent at the knee on a plain pedestal. On the same pedestal are seen two legs of the buffalo, from the truncated neck emerges the demon. The image was at least eight armed. Her lowest left hand holds the hair of the demon, while another left arm is bent and turned towards her abdomen. The trident which pierces the neck of the buffalo was evidently in the grip of one of her right hands.

An eight-armed image of Mahishāsuramardinī was found at Devadāru, East Pilāk, and now worshipped at the Devadāru Āśram. The goddess is in attitude of piercing the neck of the buffalo with a trisūla held in one of her right hand. The three remaining right hands are missing. The lowest left hand holds the tail of the buffalo, the next a bow, the third a shield and the fourth a snake. Absence of the lion-mount as well as of sharpcut curves in the *atibhanga* stance of the deity and also the theriomorphic form of the demon in the relief of the image indicate an early date for it. Though executed in rough stone, the figures are so modelled as to suggest the soft texture of flesh and skin. The heavy form and gigantic size indicates it to be belonging to the eighth century A.D.

An exceedingly charming image of ten-armed Mahishāsur-mardinī[298] of the eleventh and twelfth centuries A.D. was found at Amarpur, south Tripura. It is now worshipped in the house of Chandramohan Shil, Amarpur. The Devī stands in the *pratyālīḍha* pose. The left leg of the goddess is placed on the body of Mahisāsura, while the right leg is on the back of the lion. The image is endowed with ten hands carrying, triśula, kheṭaka, tanka, śarā, khaḍga, dhanu, paraśu, aṅkuśa, nāgapāśa and sūchimudrā. She has plunged a trident into the body of the Asura.

An interesting sand-stone image of Mahisāsurmardinī of the twelfth century A.D. is erroneously worshipped as Kālī in temple near Kamālasāgar at Kasbā.[299] The ten-armed goddess holds in her hands nakusa, triśula, śakti, chakra and abhaya, but other attributes are not clear. She wears *Jaṭāmukuṭa,* and the Jaṭās are spread over both the sides of the head in an orderly manner. The *Vāhana,* the lion is shown in the middle portion of the stele. The kneeling demon with folded hands rests on a plain pedestal. A Śivaliṅga is present in front of the demon and this is rare evidence in the field of Hindu iconography. Two inscriptions are engraved on the northern and the southern side of the temple, both are damaged.

A ten-armed Mahishāsuramardinī image which is tentatively assignable to eleventh-twelfth century A.D. was discovered from Hiripura village, Comilla, Bāṅglādesh. Now it is worshipped in the house of Anil Chandra Chakraborty of Nalchharā, Sonāmurā in Tripura. The height of image is 1.03m, the maximum width being 52 cm. The goddess is standing with her right leg stretched on the lion and left leg bent on the buffalo, which are on a plain pedestal. Two front legs of buffalo and front, and a behind legs of lion are seen on the pedestal. Her ten hands hold aṅkuśa, paraśu, dhanu, sarā, chakra, kheṭaka, khaḍga, padma, śaṅka, and triśula. The central figure is mounted on her lion in pratyaudha attitude seizing the locks of the demon by her left hand and piercing his breast with a śula. Two images stand on two side of the goddess and holds in their hands a khaḍga and a śaṅka. She wears a short necklace and a Śari fastened with an ornamental belt at the waist.

A fourteenth century A.D. rock-cut image of the Devi is discovered at Devatāmuḍā, South Tripura district. The measurement of image is 12.88m x 7.76m. The goddess of Mahishāsuramardinī with round face and bulging round eyes, is executed frontly. The heavy torso, broad shoulders and sturdy hands are mechanically joined with each other, as it were, and the total effect, that the image creates, is not of an organic whole. The goddess is standing with her right leg stretched and leg bent at the knee on a plain pedestal. An interesting sand stone image of eight-armed Vaiṣṇavi[300] of the fifteenth century A.D. from Amarpur is shown seated in the *lalitasana* pose with Garuḍa below her seat. The goddess gracefully helds śaṅkha, chakra, godā, khaḍga, dhnu, sarā.

The famous image of the four armed goddess Kālī, locally called Tripurasundarī is worshipped in the temple of the Tripurasundarī at Udaipur, South Tripura. It is a well known Śākta Pīṭha in the Tripura state, Dakṣiṇa pāda of Devī Satī fell down here. *Tripurāyām Duttapādo Devi Tripurasundarī.*[301]

On the composition the goddess under a multifoiled arch stands in the *samapadasthānaka,* posture on a short figure like south Indian *apasmārapurasha,* the latter is locally known as Mahādeva, perhaps on the analogy of Kālī standing on prostrate Śiva. The goddess wears a somewhat elongated pronged head gear and exhibits in her four hands clockwise varamudrā, ankuśa, pasā and naramuṇḍa respectively. It is believed that the image was installed in the temple in the seventeenth centtury A.D. after its renovation by Rāmadeva-Māṇikya (1681 A.D.). Stylistic considerations also point to a similar dating on the basis of the presence of multifoild arch on the back slab.

Other Minor Sects

The two other deities of the Brāhmanical pantheon, Sūrya and Gaṇapati also received worship from the peoples of Tripura though in comparison with Viṣṇu, Śiva and Devī they were less popular. Of the five all known Brāhamanical sects (Pañcopāsakas), the Saura or the worshipper of the Sun god and Gāṇapatya or the worshipper of Gaṇapati, the elephant headed and pot bellied divinity, are also considered to be the objects of great veneration for Hindus since very early times.

The Vedic solar deity Sūrya is invoked in every morning and evening through muttering of the Gāyatrī hymn. The importance of Sūrya was due to his diverse functioning in bestowing long life, prosperity and fame apart from his other activities of removing sins. Yudhishthira was graced by the God with the power of having all kinds of food just on the eve of their exile. In the *Rig-veda,* he is equated with Brahman being described as the soul of both movable and immovable objects. In the *Purusha-Sūkta* and in the *Śataruriya,* he is addressed as the bestower of salvation. Above all, the main function of Sūrya, as a cult divinity, to remove all kinds of diseases and Harimāna, i.e. certain skin disease destroying the softness of epidermics, is highly estimated in a triplet devoted to the God. Sāyaṇa in his commentary with illustration of Ṛishi Praskaṇva,[302] advocates recitation of the above triplet by any afflicated man, who was found to be cured of any kind of disease.

Removing of all kinds of diseases, specially leprosy, became the main trait of the cult god, Sūrya, who assimilated certain foreign elements, not basically different from the indigenous ones, after the immigration of some priest from Persia in the north-western frontier of India during the Śaka and the Kushāṇa rule. The historic event is conspicuous in the narrative of Śāmba found in the *Bhavishya*[303] and *Varāha-Purāṇas.*[304] Arrival of eighteen priests from Śākadvīpa, (probably Seistan) being appointed by Śāmba to worship the Sun god in a munificent temple built by him on the bank of Chandrabhāgā, is the story in the event of intercommunication of some elements prevailing in association with Sūrya in both India and Persia. Epigraphical information corroborating the Purāṇic evidence of Śāmba hailing the Magi priests to India is to be noted in an inscription from Govindrapur, assignable to 1137-38 A.D.[305] The coins of Kaṇishka and other Kushāṇa kings bearing an engraving of the Sun God Miyiro or Mihira (i.e. Mithra) of ancient Iran[306] provide concrete evidence of the advent of Iranian Sun on the soil of India. That the worship of Sun God in India was prevalent since fourth or fifth century A.D. is to be noted in an evidence of *Bṛihat-Saṁhitā* extolling efficacy of the Maga Brāhmaṇas for installation of Sun images.[307] It is not unlikely that both the Hindus and the Iranians of the same Aryan stock might have worshipped Mitra and Mithra side by side. The cuneiform inscription found in Cappadocia (as kingdom of Asia-Minor) mentions names of Indo-Iranian gods like Mitra, Varuṇa, Indra and Nāsatya worshipped by a Hittite tribe living in Mitani to the north-west of present Iraq.

The gods were also extremely popular in Persia during the Aryan period.[308] May be, the Indian Mitra under Iranian Phalnax reappeared in India with the Magi Sun worshipping sect of Persia. The healing function of leprosy among other traits of Sūrya gained momentum after the Magian settlement in India. In ancient Persia, leprosy, caused to be afflicated due to some offences committed against the Sun, was believed to be the curse of Sun. The echo of the above belief and the following custom that "a leprous Persian must neither enter the city nor have communication with any of his country men"[309] is to be seen in the story of Śāmba.

The grace of the Sun god in his divine power of removing diseases, bestowing vigour, strength and long life is advocated in the *Dhramaśāstras,* the *Rāmāyaṇa,* the *Mahābhārata* and the *Purāṇas.* In the *Brihatsaṁhitā,* a sculptor is warned against leaving careless defect on Sun icon[310] because this may destine him to be afflicted with diseases like leprosy. The lyrical poem 'Sūryaśtakam' was composed by Mayura (seventh century A.D.) out of his great devotion to Sun whose grace recovered him from affliction of leprosy. A verse in the above Kāvya carrying an implication of the said disease resembles astonishingly those found in the *Charakasaṁhitā.*[311]

The popularity of Sūrya since the time of the Vedas made way for an exclusive class of Sun worshippers. Reference to the existence of such a class comes to be known from the *Matsyapurāṇa* where the word *Sūrya-bhakta* is found beside *Śiva-bhakta* and *Viṣṇu-bhakta. Vāyupurāṇa* refers to *Rākshasadharma* in connection with Sun worship. Scattered evidences are to be found in both early epigraphs and literature shedding light on the existence of a class of Sun worshippers. Available early data are some copper coins (C. first century B.C. to C. first century A.D.) recording two names, viz. Sūryamitra and Bhānumitra on one side and with engraving of Sun radiating luster on the other.[312] All the predecessors of Harshavardhana

(7th century) are styled 'Paramādityabhakta' in the royal grants of Harsha. Prabhākaravardhana, father of Harsha, appears to have been a great devotee to Sun in the *Harshacharita* of Bāṇabhaṭṭa.[313] In '*Probodhachandrodaya*' the poet Kṛiṣnamiśra in a significant passage mentions the Śaivas, Vaishṇvas and Sauras who under the leadership of Sarasvati conducted a fierce campaign against the Buddhists, the Jainas and the followers of Chārvāka (materialists) living under the protection of *Mahāmoha*. Ānandagiri in the 13th *Prakaraṇa* of Śankaravijaya-kāvya[314] refers to different Saura classes. The sun-cult which was an amalgamation of indigenous and foreign elements, came to be professed by the people of this region since medieval period. The inscribed image of Sūrya discovered from Deulbāḍi in Tripura belongs to the seventh century A.D. An important image of Sūrya was found at Pilāk and is now worshipped in Rājesvani Āśram at Muhuripur. This image consists of a semi circular stele. The lower part of the Sun god is hidden up to thigh by the body of the car. The Sun chariot is drawn by seven horses. The central horse placed in rectangular shaped niche faces outwards and the remaining six, three on each side, are represented as prancing. Aruna is placed in front of the deity and the two side figures have their knees and legs uncurved and shown as inserted in the pedestal.

Sūrya holds, as usual, stalks of full blown lotuses in his both hands and a sword which is suspended from the waist-girdle on the left (girdle is not clear at present). He wears high *Kirīṭa-mukuṭa* with a flattened top, a simple curly wigs come upto the shoulder. At the top corners of the blackslab are seen flying Vidyādharas. The figure conforms to the iconographic tradition of the northern variety of Sūrya images. The face and garment of the deity being partially painted, the original nature of the facial treatment except its oval shape, can hardly be ascertained. Aesthetically, the modelling is some what stiff, but a sense of rhythm has been sought to be created in the composition by the soft movement of the lotus stalks, flying Vidyādharas and the galloping horses. It appears, however, from the pleasing accessories that this sculpture deserves to be placed in works of the later Gupta tradition of the seventh-eighth centuries A.D. Incidentally the Sāgardhebā Sūrya image is strongly reminiscent of an inscribed image of the same God from Mrohung (Ārākān)[315] which bears a family likeness to it. And as Ārākān Sūrya icon is palaeographically datable to the seventh - eighth century A.D.,[316] the present sculpture is also to be assigned to the same period.[317]

Sūrya image found at Pilāk is an interesting and important specimen for the study. This is the biggest among the Sūrya images so far found in Tripura.[318] The heavy and solidly built (but at the same time of reposeful, delicate and highly spiritual modelling) massive standstone image is lying in *situ* in the Thākurāni tilā mound at Pilāk. The figure, perhaps a standing one holds eight-petalled lotuses in both hands held with beautifully carved soft finger tips. The lotus in his rounded backslab is missing, though the stalk exists. The god wears a *Kirīṭamukuṭa* which seems to have flattened on the top, a dangling *Karṇakuṇḍals* and a necklace with a pendent. Locks of hair fall upto chest on each side. The square type of face instead of being ovoid, the sharp-cut eyes with heavy drooping eye lids, fleshy lips and the absence of intricate ornamentation, which are the characteristics of the later Gupta art, are all prevailing in the image. The deep shadow below the lips, soft gliding of the lines and rounded modelling of the figure which slowly and softly emerges from the backslab, the long wigs of the god and the simplicity of the ornamental devices are all reminiscent of the later Gupta tradition.

It is evidenced from the piece that sculptor took much pain to achieve success on such a crude type of stone where it was difficult task to bring out the sensuous modelling and it also proves the some earlier tradition of sculpting on heavy stone was there prior to the period with out which this type of creation would not have been possible. But this type of monumental sculpture or rock cut works of earlier period have not come to our notice as yet. This is one of the reasons to presume the influence of more powerful artists of south India who had an earlier tradition of such type of sculpting.[319]

Another large sandstone standing image of Sūrya is buried on the Pūjā-Kholā mound of Paśchim Pilāk. The height of the exposed portion of two meters, the maximum width being 1m 46cm. Wearing a *mukuṭa* and other ornaments (mostly broken) Sūrya holds in both hands stalks of full-blown lotuses. On his either sides are two standing figures, with a halo behind, one above the other. All the four are two armed, one hand resting on the thigh and the other on the waist.

They may represent wives of Sūrya.[320] By the side of the legs of Sūrya are two more figures, their upper portion alone exposed above ground. They too have a halo each carved out of the backslab.

Another two feet standstone image of Sūrya of Pilāk, is preserved on a double petalled lotus. Issuing from the lotus is the stalk of a smaller lotus. The pedestal below the main lotus was relieved with seven horses (within separate compartments) of which five are extant—three prancing on the sinister, the central squatting and one prancing on the dexter. The height of the available portion is 43 cm.

A sand-stone image of Sūrya of the eleventh century A.D. found somewhere in Tripura presents some development in the treatment of the iconic type. This image is now preserved in the house of Māhārāj Kumar Sahadev Bikaram Kishore Debvarman of Agartala. The chariot is drawn by seven horses. It is interesting to note that two swords are carved on both sides of the Sun-god. Piṅgalā to his right and Daṇḍin to his left and well carved. His consorts Usā and Pratyūṣā are also presented with their arrow-shooting-kneeling posture. Saṁgā and Chhāyā are also visible standing in their usual poses. Maheśvetā stands between the Sun god and Aruna.[321]

The images of Sun god discovered in Tripura indicate the wide worship of Sun god from eighth to the fifteenth century A.D.

Gaṇapati

Gaṇapati is the master of this world. He is the deity of the Gaṇas in the *Rig-Veda,* i.e. the terrible and the wild followers of Rudra and therefore he was placed at the head of a non-vedic deity.[322] A host of *Vināyakas* or evil doers come to our notice in early literature and the *Mahābhārata*. They do mischief if not properly propitiated. In course of time all these Vināyakas were singled out into one in the form of Gaṇapati whose chief function was changed from creating obstacles to bestowing success.[323] Thus, Gaṇapati came to be identified with Brahma, Brahmanaspati or Brihaspati[324] and was elevated to the position of a Vedic deity. The hymn of Brahmanaspati is also called Gaṇapatisūkta and Gaṇapati being equated with Brahma become the lord of wisdom and ruled over all the manifested and unmanifested aspects of Brahma. His intimate allegiance to Veda and Vedic Brahma helped to develop myths in the Purāṇas around the elephant headed god. The story of Gaṇapati's writing of the *Mahābharata* at the instance of Vyāsa was a later addition. Probably worship of Gaṇapati was initiated by the people living in northern and north-western India where the primitive Aryan tribes living in deserts, mountains and forests felt need of such a guardian deity. In the *Śānti-parva* of the *Mahābhārata,* Gaṇas are mentioned as dwellers of such places.[325]

Gaṇeśa is universally regarded as the eldest and the most favourite son of Mahādeva. But he is one among the host of his attendants and is Brahmachārin. Still, he is also regarded as the god of the Sūdras in the scriptures:

"Viprāṇāṁ daivatiṁ Śambhuh
Kshatriyāṇām tu Mādhavah
Vaiśyānāṁ tu bhaved Brāhmā
Śūdrānāṁ gaṅanāyakaḥ"[326]

In fact, the worship of Gaṇeśa among the people of upper class get affiliation in a late period. Only modern *Smritis* like Kātyāyana[327] resorted to his worship with mothers. *Mānava-Grihya-Sūtra*[328] gives an account of *Vināyakaśānti* which was to be performed in connection with wanding off a kind of malevolent spirits. Materials prescribed for Vināyaka-śānti in the *Yājñavalkasmriti*[329] are very impure substances like wine, raw and cooked fish and flesh. Prohibition against receiving invitation in the Śrāddha ceremony of the people performing *gaṇayāgas* is repeatedly referred to in the *Manusmriti*[330]. So, worship of Gaṇapati gained recognition in association with evil art of magic and *abhichāra* works. Archaeological evidences regarding Gaṇeśa worship are attested by the elephant device on the coins of Indo-Scythian and Indo-Parthian rulers. The literary evidences available in the *Kādambarī* of Bāṇabhaṭṭa give an estimation of Gaṇeśa among the divine groups of the Gandharvas and Kinnaras[331]. Scanty evidences with regard to the existence of Gaṇapaticult in Tripura put forward no concrete idea but a few number of images from different parts of the region provides an idea of his position and prevalence of worship.

An inscribed image of Gaṇeśa from the village Mandhuk of Tippera and dated in the first year of Gopāladeva[332] has not only thrown a flood of light on the prevalence of Gaṇeśa-worship in the far eastern frontier of Tippera district, but also is an unquestionable evidences of the Pāla rule over South East Bengal during the reign period of Gopāla II. The image is of a four-armed deity, executed on an asymmetrical slab. The pot bellied elephant-headed god, seated on a lotus throne with left leg drawn up and the right knee raised, seems to hold a rosary in the upper right hand which is broken and the other hand just below, conveys an elephant tusk. The emblems held in his left hands are missing now, but there is trace of a tray of sweetmeat (*modakapātra*) into which the tip of his proboscis was applied. The other remaining attribute might have been a sapling of a sugar cane (*Ikshudaṇḍa*). The figure is moderately executed carrying matted locks of hair and snake forming the holy thread (*nāgayajñopabīta*). Below his lotus seat on the pedestal, there are engravings of his vehicle rat (*Vāhana*), effigies of donors and a record of three lines in between.

Siddhaṁ II Śrī Gopāladevarāje (rājye Saṁvatsare)

mātāpitir pūrvāngama (mam) Krtvā -

Sakala Sattvarase (Sih) (anuttara) Jñānalābhau (lābhāya)
devadharmo'yam - Vrddha sārtha jambhalamitrena

Kriyatām (Karita) iti II Siddham II.

It means that this meritorious offering is caused to be made by the old merchant Jambhalamitra for the attainment of superb knowledge by the creatures, headed by his parents, during the first year the reign of Śrī Gopāladeva.

While analysing the record, it is stateted that the deity installed by the donor Jambhalamitra during the first year of Gopāladeva, was apparently a Brahmanical divinity, Gaṇeśa, but the phraseology of the inscription bears the tradition of a Mahāyāna record aspiring after enlightenment and well being of all creatures headed by his parents. Even the name of the donor Jambhalamitra signified a name of a Buddhist deity, viz. Jambhālā.[333]

The present act of donation is a parallel instance of another Vināyaka (Gaṇeśa) image dedicated by a merchant Buddhamitra during the fourth regnal year of Mahīpāla I, the grandson of Gopāla II.[334] It is curious that the name of the donor's father's name is in the previous record from Mandhuk. Judging in the light of intervening period between these two acts of peity and from the mention of the reign monarches in both the records, it seems not to be unlikely that Jambhalamitra, donor of the first record and the father of Buddhamitra in the latter was one and the same person.

The image dedicated by Buddhamitra is a seated one being endowed with emblems like a radish, a rosary in the right hands, an axe and a tray of sweetmeat in the left hands, respectively. The trunk is applied to the tray of sweetmeat and the left task of the elephant head is in the broken manner. The god is decorated with a serpent thread and a small figure of his Vāhana is found on the pedestal.

The iconographic description of the god follows up the description of Vināyaka found in the *Viṣṇudharmamottara.*

Vināyakastu Kartavya gajavaktraś-caturbhūjah-I

Mulakam Cākṣamālā ca tasya dakṣiṇahastaryaḥ II

Pātram modakapurṇam tu paraśuścaiva vāmatacḥ I

Dantaścasya na kartvyo vāmeri - punisūdana II

Pādapīṭha Krītapādam eka asanāgo bhavet I

Pūrṇamodakapātre tu karāgram tasyakārayet II[335]

It is generally believed that the image is that of Brahmanical Gaṇapati, but the record on the pedestal follows the pevious tradition found in that of Jambhalamitra. Possibly the donors of the images were followers of Buddhism, but devoted to Brahmanical deity Gaṇapati because of their belongingness to merchant community. And Gaṇapati is the deity par excellence of the business magnate.[336]

A seated image of Gaṇeśa with four arms is found carved among a group of statues on the Unakoti hill, Dhalay district, Tripura. The date of the sculpture seems to be the eleventh - twelfth century A.D.[337] The god is accompanied by two unusual elephant headed attendants with four tusks and four and six hands respectively with weapons other than those of Gaṇeśa. The main figure is drapped with a dhoti tightened to his waist with a serpent felt. Emblems in his hands are defaced. His two attendants were probably some local deities associated with Gaṇeśa. Gaṇeśa is seldom found in supreme position like the present one and usually occupies a subordinate place of an associate in company of important deities.[338]

In the sculptures of Unakoti, another finely executed image of four-armed Gaṇeśa[339] made of sand-stone is shown seated and he holds parasū, śaṅka, aksamālā and vara-mudrā. This Saḍa-bhuja Gaṇeśa has three tusks and stands in *Sthanaka* pose. The image is datable to the eleventh and twelfth centuries A.D. Another seated image of Gaṇeśa with eight arms is found in Unakoti hill. It has four tusks. In the two hands on the right, the God carries the *padma, chakra,* and other two hands on the left holds the triśula and śaṅka. Next one right hand and one left hand hold *aksamālā* and last right and left hand raised on his waist.[340]

A stone image of four armed Śakti - Gaṇeśa[341] of the eighth and ninth century A.D. originally discovered from Thakurani tilla mound, Pilāk now housed in the west Pilāk club. This type of Śakti Gaṇeśa seems to be associated with Vāmāchāri Tantrik variety of worship and few of this form of images are actually met with in the Gupta and post-Gupta art and is thus of great interest. This is the only image of Śakti-Gaṇeśa so far discovered in Tripura, though Gaṇeśa is seated on a crudely carved double petalled lotus in *lalitāsana* with his consort sitting on his left lap. The god covered the whole stela. The long trunk softly curled over the pot-belly to reach upto the right knee (which is peculiarity of the Gaṇeśa images of Tripura, belonging to this period), which brings the effect of rhythm and gliding softness in the modelling. The sculpture is so badly defaced and abraded that only outlines of the modelling is recognised and is difficult to make a proper appraisal of its artistic qualities.

Another stone image was brought from Thakurani tilla in west Pilāk in 1956. This represents the four-armed pot bellied Gaṇeśa seated in *lalitāsana* on a double petalled lotus rising above a long stalk. The trunk is turned towards his lower right hand. Below the lotus, at a lower level, is a mouse.[342]

References

1. Ganchaudhuri, J.N., *Tripura: The Land and Its People,* Delhi, 1980, p. 182.
2. Roy, N.R., *Bāṅgālir Itihāsa* : Adiparva, reprinted, Calcutta, 1959, p. 446.
3. *I.H.Q.*, vol-6 (1930), p. 55

4. Das, Ratna, *Art & Architecture of Tripura,* Agartala, 1997, p. 4.
5. Bhattacharya, Priyabrata, *Tripura Deva O Devi,* Agartala, p. 25.
6. Majumder, R.C., (ed), *History of Bengal,* I, pp. 26-27.
7. An inscription found upon the pedestal of an image discovered in Silua in Noakhali district, now in Bāṅglādesh reveals a script which was used in the inscription of the Maurya period. It is probable from this evidence that the region around Tripura was within Maurya rule.
8. *EI,* XXI, P-83; cf, *I H.Q,* X, p. 58.
9. Literally, it means the band of sixmen who belonged to a Buddhist sect.
10. *I.H.Q.*, X, p. 57
11. *I.H.Q.*, Vol. 6(1930), p. 55.
12. Ganchaudhuri, J., *Tripura : The Land and its People,* p. 65.
13. Watters, T., *On Yuan Chwang's Travels in India*, II, p. 187.
14. Niyogi, P., *Buddhism in Ancient Bengal,* Calcutta, 1983, p. 13.
15. Majumdar, R.C., *op.cit.* Vol. I, p. 86.
16. *Ibid.,* p. 87.
17. *E.I.*, XVII, pp. 357-59.
18. Sen, Benoy Chandra, *Some Historical Aspects of the Inscriptions of Bengal,* Calcutta, 1992, p. 278.
19. Sen, Benoy Chandra, *op. cit,* p. 255. The history of Khaḍgas after Rājarājbhaṭṭa is not known. There is no agreement among the scholars regarding the date of the line of the Khaḍga kings. They may be placed in the latter part of the 7th century A.D. on the basis of palaeographic evidence and I-tsing's account.
20. *I.H.Q.*, XXIII, p. 221.
21. *Ibid.*
22. *J.A.S (L),* XVII, 1951, No. 2, pp. 83-94.
23. The legend the *Dharma-chakra* in one of the *Maināmati* plates has been read as 'Śrī Baṅgalā Mṛgāṅkasya' the title adopted by the Deva king Ānandadeva (F.A. Khan, Maināmati, 1963, p.19). The legend 'Śrī Abhinava-mṛgāṇka' referred to above is taken as Buruda of King Bhavadeva, who issued the Charter-(Morrison, B.M., Lālmāi, A Cultural Centre of Early Bengal, p. 102.)
24. Alam Shamsul, A.K.M., *Maināmati,* 1982, pp. 51-52.
25. From the three Deva plates we get the names of four generation of Deva rulers :

Śri Śāntideva
Śri Vīradeva
Śrī Āandadeva
Śrī Bhavadeva

All these rulers bore imperial titles as indicative of their independent position. We do not know about the extent of their empire but it seems that the Deva rulers had their Headquarter in the Comilla region.

It is difficult to assign any definite date of the inscriptions. F.A. Khan places them not long after the Khaḍgas (*Maināmati,* 1963, p. 19); but some other scholars believe that the Deva was dynasty ousted by the Khaḍgas from Samataṭa, who according to A.H. Dani (*Indian Palaeography,* Oxford, 1963, p.135) has bracketed the two Maināmati plates of Bhavadeva with the Khalimpur plate of Dharmapāla.

26. *JAIH,* V, p.176.
27. *E.I,* XXVI, p. 313.
28. Vardhamānapur has not yet been definitely identified R.C., Majumdar identified it with modern Burdwan in West Bengal (*E.I,* XXVI, P. 315); while N.K. Bhattasali with Vikramapura (*I.H.Q.,* II, pp. 321-25). D.C. Sircar looks in for its location in Sylhet [*JRASB(L),* XVII, p. 901].
29. *E.I,* XXVI, 317, verse 4 : it is translated as 'a daughter of great king.'
30. In the Mathura Museum there is a similar; c.f. Coomarswamy, *History of Indian and Indonesian Art,* fig. 84.
31. Majumdar, N.G., *Inscriptions of Bengal,* Rajshahi, 1929, (Vol. III), P. I, *E.I,* XI, p. 136.
32. This verse occurs about the beginning of the other charters, e.g., Kedārpur and probably the Edilpur.
33. Gupta, K.K., *Copper Plate of Sythet,* pp. 81-192.
34. *E.I,* XXVII., pp. 51-58.
35. *Ibid.,* XXXIII, pp. 134-40.
36. *PIHC,* XXIII, 1960, Pt. I, p. 36. The plate was recovered from Dacca and is dated in 24th regnal year.
37. His name was hitherto known from the Bharella image inscription (*E.I,* XVII, pp. 349-55). For his Maināmati plates, see Khan, F.A., *Maināmati,* p. 22, and *PIHC,* XXIII, pt. I, P. 36.
38. *PIHC,* XXIII, 1960, Pt., I, P. 36; Khan, F.A., *Maināmati,* p. 13; Govinda Chandra is known from two more inscriptions of his

region. His name seems to be alluded to in the Tirumalai inscription of Rajendra Chola.

39. *E.I,* XII, 37; Majumder, N.G., *Inscription of Bengal,* Vol. III, p. 14.
40. *E.I,* XXX, 259-63.
41. Sengupta, S., *Tripura Prasanga,* Agartala, p. 19.
42. *I.H.Q,* Vol. 6, 1930, p. 40
43. Niyogi, P., *op. cit.,* p. 67.
44. Sen, Binoy Chandra, *op. cit.,* p. 93.
45. *Ibid.,* p. 86.
46. Bhattasali, N.K., *Iconography of Buddhist and Brahmanical Sculptures in the Dacca Museum,* New Delhi, 1974, p. 7.
47. *I.H.Q.,* IX, p. 282.
48. *Ibid.*
49. *J.N.S.I.,* Bombay, 1962, pp.141-142.
50. Cordier, *Catalogue, II,* pp. 159-60.
51. Paul, P.L., *The Early History Bengal,* II, Calcutta, 1930, p. 30.
52. Cordier, *op.cit.,* p. 68.

    The question of the identification of Paṭṭikarā is still controversial. It is held that it is situated within the district of Tippera 'for an important *Paragaṇā* of this district which extends upto the Maināmati hills, five miles to the west of Comilla and is still known as Pātikārā or Pāiṭkārā. In older documents this pargaṇā is called Pātikārā or Pāiṭkerā which more closely resembles the old name. An important information is found in a Maināmati grant of Laḍaha Chandra' sixth regnal year. The grant was made in favour of the God Laḍaha-Mādhavadevabhaṭṭaraka installed by the king at Paṭṭikeraka is Samataṭamaṇḍala. The second plot was also situated in the same area. From this it may be presumed that Paṭṭikeraka may by identical with Paṭṭikera and was situated with the Samataṭamaṇḍala of the Paṇḍrabhukti. Devapravata was situated in the neighbourhood of Paṭṭikera; see, Majumdar, R.C., *History of Ancient Bengal,* p. 280 and *P.A.,* No. 3, 1966, p. 22.
53. Shamsul Alam, A.K.M., *op. cit.,* p. 27. The northern half of the ridge is known as *Maināmati.* This name is the name of the queen Mayanāmati, the wife of Manikachander of local ballads. The southern half of the ridge is called Lālmāi from the fact that "it is made up of slightly micaceous, yellow-coloured sand stone and ferruginous concretions which when decomposed colour the top of the hill brick red.; see, *ASI-AR,* 1922, p. 81.

54. *Ibid.*
55. Shamsul Alam, A.K.M., *op. cit.*, p. 34.
56. *Ibid.*, p. 35.
57. *Ibid.*, p. 35.
58. *Ibid.*, p. 28.
59. *Ibid.*, p. 28.
60. *JAIH,* V, 1971-7, p. 179.
61. Morrison, B.M., *Laimai—A Cultural Centre of Early Bengal,* Newyork, 1977, p. 28
62. The maximum being 13" x 11½" x 2¾"
63. Shamsul Alam, A.K.M., *op. cit.*, p. 47.
64. *Ibid.*, p. 48.
65. *Ibid.*, p. 48.
66. *Ibid.*, p. 30.
67. *Ibid.*, p. 31.
68. *Ibid.*
69. Niyogi, P., *op. cit.*, p. 77.
70. Shamsul Alam, A.K.M., *op.cit.*, p. 29.
71. Niyogi, P., *op. cit.*, p. 79.
72. Morrison, B.M., *op. cit.*, pp. 33-34.
73. *P.A.*, No. I, 1964, p. 19.
74. Khan., F.A., *op. cit.* pp., 23-24.
75. But when it was visited earlier there was no image of Chaṇḍī.
76. Morrison, B.M., *op. cit.*, p. 60
77. Shamsul Alam, A.K.M., *op. cit.*, p. 74.
78. *Ibid.*
79. It is now in the Maināmati Musem.
80. Shamsul Alam, A.K.M., *op. cit.*, p. 76.
81. Sen Majumdar, G., *Buddhism in Ancient Bengal,* Calcutta 1983, p. 136.
82. It is now in the Tripura Govt. Museum, Agartala.
83. *JAS,* XVIII, No. 1-4 Calcutta, 1976, p. 58.
84. Bhattacharyya, Dipak Chandra, *Tantrik Buddhist Iconography,* New Delhi, p. 34.
85. It is now housed in Tripura Govt. Musem, Agartala, (Acc. No. S/49).
86. *J.A.F.,* XVIII, No. 1-4, Calcutta, 1976, p. 61.
87. It is also now in Tripura Govt. Museum. Agartala (Acc No. S/48).

88. The Niyamatpur image along with several other eighteen armed images of Chuṇḍā has been described in great details by J.E. Van Lohuizen-de-Leeuw in her article entitled 'The Paṭṭikera Chuṇḍṇā and Variations of Her Image' in the *Nalini Kanta Bhattasali Commemoration Volume,* ed., A.B.M. Habibullah, Dacca, 1966, pp. 119-43).
89. Banerjea, J.N., "*Iconography*" in Majumdar, R.C., ed, *The Age of Imperial Kanuj,* (Bombay, 1955), p. 277.
90. *JAS,* XVII, p. 68.
91. It is now in Tripura Govt. Museum, Agartala.
92. Now it is worshipping a modern temple called Vāsudevabāḍi in Jolaibāḍi area.
93. *Tripura District Gazetteers,* Agartala, 1975, Photo. IV.
94. Ganchaudhari, J., *op. cit.,* p. 67.
95. *Ibid.,* p. 67.
96. *P.A.,* No. 5, 1968, p. 165.
97. *JAIH.,* V, 1971, p. 181.
98. *E.I.,* XXVII, p. 182.
99. Morrison, B.M. *op. cit.,* p. 107.
100. *E.I.,* XXX, p. 184.
101. Morrison, B.M., *op. cit.,* pp. 108-9.
102. Niyogi, P., *op. cit.,* p. 83.
103. *E.I.,* XXVI, p. 313.
104. Bhattasali, N.K., *Iconography of Buddhist and Brahmanical Sculptures in Dacca Museum,* p. XXIX.
105. It is peculiar to note that when Jains and Ājivikas were able to establish their tenets in Bengal prior to Buddhism, no evidence or information about their foothold in Tripura has yet been recovered. Even today, Jainism is not at all a living religion as Buddhist and Brahmanical faiths in Tripura.
106. Chatterjee, Rama, *Religion in Bengal,* p. 132.
107. Bhattacharya, Satyavrata, *Śrī Śukla Yajur Vedah, Vājasaneyi Saṃhita, Śrī Manmanhidhara Krita Vedadipanam bhāshya Sahita,* Calcutta, Sak, 1799, Voll. II, XIV.
108. *Atharva Veda,* Trans. Whitney W.D., 1662, Vratya Kanda, XV, The Paryaya, pp. 778-779.
109. *Śatapatha Brāhmaṇa,* SBE, Vol-XII, pt. III, VI, II, I.

110. *The Mahābhārata*, Pn. Cr. edn., VII.
Dve tanu tasya devasya vedajña Brāhmaṇa vidhu /
Ghorā chānyā Śiva chāuya te taṇu Vahudhā Punah //
111. *Atharva Veda*, trans. Whitney Vol-II, book-V, XV, pp. 773-61.
112. Jash, P., *History of Śaivism*, Cal, 1974, p. 2.
113. Bhandarkar, R.G., *Vaisnavism, Śaivism and Other Minor Sects*, p. 103.
114. Dandekar, R.N., *Journal of Oriental Institute*, Baroda, XII, 1962-63, pp. 232-37.
115. Marshall, J., *Mahenjodaro and Indus Valley Civilisation*, Vol. I, p. 52.
116. Jash, P., *Glimpses of Hindu Cult & Culture*, Delhi, p. 3.
117. *Tripura District Gazetteers*, 1975, p. 388.
118. Ganchaudhari, J., *Tripura : The Land and its People*, 1980, p. 60.
119. Majumder, R.C., *History of Bengal*, Vol.I, Calcutta-1971, p. 404.
120. Bhanderkar, R.G., *Op. Cit.*, pp. 121-24.
121. Chatterjee, Rama, *op. cit.*, p. 135.
122. Mukherjee, Ramaranjan & Maity, Sachindra Kumar, *Corpus of Bengal Inscription*, p. 65.
123. *Ibid.*, p. 70.
124. Deopārā praśasti of Vijayasen mentions one Pradyūmṇeśvara temple along with installation of a Hari Hara. The verse runs thus :
"Lakshmivalla Bhasailajadayitayora-dvaita-litagriham/
Pradyyūmṇeśvara-sabdalan Chchhanamadhisthanaṁ Namaskurmahe//
Yatralinganabhaṅ-gakatarataya Sthivantare Kāntayoh/
Devibhyaṁ kathamapyobhinnatanuta-silpe antarayah kritah//"
125. *EHI*, II, Pt.2, APP. B., p. 170.
126. Śabdakalpadruma on Hari-Hara, *Vāmana Purāṇa*, chap-LIX, p. 520.
127. Chatterjee, B., (ed) *Culture of Bengal Through the Ages*, p. 49.
128. Sen, B.C., *Some Historical Aspects of the Inscriptions of Bengal*, p. XVII.
129. *EI*, XVII, p. 357, 11-2-3.
130. Maitreya, A.K., *Gauḍalekhamālā*, p. 9, vol-5.
131. *EI*, XV, 1919-20, p. 301
132. *Ibid.*, p. 306.

133. Bhattasali, N.K., Bhārrellā inscription dated in the 18th year of Laḍaha Chandra (Laḍaha Chandra), *EI*, Vol. XVII, p. 349.
134. Chatterjee, Rāma, *op. cit.*, p. 137.
135. *ASR*, XXI, p. 33; we have other instances of *chatur-Mukhaliṅga*, viz. one having from Sirpur, Raipur dist., Chattisgarh (*JIH*, Xi, 1962. p. 163). A. Mukha Mahādeva Chatur sculptural representation is discovered in Java and exhibited in Indian Museum, Calcutta. *ASI, AR*, 1924-25, Pl-37; cf also P. Jash.(ed), *Religion and Society*, p. 155.
136. Bhattacharjee, P., *Tripurar Dev O Devi*, p. 25.
137. Ganchaudhury, J., *op. cit.*, p. 61.
138. Majumdar, R.C. (ed), *op. cit.* p. 483.
139. An Ekamukha Śivaliṅga variety shows one human face added to the cylinder. This type of *liṅga* of the early Gupta period has been discovered from khoh. *ASI, AR*, 1904-05, Pl-XXVI, figs a-d.
140. Roy, N.R., *Brahmanical Gods in Burma*, fig. 2, 21, 30.
141. Das, Ratna, *Art & Architecture of Tripura*, Agartala, p. 46.
142. *Ibid*, p. 47.
143. *Ibid*, p. 47.
144. Hunter, W.W., *Statistical Account of Bengal*, Delhi (Reprint - 1973), Vol. VI, pp. 463-64.
145. Rowaland, B., *Art and Architecture of India*, p. 412, Fig.343; In this context we may cite the head of a king covered on the walls of Mikirhills; see R.M. Nath, Background of Assamese Culture, Pl-XVIII.
146. Jash, P., *op. cit.*, p. 21.
147. Chatterjee, Rāma, *op. cit.*, p. 159.
148. Bhattasali, N.K., *Iconography of Bhuddhist and Brahmanical Sculptures in the Dacca Museum*, p. 111.
149. *Matsya purāṇa*, vaṅg. edn. chap-ccLix.
150. Chatterjee, Rāma, *op. cit.*, p. 159.
151. Bhattasali, N.K., *Catalogue of the Buddhist and Brahmanical Sculptures in the Dacca Museum*, pp. 112-13, pl—XLII; cf. also *History of Bengal*, Dacca University, p. 442.
152. Ganchoudhary, J., *op. cit.*, p. 60.
153. Ray, Jagat Jyoti, (ed), *Rajendra Kirti-shalar Silver Jubilee Commemorative Volume*, p.44.
154. *Ibid*, p. 45.

155. The earliest example of Śiva dancing on the bull type of images has been discovered at Bamunara near the steel-city of Durgāpur in the Burdwan district, West Bengal. It is of the eight-handed variety and is the only instance of its kind; cf. also "*Viśvambhara. Felicitation Volume* of V.S. Pathak, Delhi, 1994.
156. Ray, Jagat Jyoti, *op. cit.*, p. 46.
157. *Pañcamukha aspect of Śiva liṅgas* representing Īśāna, Tatpuruṣa, Aghora, Vāmadeva and Sadyojāta. The face representing Īśāna should be on the top while the others should be on the east, the west and the north respectively, P. Jash, *op. cit.*, p. 7.
158. Das, Ratna, *op. cit.*, p. 55.
159. *Śāradatilaka Tantra,* ch. 18, *Prapañcasāra Tantra,* 26-71.
160. *EHI,* II, Pt. 2, APP, B.
161. Agrawal, V.S., *Journal of Research of the University of Uttarapradesh,* VII, No.1, April, 1960.
162. *Bṛhat Saṁhitā,* Ch. 58, V. 53.
163. *Matsya Purāṇa*, Ch. 260, VV, 12-19.
164. Tadapatrikar, S.N. Krṣṇa problems, *ABORI,* vol X, 1929, p. 269.
165. *Ṛig. Veda,* I, 116. 23. Avasyate sruvate Krṣṇiyāyu-dadathurviśva-Kāya; Rigveda, I, 117,7. "Yuvaṁnara sruvate Krshniyaya Vishiṇāpvaṁ dadathurviś vakāya."
166. *Rig-Veda,* 8,86,13.

    Avadrapso Aṁśumatimatish thadiyānaḥ Krṣṇo Daśabhiḥ sahasraih.

    commentary of Śāyana to this verse. Krṣṇonāmāsuro daśasahasrasaṁ—Khyāirasurash Parivri.
167. *Kaushitaki-Brāhmanopanishad,* Chaukhāmba, Varanasi, 1968, 30, 9.
168. Mitra, R.L., *Aitareya-Ātareya,* Bib. Ind., New series, 1876, 111, 2, 6, p. 370.
169. Mitra, R.L., Taiṭṭiniyāraṇyakaṁ, Calcutta, 1872, X, p. 770-7.
170. Śrīmad Bhāgavat, Ch-11.
171. Viṣṇu-grayatrī - "Om Nārāyaṇaya Vidmahe, Vāsudevāya dhīmahi tanno Vishṇu Prachadayāt".
172. Shastri, Govindacharya., *Pāñcharātras* or *Bhāgavata Śastra, JASB,* 1911, p. 935.
173. Sircar, D.C., Garuḍa-stambha lipi of Heliodorous; *Select Inscription,* Calcutta, 1965, p. 88.

174. *Mahābhārata,* Vaṅga End, XVIII, VI, 97.
175. Pāṇini, Sutra, IV, 3.98; Kielhorn, *Mahābhāshya,* Patañjali, vol. 1, 1892-1909, vol. 1, p. 435-36 under Pāṇini 11, 2, 34.
176. Majumdar, R.C., McCrindle, J.M., *Ancient India as Described by Megasthenes and Arrian,* Calcutta, 1960, p. 196.
177. *Ibid.,* p. 201.
178. Chatterjee, Rāma, *Religion in Bengal,* Calcutta, p. 90.
179. *Mahāsanatkumāra Saṁhita,* III. 6, 36.
180. *Pādma-Tantra,* I, 2, 36.
181. Banerjea, J.N., *Development of Hindu Iconography; JISOA,* vol. XIII, 1945, p. 102.
182. *I.H.Q.,* vol. 6, 1930, p. 40
183. Bhattacharya, D.C., *I.H.Q.,* vol-6, p. 53.
184. Bagchi, P.C., *History of Bengal,* vol-I, 1943, p. 400.
185. *I.H.Q.,* vol-6, p. 53.
186. *EI,* vol-XV, p. 301.
187. *I.H.Q.,* vol-6, p. 88.
188. Mukherji, S.C., *A Study of Vaiṣṇavism in Ancient and Medieval Bengal,* p. 21.
189. *Ibid.,* p. 21.
190. *E.I.,* vol-XV, p. 306.
191. *I.H.Q.,* vol-22, p. 269.
192. Majumder, R.C., *History of Ancient Bengal,* p. 211.
193. Bose, N.N., *Vaṅger Jatiya Itihāsa,* II, p. 215, *EI,* XXX, p. 225.
194. Josh, P., *History of Evolution of Vaiṣṇavism in Eastern India,* p. 51.
195. Mukherjee, S.C., *op cit.* p. 47.
196. "Gopi-Sata-Kelikarah Kṛṣṇo Mahābhārata-sūtradhārah etc." V-4. Belava grant. According to Dr. N.K, Bhattasali, the explicit mention that Kṛṣṇa was an 'Aṁśāvatāra' of Viṣṇu was probably due to the prevalence of a rival theory in East Bengal during the reign of the Varmans, which made Kṛṣṇa was only a 'Partial incarnation' of Viṣṇu, It is to be noted here that Kṛṣṇa was not considered till now as the 'Aṁśin, (the whole) but 'Aṁśa' (the part), but the position changed with the advent of Śrī Caitanya and evolution of Gauḍīya Vaiṣṇavism. The works like the Bṛhad-Bhāgavatāmrta of Sanatana Gosvami, the Laghu or Saṁkṣepa-Bhāgavatāmrta of Rūpa Gosvami and the 'Satsandharvas' of their nephew, Jīva Gosvami, give us a systematic composition of the

'Avatāra doctrine' of the Gauḍīya Vaiṣṇavism, chiefly depending upon the Śrīmad-Bhāgavatam of these three, Jīva has shown that Balarāma and Kṛṣṇa were not the Aṁśas of Kalās (partial manifestations) of the *Puruṣa*. According to the Gauḍīya Vaiṣṇavism, Kṛṣṇa is not an Avatara or incarnation, but the 'Bhagavat Himself' (Kṛṣṇastu Bhagavān svayaṁ). This is very interesting, indeed.

197. Mukherjee, S.C., *op.cit,* p. 48.
198. Jash, P., *op. cit,* p. 51.
199. Siddhala has been identified with the present village Siddha near Ahmadpur in the Birbhum distict, Birbhum Vivarana', part-II, H.K. Mukerjee; Law, B.C, *Historical Geography of Ancient India,* p. 260.
200. *Proceedings of the Indian History Congress,* Third Session, Calcutta, 1939, p. 313. According to D.C. Bhattacharya the temple of Bhavadeva could not be in Rādhā, but it was possibly at Vikramapura, IHC,XXII, pp. 134-35.
201. Raychaudhuri, H.C., *Materials for the Study of the Early History of the Vaiṣṇava Sect,* University of Calcutta, 1936, pp. 72, 95.
202. P.A., No-3, 1966, Karachi, pp. 22-55; Sircar, D.C., *Epigraphic Discoveries in East Pakistan,* Calcutta, 1975, pp. 41-59.
203. Sircar, D.C., *op.cit.* pp. 51-52.
204. *Ibid.,* pp. 70-75, Maināmati plates of Laḍaha Chandra, Regnal year-6.
205. *Ibid.,* p. 52.
206. *Ibid.,* pp. 57-58.
207. Paṭṭikera is identified with Paiṭkārā parganā extending upto the Maināmmati hills, five miles to the west of Comilla, Bāṅglādesh, *History of Bengal,* Vol. 1, p. 258.
208. Sircar, D.C., *op. cit,* p. 81.
209. *I.C.,* VII, No-4, pp. 405-16; *Bhāratavaśa,* 1341, B.S., P-768-775.
210. *El,* vol-17, H.C, *I.H.Q.,* vol-16, p. 631.
211. Mukherjee, S.C., *op. cit,* p. 38.
212. *Ibid.,* p. 38
213. Banerjea, J.N., *Development of Hindu Iconography,* 2nd ed., p. 324.
214. Ganchaudhuri, J., *Tripura : The Land and its People,* p.59.
215. *Ibid.,* p. 59.
216. B.S., LVII., 31-5.

217. Utpala explains it as the hand facing the visitor (turned to the front) with figures raised upwards: Drastur abhimukha Ūrdhv-āṅgulih, Śantidah Karah, it is apparently the same as the abhaya-mudrā of the Buddhist art.
218. Besides the four *vyūhas,* the names of the twenty secondary ones are Keśava, Nārāyaṇa, Mādhava, Govinda, Viṣṇu Madhusdana, Trivikrama, Vāmana, Śridhara, Hṛṣikeśa, Padmanābha, Dāmodara, Purusottam, Adhokṣaja, Nṛsiṁha, Achyuta, Janardana, Upendra, Hari and Kṛṣṇa.
219. Rao, G.N., *EHI,* Pt. pp. 227-28.
220. Jash, P., *op.cit.* p. 56.
221. Of course in some iconographic reliefs, a god of one sect is shown laying under the feet of a deity belonging to a different sect, showing definitely a sectarian bias.
222. Rao, G.N., (*E.H.I.*) mentions some other varieties of *Śayana* image of Visnu, such as Yogāśayaṇa, Bhogāśayaṇa, Vīraśayaṇa, Abhicārikaśayaṇa, Jalasayin and Vaṭapātraśayin. All these aspects are ideologically similar to the Ananta Śāyaṇa form which represents the god recumbent on the folds of Ananta or Adi-Nāga.
223. Jash, P., *op. cit.,* p. 56.
224. *M.A.S.I.,* No-55, p. 59, PL XL11-4-5.
225. Ganchaudhuri, *op.cit.,* p. 59.
226. *Tripura Unakoti,* Directorate of Education, Agartala, 1972, Plate-VII.
227. *Tripura District Gazetteers,* 1975, plate-V.
228. *Ibid.,* Plate-V
229. *JAS,* vol-XVIII, No-1-4, 1976, p. 54.
230. Bhattacharjee, Priyabrata, Curator of Govt. Museum, has been mentioned in his book (Tripura Dev o Devi Mandir) that the image is god of Sūrya, but Debala Mitra (*J A S,* vol-XVIII, p. 64) identified the image with Viṣṇu.
231. Das, Ratna, *Art & Architecture of Tripura,* p. 43.
232. *Tripura District Gazetteers,* op. cit., p. 48, plate-V.
233. Das, Ratna, *op.cit.,* p. 49.
234. *Gitā-Govinda,* Canto-1, verses, V-XV Cf. also appendix-III.
235. *Tai.Ar.,* X. 1.6.
236. *Māha, up.* III, 17.
237. *Mbh,* XII, 34-36, 337.

238. *Harivaṁśa,* III, 41-47.
239. *Bhāgavata-Purāṇa,* VII, 8, 10.
240. *Mātsya Purāṇa,* Adhyaya, 260, 31-34.
241. *Agni-Purāṇa,* Adhyaya, 49,4.
242. Eastern India hardly hears any icons representing eight, twelve, sixteen or thirty-two hands. The Jaina temple of Vimalasah at Mount Abu contains a twelve handed Nṛsiṁha (K.B. Dave, *Gujaratnu Murtividhan,* p. 17), the *Parameśvara-saṁhita Kriyakāṇḍa,* Adh, (23, 45-47) mentions sixteen handed, while the *Nāradiya Mahā Purāna Pūrva Kāṇḍa,* (71, 62-66) speaks of thirty two hands.
243. *J.A.S.*, vol., XVIII, No. 1-4, 1976, p. 74.
244. *Ibid,* p. 64.
245. Das, Ratna, *op. cit.*, p. 35.
246. Jash, P., *op.cit.*, p. 113.
247. Bhattashali, N.K, *IBBS,* in the Dacca Museum, Pl. XXXVII-b.
248. *ASI, AR,* 1921-22, Calcutta, p. 85.
249. Ganchaudhari, J., *op. cit.*, p. 60.
250. Dixit, K.N., *ASI, AR,* 1921-22, p. 80, Pl-XXVIIIb; *EISMS,* Pl-XLVI-b.
251. Das, Ratna, *op. cit.*, p. 57.
252. Chatterjee, Rāma, *Religion in Bengal,* Calcutta, 1985, p. 173.
253. *Rig Veda,* X, 29.
254. *Ibid.*, 110,9; 111, 3, 11, Yame dyāvāprithivi jaṇitri ubhā pitarā *Mahayannajayatgni.*
255. Williams, Monier, *Religious Thought I live in India,* London, 1883, p. 182
256. *Rig Veda,* X, 72, 4-5.
257. Atharva-Veda, VI, 4, 1.
258. *Rig Veda,* X, 125.
259. *Ibid,* II, 14, 15.
260. *Ibid.*, II, 8, 7.
261. *Muṇḍakopaṇishad,* 1, 2, 4.
262. *Kenopoṇishad,* III, 55.
263. Mitra, R.L., Taittriya-Āraṇyaka, Calcutta, Asiatic Society of Bengal, 1872, *Namo hiraṇyavāhave hiraṇyavarṇāya hiraṇyarūpāya hiraṇyapatiye, mbikāpataye umāpataye paśupataye namo namoḥ//*
264. *Ibid.*, X, 1.

265. *Ibid,* X, 1.7.
266. *Ibid., X, 1, Viśeheṇa rochate svayameva prakāśate vairochaṇa.*
267. Durgāstavas in the *Māhābhārata,* Pn. Cr. edn. VI, 23, IV, 6.
268. Dutta, M.N., *Harivaṁiśa,* Āryāstava, ed, and tran, Calcutta, 1867, Chap LIX.
269. *Ibid,* LIX.
270. Marshall, J, *Mohenjodoro and Indus Valley Civilization,* London, 1931, pp. 50-51.
271. *Ibid,* pp. 51-52
272. Chatterjee, Rāma, *op. cit.,* p. 176.
273. Majumdar, R.C., *History of Bengal,* Vol. 1, p. 407.
274. Chatterjee, Bhaskar, *Culture of Bengal Through The Ages,* Burdwan, p. 57.
275. Hazra, Dr. R.C., *The Devi Purāṇa,* New Indian Antiquity, Vol. p. 13.
276. Majumdar, R.C., *Bāṅglādesher Itishāsa* (Prāchina Yuga), Calcutta, 1317 BS, p. 148.
277. *Kubjikā Tantra* (paṭala VII) manuscript No. 3174 (RASB); the same quoted in the Praṇatoṣani Tantra Vasumati, p. 234.
278. Sarkar, J.N., *India Through the Ages,* Calcutta, 1951, p. 35.
279. Sarkar, H.B., *Some Contributions of India to the Ancient Civilization of Indonesia and Malayasia,* Calcutta, 1970, p. 25.
280. Chatterjee, Bhaskar, *op. cit.,* p. 56.
281. *EI,* XVII, p. 357.
282. Dev Sarma, Chandra Daya, *Silālipi Sangraha, Agartala,* 1968, p. 4.
283. *Ibid.* p., 28.
284. Bhattasali, N.K., *Iconography of Buddhist and Brahmanical Sculptures in the Dacca Museum,* p. 204.
285. *Brahmavaivartta Purāṇa,* Vang edn., L VII, 17.
    Sarvān mokshān prāpayati janmamrityujaradikaṁ/
    Charācharaṁiścha viśvathān Śarvānī toana kīrttitā//
286. *Tripura District Gazetteers,* Agartala, 1975, plate-IV.
287. Singh, Chitralekha & Nath, Prem, *Hindu Goddesses,* New Delhi, 1995, p. 227
288. *Śabdakalpadruma,*
    Durgodaitye mahāvighne bhavabondhe kukarmaṇi/
    Śoke duḥkhe cha narake yamadande cha jaumani//
    Māhābhayeti Roge remase Devi durgeshu Durgśvari namo stute//

289. *Mārkaṇḍeyachaṇḍi,* 11/49-50.
290. *Ibid.,* IV, 11.
291. *Devī Purāṇa,* Vaṅga edn, LXXXIII, 62, 63, Devi Bhāgavataṁ, Vaṅg, edn., III, 24, 5-6.
    Nagara'tra tvayāmātaḥ sthātavyaṁ mamo sarvadā/
    Durgā devīti nāmnā vai tvaṁ śaktirīha saṁisthitā//
292. *ASI, AR,* 1921-1922 (1924), Calcutta, pp. 86-87.
293. Das, R., *Art and Architecture of Tripura,* p. 47.
294. *Rig-Veda* , VIII, 8, 12.
295. *Hindustan Standard,* Calcutta, 26th October, 1959, Durgā Puja, Durga Das Patra, in letters to the Editor.
296. *JAS.*, Vol XVIII, No-1-4, Cal, 1976, p. 62.
297. *Ibid.,* p. 65.
298. Ganchaudhuri, J.N., *Tripura : The Land and Its People,* 1980, Delhi, p. 63.
299. Bhattasali, N.K., *op. cit.,* p. XIX.
300. Sengupta, K.P., (ed). *The Rājmāḷa,* Vol-III, Agartala, p. 163.
301. Sircar, D.C., *The Śākta Piṭhas,* Delhi, 1973, p. 47.
302. *Rig-Veda,* 1, 50, 1-13.
303. Udyannadhya ...... ahaṁ dvishateradhaṁ/Com. of Sāyaṇa to hridrogaṁ hridayagatamāntaraṁ rogaṁ Harimāudaṁ : Śarīragafaṁ Kāntiharanaśīlaṁ Vāhyaṁ ragaṁ. *Bhavishya purāṇa,* Venk. Press, Chap. 117.
304. *Varāha Purāṇa,* Bib. Ind, Chap. 117.
305. Keilhorn, *Inscription from Govindrapur of Gaya,* Vol. II, Sl. 2, p. 333.
306. *Sahitya-Parishad Patrika,* B.S. 57, saṁkhya I and 2, p. 25.
307. Chatterjee, Rāma, *Religion in Bengal,* p. 209.
308. Davoud, Prof. Pourne, Mithracult, *JBORS*, vol. XIX, 1933, p. 255.
309. Beloe, William, *History of Herodotus,* Eng. Tran. vol. I, 142.
310. *Bṛihat Saṁhitā* of Varahamihir, LT III, 46-52.
311. Quackenobs, G.P., *Sūryaśatakaṁ,* In the Skt. Poems of Mayūra, New York, 1917, Sl. 65, P. 115. cf. the Passage in the *Charaka Samhitā* Pub. NSP, 1922, p. 215, "Teshāmimāni ... dushṭira saṁrohaṇaṁ cheti."
312. *Pañchopāsanā,* p. 303.
313. Kane, P.V., *Harshacharita of Bāṇabhaṭṭa,* Ullāsa, IV, p. 3, nisargate eva cha ..... mantramādityahṛidayaṁ.

314. *Pañchopāsanā*, p. 306.
315. Ray, N.R., *Brāhmaṇical Gods in Burma,* pp. 1-24.
316. *AR, ASB,* 1923, p. 28.
317. It is mentioned earlier that Indian colonists and traders from Bengal presumably went to Ārākan and Burma via land routes through the Southern part ot Tripura. It may be tentatively assumed that the same tradition was responsible for creation of art of these regions with local variations.
318. The backslabs of the figures of this group excluding the Narasiṁha which has been found upto the knees, measure 3m and 29cm. high and 1m and 68 cm wide. Major part of the front side of the Sūrya image being buried below ground, the details have not been recorded.
319. Das, R., *Art and Architecture of Tripura,* Agartala, p. 34.
320. *JAS,* Vol. XVIII, No. 1-4, Calcutta, 1976, p. 66.
321. Ganchaudhuri, J., *Tripura : The Land and Its People,* New Delhi, 1980, p. 64.
322. Vrātebhyo Vrātapatibhyaścha vo namo namo ganebhyo gaṇapatibhyaścha, Tai-Sam, IV. 5.
323. Bhattacharya, Haridas, *The Foundation of Living Faith,* Vol. I, Calcutta 1938, p. 237.
324. Atharva Veda, 1, 21.
325. Mitra, Haridas, *Gaṇapati,* Visva Bharati Annals, Vol. VIII, 1958, p. 19.
326. *Ibid.,* p. 33.
327. *Kātyāna Smriti,* 1, 11-14.
328. *Mānava-Gṛihya-Sūtra,* 11, 14.
329. *Yajñavalkasmṛiti,* VII, 71-94.
330. *Manusmṛiti,* III, 46.
331. *Copper Plate of Vaidyadeva,* G.L., p. 127.
332. Sircar, D.C., I.H.Q, XXVII, 1952, p. 55.
333. *Ibid.,* p. 57.
334. Sircar, D.C., Nārayaṇapura Viṇāyaka Image Inscription of King Mahipāla I, Regnal Year 4, *Indian Culture,* vol. IX, 1942-43, p. 121. cf. also *Pālā Yuger Vaṁśanucarita,* p. 14 and *Śilālekha-Tamra-Śāsanadir Prasaṅga,* pp. 81-84 of the same author.
335. Sircar, D.C., *Indian Culture,* pp. 121-125.
336. Jash, P., *Glimpses of Hindu Cults and Culture,* New Delhi, 1997, p. 153.

337. Getty, Alichary, *Gaṇeśa* - A monograph on the Elephant Faced God, Oxford, 1936.
338. Chatterjee, Rāma, *op. cit.*, p. 226.
339. *ASI, AR,* 1921-22 (1924), Calcutta, pp. 86-87.
340. Bhattacharjee, Priyabrata, *Tripurar Dev O Devi,* Agartala, p. 30.
341. *JAS* Vol. XVIII, Nos. 1-4, Calcutta, 1976, p. 65.
342. *Ibid.*, p. 64.

4

TRIBAL RELIGION

The word 'Tribe' has come from the Latin word 'tribus'. It means an inhabited place. It denotes a group of persons coming from a common ancestor and forming a community. The Tribes in India can broadly be divided into the following three groups:

1) The Tribes of north western frontier (Baluch, Pathan, etc.)
2) The Tribe of north eastern frontier (Tripuri, Naga, Khasi, etc.)
3) The interior Tribes (Munda, Santhal, Bhil, etc.)

Territorially, Tripura belongs to north eastern frontier and the land is predominantly inhabited by 19 different types of Tribal communities. These Tribal communities have been classified into following two broad groups.

1) Mongolian, comprises - 15 (fifteen) tribes.
2) Non-Mongolian, comprises - 4 (four) tribes.

Out of these above 19 tribes, Chākmā and Magh are Buddhist fold tribes and rest are of Hindu fold tribes. But now a days, Lushais and Kukis are converted to the Christian religion. The tribal religion of Tripura is essentially polytheistic and is expressed in pūjās and festivals both at the family and community levels. The Tribes of Tripura give preference to the nature deities, spirits and ancestors to carry on struggle for existence. The Tribal culture is related to religion. It is their music, dance, sculptures, craft and literature which found expression in religious rites and rituals. So, here in Tripura the cultural identity and religious identity of the tribal people go together.

A graphic description of some existing tribal religious practices and also rites and rituals will strengthen our contention. One should, however, mention that even in the temple, which is naturally Brahmanical and Sanskritic through and through, there are still elements of the original tribal cult.

To a large extent the history of Hinduism consists of its encounter with tribal religions and their continuous integration. 'Sanskritization' is the name given to this process of "Partial acceptance of communities, which upto now had been outside the folds, into the religio-social community of the Hindus, whose system is based on Sanskrit texts."[1] This process of 'Sanskritization' is not acceptable to all the scholars since it generally leads to the adoption of Sanskrit as a sacred language. They, therefore, use the term 'Hinduization'. The sociologists, on the other hand, prefer to use the term, viz., 'Great Tradition' and 'Little Tradition'.[2] Without going in details in this regard, it may, however, be noted that the process of Hinduization is basically made possible due to three characteristics of Hinduism—the fundamental doctrine that all divine powers are manifestations of the one, the lack of a binding doctrinal authority and the open caste hierarchy. This not only enables new gods to be accepted into Hinduism and to be identified with the gods already present, but also the continuous creation of new castes, or rather the recognition as castes of tribal groups which have been Hinduized only very superficially.

Thus, the process of Hinduization is basically effected in two directions. On the one hand, gods of tribal religions, with their symbols and cult, are accepted in Hinduism, i.e., in some way or another, affiliated to or even incorporated into the temple cult. On the other hand, tribal cults take up Hindu elements — names of gods and goddesses, rites, conceptions — and through this, ephemeral though this assimilation may be, are 'reputable' for Hinduism. The area in which the process of Hinduization mainly occurs is folk religion. This is the religion of a Hindu village which geographically, as well as in a more abstract sense, lies between the tribal religions and Hindu temple cults. Hinduization of the tribal deities and vice versa to the greatest extent possible is reached in various temples as well as in folk religions in Tripura.

Pūjās and festivals constitute the major part of the Tribal religious life. Pūjās are regulated ways of devotion shown towards Gods and Goddesses, spirits and ancestors to satisfy their anger or to achieve material gain. The water of holy pipe, chanting of *mantras* in the indigenous language, sacrificial animal, wine and *Ochai* are the essential components of puja. The *Ochai* performs to his ancestral procedure. The aim behind majority which might fall upon them or for food production or crops and also to achieve *pūnya*. Beside some pujas are arranged to drive out the evil spirits from a body of diseased person. The *Ochai* conducts puja as a *shaman* to cure a patient from illness.

Another most important universal feature of tribal faith in Tripura is that it ranges from the animism and super natural worship to the deepest anthropomorphism. It is a fact that the rites and rituals of the tribal people vary from those of the stately temples of Agartala to those of the Tipras, the Riangs, the Noatiās, the Jāmatiās, the Uchais, the Kalais and the Ruipinis who worship their indigeneous pre-Hindu fourteen Gods and Goddesses with conventional tribal rites and beliefs and practices. But it should be remembered that the form of worship springs from true love, therefore, no differences in the field of tribal religion from the Brahmanical faith.

However, besides pūjās to the Brahmanical Gods and Goddesses in their day to day life, there are countless Gods and Goddesses belonging to animism along with rituals of all kinds in which sacred natural objects representing them are adored. Most of the tribal peoples of Tripra are Hinduized or Buddhized or Christianized but many of them seem to be knitted together by tribal beliefs and practices and they are preserving vestiges of tribal faith or religion even to day. Through the centuries many of the Tribal peoples along with the ruler of Tripura have without doubt been drawn into the main stream of Hindu way of life along with their Pantheon of Gods and Goddesses. The sacred Scriptures, the Epics, the Purāṇas and the socio-religious system of Bengali-speaking Hindus were highly accepted by the tribals of Tripura. It is true that Tribal people of Tripura have accepted the Hindu faith and have contributed to building up Hinduism. In this connection it may be mentioned here that the previous census reports of 1901[3], 1911 and 1921[4], have already informed that the tribal people are in the fold of Hinduism and it is not a possible task to separate Hindus from animist. In case of Tripura, Hinduism takes a different shape where we find that animism is deeply influenced by the '*Sanātana Dharma*'. The relation of tribal communities to Hinduism is not alike to Christianity on the religious point of ground. Christian tribal peoples are fast giving up their old custom and adopting the western mode of life. Many of their present customs are mixture of their old customs and western pattern of life. A good number of Khasis, Lushais and Kukis are said to embrace Christianity. Buddhism has undoubtedly brought the message of peace of love to the converts. The Maghs and Chākmās are Buddhists. It is clear to picture of tribal religion of Tripura, most of the tribes are Hindus, a few are Buddhists and recent a few tribes convert into Christianity.

The polytheistic religious structure of tribal people recognise a number of deities, spirits and other supernatural agencies which may be put under the following categories.[5]

1. The worship of the deities, spirits etc. which have come from their traditional culture are the Kerpūjā, the Lampra Pūjā, the Maylwngma Pūjā, the Naksu Pūjā, the Burasā Pūjā, the Mahādev Pūjā, the Garia Pūjā, the Chauddadevatā Pūjā and Mwytamwng Or Twymakermwng.
2. The worship of the deities, spirits etc. which have been borrowed from the neighboring castes and communities as a result of neighbouring acculturation are the Sani Pūjā the Trinath Pūjā, the Laxmī Pūjā, the Sarasvatī Pūjā, the Rakshakālī Pūjā, the Rathajatra festival and the Janmaṣtami festival.

The deities may be grouped under two classes namely-malevolent and benevolent. The benevolent deities are :

1. *Mwtay Katar* : The Supreme deity.
2. *Hakwcharmama* : Tripura Sundari.
3. *Maylwngma* : A female deity who rules over rice and crops.
4. *Khulwngma* : The Goddess of cotton and weaving.
5. *Garia* : The fulfiller of one's wishes.
6. *Akatha, Bikatha or Sukundray, Mukundray and Twybuk* : Jointly worshipped in the Lampra Pūjā. They are auspicious deities.

7. *Twyma* : The Goddess of Water.
8. *Sangrang* : Goddess of Wealth and Prosperity.
9. *Nagusu* : The Goddess who is the protector of the homestead.

The malevolent deities are :

1. Burasā : A male deity who causes diseases and suffering to others.
2. Haychukmā : The Goddess who rules over the animals and the forests.
3. Thunnayrag and Banirag : The collectors of death news.
4. Swkal/Mang : Witches.
5. Srijamdu and Srijadu : They cause barrenness in the woman.

Besides these, there are seven types of Swkals (evil spirits) who are known for their evil eyes. They are :

1. Jahari; 2. Prahari; 3. Premchari; 4. Dakini; 5. Jogini; 6. Magini; 7. Magadhchari.

In addition to the above mentioned seven malevolent deities, there are eighteen more. A patient may be cured by their propitiation. These malevolent deities are :

1. Sunamati; 2. Kahanmati; 3. Aychuti; 4. Aluti; 5. Berua; 6. Kherua; 7. Narite; 8. Nakete; 9. Lankhete; 10. Patalkainya; 11. Surung Kainya; 12. Hadini; 13. Medini; 14. Sukala; 15. Rangkhal; 16. Susugiri; 17. Tangburi; 18. Balsingraja.

Lampra Pūjā

One of the most important religious functions of the Tripuris, Noatias and others tribes of Tripura, is the Lampra Pūjā. In the Kakbark "*lam*" means *lane* or 'way', 'road', "*Pra*" means 'branch'. So *Lampra* literally means cross roads. It is believed that the abode of the deities are in the bamboo plants where two roads are merged. The religious activities of the Tipras begin with the Lampra puja. So the community worshipped the deity as "Holy God", i.e. the "*Supreme God*" or "*Narāyāna*". The supernatural powers i.e. the sea and the sky are worshipped as *Akatha* and *Bikatha* respectively.

There are six deities for worship in the Lampra pūjā. These deities are :

1. Akatha 2. Bikatha 3. Sukundray
4. Mukundray 5. Twybuk 6. Sangrang.

This puja is performed at the household level, village level, regional level and community level for the welfare of people at the respective levels. But there are two types of the Lampra pūjā. One is held in the morning (till the sun in the mid sky). It is known as fuwayni Lampra. It means the morning Lampra. It is obligatory to be performed with important affairs like birth, marriage, death etc. But in each type of pūjā only four deities are worshipped. These deities are 1. *Akatha* 2. *Biktha* 3. *Twybuk* and 5. *Sangrang.*

Other Lampra is held in the afternoon when the sun begins to descend. It is known as Sarini Lampra, means the afternoon Lampra. It is in performed in case of ordinary matters like widow marriage, the marriage of a divorced women, ceremonial friendship etc. The Sukundray, Mukundray, Twybuk and Sangrang are deities of the Sarini lampra. But Twybuk and Sangrang are worshipped in both the pūjās.

To make the structure of the deities, two pairs of bamboo poles measuring 61 cm. in height are planted in the ground on the courtyard. Afterwards, two other bamboo poles are tied horizontally, like a Latin cross. This particular bamboo is called "Lampra *Owathap*" *Owathap,* meant bamboo clump. As the object of ritual the bamboo made "Owathap" is needed in every pūjā of the Tripras after some addition or alteration regarding sizes and decorative works around the bamboo poles in times of making it. The bamboo poles are symbolic representations of the deities, E.T. Dalton remarks, "a trace of their old faith is to be found in their present religious festival and worshipping it"[6] Anthropologically we may call it animistic representation of the deities which is a characteristic manifiestation of animistic belief of the Tripras even today and these bamboo poles fully prove in the presence of the worship of supernatural deities and spirits among the Tipras. In any case, we have no ground to believe the idea of full standing image prevailing among the Tipras during ancient period. The real fact is that the bamboo itself is worshipped in its natural form and the deities of Tripras are not personified and endowed with human shape.

The bamboo worship was not only earliest form of divine ritual, but it was existing long before the creation of temple and images of the Gods and Goddesses. But one should notice that only green bamboo is regarded as sacred. The dry one is deprived of all its sacred nature. Even the Turi Tribe of Gujrat place two small pieces of bamboo in the room of confinement, so that no malevolent spirits can have its influence on the new born baby."[7] The green bamboo is the "Vāstu Devatā" or the God of residential house of the Bengalees. The pūjās of Vāstu Devatā is observed on the Pous Sankranti day. On the occasion of the Vāstu pūjā is found that a slender bamboo pole, with branches and leaves, in placed and purified by cowdung on the previous day. Decorations by rice powder, turmeric powder etc. are made on the ground around the pole. The article needed for the worship are made of fruits, unboiled milk etc.[8] Generally the *Ochai,* the priest of Tripuri always conducts the "*Tampra pūjā*" and the symbolic bamboo made *Owathap* is also constructed by him. Borua is the name of the helper who assists the *Ochai* in times of pūjā.[9] The *Ochai* is required to observe fasting to officiate this pūjā. This pūjā is performed in two ways (1) by sacrificing a fowl and (2) by offering Naibaday. But at present the practice of offering of Naibaday is in vogue in their community. The articles generally required for this puja are the Banana leaf, Dhup, flower, Tulsi leaf, fowls or pigeon, eggs, earthen pots, cotton, *Risa* and wine and a Naibaday consisting of Banana, sugarpole, atap rice etc. When every thing in order, the *Ochai* kneels on the ground and starts the pūja. Chanting the *mantras* the *Ochai* begins the pūjā by sprinkling water from the bamboo pipe or a jhāri (a sacred pot made of brass). Afterwards, two fowls or pigeons are sacrificed and their blood is decidated to the deities on the undried rice which are on the banana leaf in front of the *Owathap.* During the pūjā the *Ochai* chants *mantras, "Hengnai dengnai nachiri chiri chiriadung, balae Akhata bala Bikhata tuituibu elakhkhiraja dung balae nusa Kamalapati nasu Jaduram, hamaychai tangnai tuibuk laktạị aiugalagay, tangmani aiugamana tangthum langnay.*"[10]

"The inner meaning of the *mantras* is as follows. Let the couple Jaduram and Kamalapati be laborious and happy in their married life. Let their life be as long as a river and unaffected by anything like an undecaying stone." However, the *Ochai* offers the heads of the sacrificed fowls or pigeons along with the entrails to the deities and some quantity of wine is also offered. The heavy knife is washed and placed in front of the *Owathap*. It is interesting to observe that the *Ochai* touches the heavy knife with his right hand and the same time he touches his right ear when the spelling of *mantras* is continuing. This type of activities is performed thrice continuously. Regarding animal sacrifice a certain thing is to be remembered. The *Ochai* does not completely sever the neck of the fowl or pigeon. Cutting the half portion of the neck of the fowl or pigeon the *Ochai* offers the blood to the deities. Afterwards, the fowl or pigeon is completely beheaded. As soon as the sacrifice is over the *Ochai* sprinkles water and wine over the heads of the fowls or pigeons. It is a fact that in case of lesser deities, the neck of the sacrificed animal is half cut like the Muslims Zabeh or formalized slaughter. But in case of higher deities, the neck of the animal has to be completely severed.

The *Ochai* can forecast the pūjā if it is performed rightly or not. He takes two jack fruit leaves in his hand and tosses them in the air in front of the *Owathap*. If one of them falls flat on the ground, other fall back on the ground, it is a good sign. Thus from the reading of the jack fruit leaves the *Ochai* declares that the deities have been pleased with the devotees and they will do good to the familes. If the reading is auspicious the *Ochai* will order the devotee to sacrifice two fowls in the name of the deities so that they may be pleased. Generally, the fees of the *Ochai* is not paid in cash, he is offered rice instead of it.

The purpose of the pūjā

The Lampra pūja is performed for the various kinds of welfare purposes. With this pūjā any kind of impurity or the period of mourning is ended.

The Lampra Pūjā has an important place in the socio-religious life of Tripuris, Jāmātais and other tribes. This pūjā must be performed to mark every important stages in man's life-birth, marriage and death. The manifold purposes of the Lampra pūjā may broadly be divided into two categories; (a) essential and (b) general purpose.

1. After the birth of a baby when its umbilical cord comes off or drops down the Lampra puja is performed in the name of the baby.

2. Before settlement of one's marriage Lampra pūjā is performed for the welfare of the couple.
3. In the case of Sraddha ceremony (funeral ceremony) the Lampra pūjā is performed to end the mourning period for the peace of the departed soul.
4. The Lampra puja must necessarily proceed the performance of the pūjā of any benevolent deity.

The general purpose for which the Lampra pūjā is performed are many e.g. before the starting of new work, or for the success of any important task, for the construction of new house etc. The individual household performs this pūjā once in a month for the general welfare of the family. If any one of the village dies the village headman is required to perform the Lampra pūjā on behalf of the villagers. So that the soul of the dead does not bring any harm to the villages.

Generally, the *Ochai* officiate this pūjā. He is required to observe fasting to officiate this pūjā.

The Mailoomā and Kholoomā Pūjā :

The pūjā of the Tribal community of Tripura are basically worship of natural forces as the Gods and Goddesses like the other Tribal communities of the north east India. The earth is the mother Goddess throughout the primitive world. She is the giver of blessing for increasing the productivity of paddy and crops. The goddesses Mailoomā and Kholoomā are the two benevolent female deities worshipped in each Tripuri, Jāmātias and other tribal house. The word Mailoomā (mai = paddy + loo = land, ama = mother) means the deity who rules over paddy fields. The word Kholoomā (Kho = cotton + loo = land + oma = mother) means the deity who rules over cotton crops. As weaving, the art of preparing clothes etc. are related to cotton, Kholoomā is also considered as Goddess of wisdom. In short, she is called the Goddess of wealth (Dhena - Devi). The practice of worship of the Goddesses of wealth is considered to have been prevalent among the people of Indus valley civilization about Circa 2500 B.C. It is also known from the Egyptian and Babylonian archaeological evidences that the Mother of the World, i.e. the Mother Goddess was worshipped as the Goddess of paddy or corn. This tradition of worship of the presiding deity of crops has been a very old one. The adoration of some Gods and Goddess among the Tripuris shows that the old tradition of human civilization has been preserved with enthusiasm and reverence among the Tripuris.

Afterwards these two deities are extremely related with the fertility cult. The worship of the deities of paddy land and cotton clearly shows the importance given by the earlier people to these two basic needs of humanity. The concept of Mailoomā similar to the concept of Laxmī (Goddess of paddy and wealth) among the neighbouring Bengalees. Besides this, the concept of Kholoomā being the deity of learning as she rules over cotton which is related to the art of weaving is similar with the concept of Sarasvatī (Goddess of learning).

The Moiloomā and Kholoomā are performed twice in a year. The first one is performed in the month of *Baiṣakh,* on the day of Senapūjā, the day on which the image of Garia is immersed. The second pūjās elaborated on the first day of eating new rice. In the society the festival of eating new rice is called "*Maikatal - Chamani*" which takes place after the collection of Jhum corn every year. Jhum is a kind of cultivation carried out on hill slopes, a mode of cultivation adopted by most of the tribes of Tripura. At the time of the said new rice festival, both the Goddesses are worshipped. The time of the pūjā is not fixed every where. In some place harvesting of paddy is done in the month of *Bhādra* or *Āswin.* So the second time puja is performed between the month of *Bhādra* and *Āswin.*

The symbolic representation of these deities is different from the others in shape, material and character. The bamboo made *Owathap* or any bamboo structure is not generally needed. As a symbolic representation of the two Goddesses, two earthern pots (*Rankdak*) are placed side by side and offerings are made to both jointly. To worship the two Goddesses together has been a regular practice in some of the families in town even now-a-days. The both deities worship is also called as "*Randak* Pūjā" Both the earthen pots are to filled in with new rice and a few pebbles are placed there on the body of both the earthen pots the "*Svastika*" designs, a well known symbol of benediction are drawn with vermilion and the necks of the same earthen pots are adorned with garlands. Some cotton also is to be placed on the earthen pot to represent the Goddess of cotton "Khulumā". After the adoration, the earthen pots along the pebbles are carefully preserved. The top part of a banana leaf is divided into two pieces to place both the pots on its side by side and decorate the same with flowers. Grains of the new rice, thoroughly cleaned, are then offered there with sugar, molasses, sugar cakes etc. They believe that their families will prosper in both wealth and progeny if these two earthern pots remain filled to the brim. Some egg shaped pebbles painted with vermilion are placed in side the earthen pots. These pebbles are considered to be symbols of good fortune. The offerings are placed side by side on seven or nine pieces of banana leaves. Fowls are also offered, but some different from the Lampra pūjā. *Ochai* offers only blood of fowls to the Lampra deity. But there the neck of the sacrified fowls are completely severed and the heads are dedicated to the deities placing them on the banana leaves. A bottle of wine is given to each of the deities for their satisfaction. Recently it has been observed that "two boiled eggs, boiled meal of the two cocks and some rice are given to the concerned deities"[11]. The Tipras propitiate the deities for the welfare of their household during the house-inauguration, marriage ceremony, sowing in Sravana, harvesting in months of Pousha and in times of "Navānna".

Tuimā

The deity is performed by community level, regional level and village level organizations along with certain individual families for the welfare of the members. The Gods and Goddesses of the Tribal people have no concretized visual symbols of abstract concept or no ideas for each one of which there is Dhyana or mental vision. Therefore the abstract symbols of the nature deities are made with the help of the bomboo poles, bamboo leaves and cotton thread etc. The bamboo made structure of a deity to some extent may be called an altar or a pedestal of the deity, but if we identify it as the abode of the deity "Matainakh", surely, this will also be justified. The traditional symbols of the deities are made in a peculiar way instructed by the *Ochai* who has to follow the specific designs in the time of constructing the certain deity. The number and shape of bamboo poles vary from one structure to another. However, on the river four bamboo poles are planted, the heads of which are rising on the surface of water in a small squarish areas, the four bamboo poles are tied together with the help of another four pieces of bamboo poles. In the middle of this structure a platform (Machang) is constructed. On the surface of the platform the symbols of Tuimā and Sangram are made by the well decorated bamboo poles in the befitting manner. A banana leaf is placed in front of the symbolic representation of the deities on the platform. The ingredients of the puja consist of four ducks, four eggs and four naibedya containing undried rice, banana and sweets in a small earthen pot. In the community level puja one is sacrificed on the bank of the Gomoti river, one on the Bijay river of Bishlagor, one on the Khowai river and one buffalo and male goat are sacrificed at Matabari of Udaipur. Besides, this buffaloes, male goats or chickens are sacrificed in the pūjā of each regional level organizations for the welfare of the people of each regions. The pūjā which is held in the village is called Luku Samwng. The Kakbark word Luku Samwng is derived from the words Luku = village Council + Samwng = work.[12] So it means the work of village council. Here importance has been stressed on the work of the village council than the sacrificed animal.

According to the tribal custom the Tuimā pūjā is to be observed as precautionary measure against the disease. Besides, for the welfare of the fields productivity, fertility and protection of the child from the danger of water the Tuimā Pūjā is performed. This pūjā is a no doubt an archaic ceremony which originated from the idea that the life was created from the water. The supernatural power who resides in the rivers water was identified as the mother Goddess Tuimā. They consider that the worship of Tuimā will make life substantial and there will be no scarcity of water[13]—William Crooke observed that the Tipras worshipped Tuimā to the nearest bathing place and they "are now claiming to share the water of Gangās through some under ground passage and to be identified with her."[14] This puja is performed also to remove the sufferings from diseases and illness at the courtyard of the house of the Tipras and Noatiās whenever necessity is felt.

Sangram

The God of Sangram is recognised as consort of the deity of Tuimā. The God of Sangram and Goddess of Tuimā are identified with two major forces of nature, the mountain, and the water control a sub-ordinate hierarchy of deities and spirits under them. Similar to Brahmanical Hinduism, there is a duality of these God and Goddess, and has a qualifying term of address of "*mā*" and "*fhā*" which means "*mother*" and "*father*" respectively.[15] Sangram is the God of wealth and prosperity. If any member of a family suffers very frequently from diseases and illness then the worship of the Sangram deity takes place to overcome the sufferings. It is a household deity. At the courtyard of the house the Sangram deity is worshipped. For this deity two fowls are required as offerings and two eggs also. It is believed that if their satisfaction is made by paying reverence to them, the whole supernatural world will not do any evil to human society.[16]

Bichukmā / Haichukmā / Hakamā Pūjā

Baichukmā is generally known as Haichukmā or Hakamā who is the spirit of the forest, malevolent in character. Another significant aspect of the deity is that she is the consort of Birasā. Although she rules over the forest, but as a household deity she has power to control the domestic animals also. It is found that Baichukmā is worshipped with a certain view. In most of the cases she is worshipped when a domestic animal is lost. The worshipper believes that the proper worship will bring back the lost animal.[17] Another reason is that the deity wards of the danger a the time of hunting and collecting fire wood. The *Ochai* performs the pūjā outside the courtyard, generally, in the forest. The *Ochai* constructs an *Owathap* as the symbolic representation of the deity. The offerings consist of two black fowls, a pig and bottle of country wine.

Burasā Pūjā

Burasā is a malevolent male deity. It is believed that Burasā was human being in the past. He turned into an evil spirit as he learnt only the evil sides of Ochaiship. The name Burasā is derived from the Kakbark word, meaning small statured old man. This may be due to the fact that Burasā assume any form that is the semblance of a child or the form of old man.[18] It is believed that Burasā does not kill any one. Although he is fun loving, he has a sadistic streak in him. They believe that the severe pain of a child or fever are caused by the deity Burasā. It is said that he is husband of Bichukmā and the deity of the forest. The puja is rendered so that the patient may be cured by blessings of the supernatural spirit. So it is performed only if the *Ochai* feels the necessity of it. The pūjā may be held in day light or in sylvan semidarkness of evening out side the boundary of the village.

On a certain occasion the *Ochai* observes this ritual in the deep part of the forest. The *Ochai* is accompanied by the male members of the family. The women and children are not allowed to visit the place of pūjā. A bamboo made *Owathap* is needed for the ritual purpose. Like the other pūjās the *Ochai* sacrifices two fowls or a pig along with the eggs. Thereafter, the head of the animal, pieces of meat of the sacrificed animal, are given to the deity along with the wine of bottle and longi (rice beer). The pūjā is rounded off with a feast in which the entire members of worshipper's family take share, but nobody is allowed to bring the meat of the sacrificed animal from the forest in to the village.[19]

Saklakmatai Pūjā

God of health Saklakmatai is worshipped in the last part of *Māgh* or in *Fālgun* as the benevolent deity. The deity is offered home made cakes along with fowls and eggs. It is very interesting that a he goat is sacrificed to the deity in the evening. The deity looks after the health of family members of the worshipper.[20] Like the other deities Saklakmatai is propitiated by the *Ochai* and wine is also served to the deity properly.

Thomnairok and Banirok Pūjā

The supernatural deity of death is worshipped as Thomnairok while Banirok is identified as the messenger of death-news. They are worshipped in the hope that they may keep good health all the year round and they will protect the danger of death. Thomnairok may be worshipped in the courtyard when Banirok is worshipped in the forest, out side the village.[21] But it is also found that they are worshipped jointly in the courtyard during the Ker pūjā as Nagray (the guests). On the appointed day, the *Ochai* makes the symbolic representations of the deities by the help of green bamboo poles. When every thing is in order, the *Ochai* sacrifices a he goat or she goat along with two chickens or two eggs for the pleasure of Thomnairok. Two fowls or two gooses are killed as offerings for Banirok. Afterwards, indigenous wine is offered to the deities.

Chhakal Jook Pūjā

The spirit has overwhelming influence among the Tribal people. Moreover, they believe that the witch causes disease and various harms.

The guardian deity of witch is called Chhakal jook who is nothing but the evil spirit of nature.[22] The Tribal people believe in the art of witch craft. They engage an *Ochai* to cure the long continued diseases. In front of the symbolic representation of deity, the *Ochai* offers the dried meat of the tortoise and pork along with the wine as offerings. The worship of this deity takes place in the forest outside the village.

Sirijumdu and Sirijadu Pūjā

These two evil spirits cause barrenness of the women. They are worshipped along with the other deities of malevolent character. Two fowls and two eggs are sacrificed to them. Besides these pūjās to the nature deities and spirits in their religious life, there are countless pujas of various kinds in which the supernatural forces as the nature deities and spirits are adored. The Para Kainai Pūjā, Satbhabi Pūjā, Kharangma Pūjā, Mautikhanai Pūjā, Khuruksonai Pūjā, Khowai Chanaima Pūjā, Bishchini Shamanung Pūjā, Bonai Sinipuja, Chongrangma Pūjā and Chuamakhlae Pūjā are also closely related with the Tipras, the Jamatias and other tribal people.[23] Dr. Kartik Lahiri is of opinion that *Kularbhanga Rajā, Kubukolandrājā, Tuibuk Kalakshirājā, Kalpurā, Santhalirājā, Jumpurā,* may be the names of the deities included into the supernatural world of the Tribal people.[24]

Moreover, the other deities included in the pantheon of invisible supernatural deities consist of Langthari, Binaigar, Khum chakkara, Samagar-Hardi, Musikha-Khusika, Dagrai, Surbai, Alak palak, Duwari, Pahari and Balong etc. In fact vast members of deities exist in the kingdom of spiritual world of the Tribal people who are not receiving due honours regularly because according to the need of the peoples the religious ceremony is held in honour of the certain deity occasionally.

Nakchumatai Pūjā

The deity Nakchumatai basically is a spirit of the house or guardian spirit of the homestead. The term Nakchumatai (Nak = House + Chu = Corner + mwtay = God) means the Goddess of house. She is a benevolent deity who is supposed to remove the evil spirits from the house and cause of illness. In the times of construction of a new house the worship of Nakchumatai is also performed. "The house owner wants to know from the *Ochai* wheather the site is good for building a house or not. To be sure that the *Ochai* performs some rituals. This is called Semanaio[25]. The pūjā is performed by Ochai after the *Randhak pūjā* is over as a part of the *Gariāpūjā*. A bamboo post of an arm length approximately and the bamboo canes are planted side by side. A banana leaf is kept in front of the planted bamboo and handful of rice is put on the banana leaf. Thereafter, the *Ochai* cuts partially the throat of a chiken and hold it on the rice to pour the blood. Now the *Ochai* completely severs the head of the chicken and he examines the entrails of the sacrificed chicken for conformation of the site selection whether it has been good or not. After cutting the rectum of the chicken the entrails are also checked.[26] In this connection it may be added that a — 'Yayamphra' is constructed by the *Ochai* and placed on the south eastern corner of the house as the symbol of Nakchumatai. The "Yayamphra" is covered by a piece of white cloth during the pūjā. Besides, four bamboo poles are planted in the four corners of the "Yayamphra" to fix the canopy over the symbolistic representation of the deity. Moreover, three pieces of spilt bamboo are also planted in front of the door of a house on the courtyard. These are marked by a taboo which suspends all outside activities for the period of puja. Even the peoples of the house are not allowed to come out of the house as long as the taboo remains in operation. The outsiders are also prohibited to enter the house, they have to observe it strictly. The *Ochai* breaks these pieces of bamboo when the puja is over. The taboo is thus related essentially to the religious ceremonies and form together the base of all ritualistic behaviour, a fundamental trait of the Tipra's religion, but is universal to all North-Eastern religion. The taboo is observed so that supernatural powers are kept in their proper mood to bestow bless on the people.

The special offerings of the Nackhumatai pūjā consist of Chyrak and Chuakama. The Chuakma is prepared in a bamboo pipe with the help of scum of wine from 'Longi' (earthen pot contained rice beer) and water. The particular wine is called chawak which is kept in a bottle.

When a man has sudden attack of diarrhoea, vomitting, fits, headache etc. he promise gifts to the Nakchu. In such cases he offers something to the woman possessed by the Nakchumatai. It is believed that with the acceptance of offering the patient recovers. The offering may range from a banana to a sugarcane etc.

Matai Katar & Matai Katarmā

Matai Katar is the supreme deity and Matai Katarmā is his consort.[27] These deities are worshipped for the enhancement of prosperity and security. They are worshipped house hold wise or community wise. For these deities a goose is required to be offered; sometimes a he goat is also offered in case of a promise. Along with this offering, banana, undried rice, vermilion, betel leaf and nut etc., are required. This pūjā takes place outside the house.

Akhatra & Bikhitra

They are the sons of the Matai Katar and Matai Katarmā.[28] These Gods are very famous in Tribal community of Tripura. These are worshipped to get relief from all problems, to win war, to win a case at the court etc. So they are known as a rescuer Gods in this community. It is similar to the *Brata* of '*Bipad Tāriṇi*' of West Bengal.

Chomlai

Wine is deeply related with Tribal society. With full respect of the God, they prepare wines. Otherwise the prepared wine gets spoiled. They believe that if the Chomlai God can be pleased, then good wine is prepared. And if he gets angry then the wine gets spoiled. For the God, seven Wyathap, various leaves and flowers and needed. Moreover a earthen pot, 1 kg Ari rice are needed. For this deity a pig is required to be offered. After that the *Ochai* ties Lakpoi (sacred thread) in every devotees hand and spreads holy water on all devotees head. He is worshipped to get relief from all problems, to bring peace in the house.[29]

Longtarai

The Tripuris believe that God Longtarai dwells in a royal rock palace.[30] The palace has hundreds of door. It is a 5-storey building. He lives in the 5th floor. He is multi-form God. Sometimes he forms himself as a goat or some other animal. He is worshipped to get the crops protected from animals and other things.

Narsing

Tribal people of Tripura believe that this God has half its body as human and rest of lion. He believed to be the creator of this earth.[31] He is so powerful God of the community. They believe that it is quite difficult to satisfy him. He always saves weaker person. He is worshipped to get relief from critical disease.

Kharchi Pūjā

Tripura is often called the Land of Fourteen Deities, therefore the worship of the fourteen deities, which is popularly known as Kharchi pūjā is an important festival in Tripura. This festival is held sometimes in June - July on the Suklāstamī day which lasts for seven days. The Kharchi pūjā is held at old Agartala, 8 km. from the state capital Agartala. Old Agartala was the capital of the Mānikya dynasty and there was a temple of Chaturdaśa Devatā where the Kharchi pūjā would take place. The fourteen head images are worshipped at the time of Kharchi pūjā. Among the fourteen head images, the thirteen are made of brass while one is made of silver only. They are all more or less equal in size measuring probably 22 cm. in height alongwith throat and crown. During the pūjā each head image is placed on a wooden made *Pira* (altar) rectangular in size. The *Pira* measuring 25.40 cm x 15.24 cm. is given as an *Āsana* to which the deity is kept. The heads display wide forehead and hair indications are nil, the eyes are long horizontal ones and eye brows are not marked. The face is oval and nose is long and semi-pointed. The mouth is indicated by a light longitudinal cut. The head bears an ornamented crown consisting of beaded decoration. The faces are all expressive and workmanship is not of a high order.

The original Kakbark names of the deities consist of Mataikatar, Matai Katarmā, Mailoomā, Kholoomā, Akhtra, Bikbitra, Tuimā, Sangrang, Kalaja, Garia, Nakchu Matai, Bichukmā, Sirijembdu and Thoumnairog.[32] According to Śrī Rājmalā the Brahmanical names of the fourteen deities are Hara, Umā, Hari, Mā, Bāni, Kumar, Gaṇeśa, Brahma, Prithī, Gaṅgā, Abdi, Agnī, Kamesh and Himādri.[33] Besides, Rajaratnakar, the Sanskrit Rājmālā also describes a list of the fourteen deities in the following verse : "*Haromā Harimā Vāni Kumaro Ganapa Vidhin Ksmabdhi Gaṅgā Sikhi Kamo Himadrisca Caturdaśa.*"[34] But it is fact that the fourteen deities of the Tipras have been identified with the great deities of Brahmanical pantheon is mostly imaginary.[35]

The Tripuris recognize one super natural supreme God called Mataikatar (means greatest God) who is believed to be the creator of universe. The supreme being Matai Katar with his wife Matai Katarmā are supposed to control all other deities like the other tribal religions of the North Eastern India. Judging by their religious beliefs, the Tripuris have to be called the worshippers of natural deities in case of Kharchi pūjā as well as day to day life. The other deities whom the Tripuris pay reverence during the Kharchi pūjā are the following : Mailoomā (Goddess of Earth), Kholoomā (Goddess of Cotton Tree): Akhatra (God of Sea), Bikhitra (God of Sky), Tuimā (Goddess of Water), Sangran (God of Mountain), Kalia (Spirit of Ancestor Deity), Garia (God of wealth and war), Nakhu Matai (Tutelary spirit of the families), Bichukmā (Goddess of forest), Serijmdu (spirit of barrenness of the woman), Thoumnairoy (God of Death). Similar to Brahmanical religion, there is a duality of God and Goddess in the religion of Tripuris and each of these Gods and Goddesses has a qualifying term of address of Fā and Mā which means Father and Mother respectively. It is good to remind ourselves that the sea, the sky and the mountain seem to be the man Gods and the earth, water, cotton, tree, become the woman Goddesses and so on.

There are more than one legends current in the state of Tripura about the fourteen deities of the Kharchi pūjā. These legends point to the antiquity of the said pūjā connected with the fourteen deities.

The chronicle of the royal house of Tripura, Rājmālā, describes the origin of the fourteen deities. It is said that the king Tripura was extremely inimical and crude. He was killed by the God Śiva for his irreligious habit. Afterwards, Trilochana was born by the blessing of Lord Śiva as a son of widow, Hirabati. It was Trilochana, successor of Tripur who brought the fourteen deities from an island accompanied by the *Chantai* and *Dearai* and the worship of the fourteen deities was performed by Trilochana.[36]

Still another legend associated fourteen deities with the queen Harabati, the mother of Trilochana. One day she was fetching water from a hilly stream, all of a sudden, she heard a few voices : "Mother, Mother, save us". At last queen came to know that the fourteen deities were resting on the branches of a *Shimul* tree and they had been attacked by a terrible buffalo who was sleeping under the same tree at that time. The queen protected the deities against the buffalo by throwing her *risa*[37] over the body of the animal and the buffalo was killed by the queens men. The deities came down from the *shimul* tree and began to drink the blood of buffalo.

It was a rainy night of Āsāḍa (July - August) and queen's men were carrying the deities on their backs making a peculiar sound 'Ehune'. At last the deities were brought to the royal palace where a room was allotted for them and they were worshipping since then. It is very interesting that the baby Trilochana was sent to the room of the fourteen deities to play with them. One day, suddenly the queen noticed that Trilochana was coming out from that room in bloodless appearance. She peeped into the room and saw a he goat was sacrificed by one of the deities. Afterwards, the deities began to drink the blood. Then, completing their drinks they revived the he-goat in the form of a child who was no other than Trilochana himself. At the sight of this scene, the queen realized desidered to drink blood. Henceforth, she made necessary arrangements for a he-goat in every day.[38]

Iconographic identification of these images of brass are uncertain. Indeed curious and interesting but equally significant are two horns which are shown behind the crown. Besides, the identification of the head-images in not possible even in the field of genders also. The head images bear no attributes according to the Brahmanical iconography so that they may be identified as the Brahmancial Gods and Goddesses. It is a fact that the broken head image may not be supported by the Brahmanical iconography as the object of rituals.[39]

It is generally believed that the head-images of the fourteen deities are not isolated from those of Tripuri Gods and Goddesses. Though the *Chantai* along with his assistants were obliged to succumb to accept the Brahmanical names of the fourteen deities the practice of planting bamboo poles to make structure of a deity is also prevalent in the religious ceremonies of Kharchi pūjā. For it is possible to find out a pole of bamboo which is planted on the ground behind each of the head-image as the representation of Tribal God and Goddess. So it is a fact that the fourteen head-image is a secondary formation. It is possibly the influence of the primitive Gods and Goddesses. This kind of animistic representation of fourteen deities is depicted on a coin of Ratna Māṇikya : "Obverse : Within horizontal line almost - dividing the obverse into two semi-circles. The upper semi-circle contains a number of vertical lines overlapped by another concave curve. This motif apparently bears a close resemblance to Tughra style of Arabic writing on the coins of Sultans of Bengal. But at the lower semi-circle of the reverse, there is a legend in Bengali characters which reads : Śri Chaturdaśa De(va)! Charana-para/Śaka 1386". The word "Caturdaśa Devatā" is met for the first time of the coin of Ratna Māṇikya the king of Tripura and the name has not come to have in use prior to the reign of Ratna Māṇikya. Besides, from the study of the coin of the king, it is known that Ratna Māṇikya issued this particular type of coin which become an unique bearing of the Brahmanical Sanskritised name - "*Caturdaśadevā*" associated with the fourteen bamboo poles as the animistic representations of the deities. Therefore, it may be suggested that the fourteen deities of the Kirata peoples have been identified with the higher deities of Brhamanical pantheon, probably as early as the c. 13th to 15th century A.D. In this connection S.K. Chatterjee also pointed out that "thus a piece of numismatic and epigraphic evidence of the highest value, indicating the final transformation of the Mongoloid (Bodo) pantheon of an important section of the Indo-Mongoloids into the orthbox Hindu pantheon of the Purāṇas."[40]

It thus shows that the religions of the tribes, the original inhabitants of the land, who, even today, live with their very own social order and religion. As oppesed to Brahmanical religion, the tribal religions have no anthropomorphic representations of deities which would be relevant to the cult.

The Kharachi Pūjā is performed by the indigenous priests of the Tipras. The chief priest is called *Chantai*. The assistants of the *Chantai* are as follows :

Galim : 14, Naran : 4, Barifang : 8, Riakchu : 8, Khapuritinai : 1.

The ceremonial worship generally starts one day before the Kharchi festival. At first the Lampra pūjā is — celebrated and traditionally the symbolic representation of the deity is constructed by the green bamboo poles. Afterwards, the Bukhukchinirok pūjā is observed in the middle of the day. The seven bamboo poles measuring 1 mtr. 30 cm. are planted on the ground and at the top of the each of the poles, the branches of the Banatulsi are kept. These seven poles of the green bamboo are the symbolic representations of the deities who are no other than the seven sisters in which one is married and the rests are unmarried. The opinion of K.C. Singha[41] is that they are seven witches or Dākinis. The fourteen eggs, three he-goats, and two ducks are required as offerings to the deities.

When the worship of Bukhukchini is over, the most important Ghat Dekhani ceremony is performed. The assistants of the *Chantai* taking the head-images move to the Howrah river for ceremonial bathing of the deities. After the bathing is over, the deities are carried back to the temple. At that time the assistant priests bearing the umbrellas on their heads make a peculiar voice 'ehune'. In Śrī Rājmālā, it has been recorded that a curious religious ceremony called Nishi pūjā would be observed at night in the courtyard of the temple of Chaturdaśa Devatā. In fact, it is said that the human sacrifices were offered to the fourteen deities during the historical period to the region of Mahārājā Govinda Māṇikya who is said to have ceased the human sacrifices from the religious rituals of the tribal peoples of Tripura. The Kharchi pūjā is celebrated in the newly constructed temple which is shown outside the main temple. The ingredients which are closely connected to the worship of the fourteen deities are cited below :

Ingredients of the Kharchi Pūjā

Buffalo : 1, *Risa* : 14, He-goat : 14, Eggs : 28, Dira : 14, Bamboo Pipes : 14, Bamboo-poles : 14, Spinner : 1, Big basket : 1, Small, Basket : 1.

Umbrella

Bamboo made : 1, Pieces of white cloth : 14, Lamp stand : 14,

Small Earthen

Water Pot : 28, Duck : 4, Pigeon : 4, Jhari or Brassmade water pot: 1, Wooden-stick : 1, Small spud : 14, Wooden sandal : 2, Mortar for grinding corn : 1.

Cotton thread, Cotton, Takkal, Turmeric, Vermilion, Wine, Banana leaves, Undried rice, etc.

The traditional religious beliefs and customs that followed during the Kharchi pūjā are the sacrifice of animal and egg to the beloved deities. It deserves mentioning here that the *Chantai* or the chief priest, offers nothing to the deities according to the "*Purohit Darpan*" or "*Aryachar Paddhati*" but to follow the primitive method of his ancestors. Like the *Ochai,* the *Chantai* does not sacrifice the animal. He chants the *mantras* as per conventional tribal way and his assistant priest sacrifices the animal. From the field investigation of the Kharchi pūjā, it has been found that the holy priest *Chantai* and his assistants are still dogmatic to follow their primitive practices.

Ker Pūjā

The Ker Pūjā is performed according to the command of the chief priest *Chantai.* Fearing the supernatural forces the *Chantai* strictly follows some rules and there is a proclamation that the person who breaks these taboos shall be punished by the supernatural powers.[42] Morever, it is a fact that the *Chantai* is in the higher position during the Ker pūjā who has power to punish the taboo breakers and his judgements are also applicable in case of the king of Tripura if he does any wrong during the observance of taboo for this ritual. A taboo means a forbidden activity, something that is not permitted, something which stands against divine approval and is not allowed by norms of religious behaviour. There are several taboos associated with the Ker pūjā. The *Chantai* becomes the supreme authority who can punish every body if any one breaks the taboos included in the Ker pūjā. Now-a-days Rajandar, in front of Ujjayanta palace (West side only) Jagannath-dighi along with its four banks, Durgābari are selected as the restricted area for the Ker pūjā in which the taboos will be effected. The taboos are seriously followed within the above mentioned area. No body is allowed to enter into the said area and the people who are living within those areas are not expected to come out of their houses as long as the Ker pūjā continues and thus they have to store their wants well in advance. The taboos of the Ker pūjā operate for nearly 32 hours (2 nights and a day). Besides, the other taboos related to the Ker puja are as follows:

a) It is prohibited that a diseased person may remain in the area of pūjā and side by side the pregnant women is not allowed to stay there also.

b) The birth of boby or the death of a person have to be controlled within the holy area of the Ker pūjā.

c) It is necessary to keep the area of the taboo undisturbed. The musical performances, dancing and making un-necessary noise are absolutely forbidden so long as the puja is continued.

These kind of taboos are effective not only in the case of Tribals of Tripura, but the whole north east India. The tribes of the different countries of the world are also following the taboos when the nature deities, spirits and ancestors are propitiated by them. It is a fact that the *Chantai* believes that the trespassers are supposed to bring evil external influences and thus pollute the sanctuous atmosphere of the holy Ker pūjā. The supernatural power are supposed to be enraged by this also. On the evening of the selected day the *Chantai* along with his assistants arrive at the palace gate by a jeep and they are received by the employees of the Royal house as well as the in-charge of Devayatan section, Govt of Tripura, with due honour. The priests are given shelters and fooding according to their need. Then as a signal of the beginning of the Ker festival, a bomb is burst open to inform the citizens of Agartala that the ritual is started. Next morning nearly at 6 A.M. wearing the Royal dress the *Chantai* comes out along with his assistants from the resting place. The dresses of the *Chantai* consist of a turban, a colourful Royal lose shirt, a white slacks, a modesty scarf and a golden sacred thread in which the symbols of the deities are engraved. The *Chantai* goes in a procession of his assistants along with the Royal employees and the defence force of the Government of Tripura to show the honour to the ancient throne of the Māṇikya dynasty which is made of ivory and silver. Afterwards, the *Chantai* is followed again by the same procession when he goes to pay reverence to the Goddess Maṅgal Chaṇḍi who is worshipped in a temple of the palace compound. After ceremonial reverences are paid to the Maṅgal Chanḍi, the *Chantai* is taken in front of the procession and the procession breaks out after crossing the road which stands in front of the Ujjyanta palace.

The *Chantai* selects holy place on the bank of Jagannath dighi. A land of rectangular shaped is well cleaned for the purpose of pūjā in which the bamboo poles are planted in the ground as the symbolic representation of the nature deities, spirit and ancestors. The articles for the construction of the symbolic representation of the nature deities, spirits and ancestors consist of the bamboo poles in different shapes and sizes, the pieces of split bamboo, the long pins of stick of bamboo, the ropes of bamboo cane, the bamboo pines of floral designs and the bamboo poles which are decorated by the geometrical design around its body from the top to bottom.

Ingredients of ritual

Small earthen pot : 28, Small earthen dish : 28, He-goat : 15, Egg : 28, Pigeon : 8, Duck : 4, Wine : 2 (Bottle), Longi : 2 (Pitcher),

Cotton : Cotton thread (Red & White), Undried rice, Turmeric, Banana, Batasa, Pieces of white cloth, a bag of dried rice, Vermilion, Bamboo pipes, River clay, *Risa* and Mustered seeds.

Special Leaves of ritual

Banana, Chhan, Chatir, Dumra, Laridam, Chākamā, Kumplai.

The *Chantai* stands on the ground in front of the *Owathap,* the symbolic representation of the Lampra deities, when a jari is shown in his hands. The Jari is a sacred pot made of brass like a Kamandulu or a jar with a curved pipe on the middle of it. The Jhari is filled with water and a branch of Kumplai tree along with its flowers and the leaves. Chanting the *mantras* the *Chantai* sprinkles the water on the banana leaves, standing before the *Owathap* the Galim takes his position on the left side of the *Chantai* holding a Kharga in his hands. The *Chantai* drops a considerable quantity of water on the Kharga, pigeon and eggs. With deep devotion the Galim chants the *mantras* while he half cuts the neck of pigeon and the blood is sprayed to the symbols of the deities. Afterwards, he completely severs the neck of the pigeon. Now the *Chantai* drops the water from the Jhari to the head of pigeon, *Owathap* and Kharga. During this ritual a bamboo made instrument for music begins to sound which is locally called "vomra". The vomra is an instrument which is used to ward off the evil spirits from the holy area of the Ker pūjā.

In this way the Goddess Tuimā and Sangrang have to be propitiated by sacrificing the he-goats, eggs, and pigeon etc. In case of a he-goat the Galim severes completely the neck of the he-got and the blood of the sacrificial animal has to be sprayed on the symbols of the deities. The *Chantai* along with the Galim following the way prescribed by the ancient tradition adores Matai Katar, Matai Katarmā, Mailoomā, Kholooma, Kalaia, Garia, Nakchumatai, Hichukam, Sirijumdu, Thumanirag, and Banirog, Jampiraj, Bukhuksinirog,

Balang, Chinui Hapang and Chinui Tui Chha Matai by sacrificing the he-goats, eggs, ducks and pigeons with due honour. So far as the Ker pūjā is concerned, the worship of Banirog and Thumnairog hold a high position among the pūjās of the other deities. A special Matainakh (temple of deity) is constructed with the four bamboo poles and a red coloured canopy. The symbolic representation of Thumnairog and Banirog and made with the green bamboo poles which are well decorated with geometrical designs. The symbols are placed on a piece of white cloth below which a red piece of cloth is also present. The symbols of the deities measure 1m. 40 cm. in height. The symbolic representation of Banirog is tied with the red thread of cotton while the Thumanairog's symbol is fastened with white thread of cotton.

It is an actual fact that Thumnairog and Banirog are called 'Nagray'. In the Kakbark 'Nagray' means 'guest'.[43] It is believed that both the supernatural deities of the sylvan forest visits the urban area as the guest of the Royal house of Tripura. Thumnairog is the spirit of death while Banirog is the messenger of the death news. The state level puja of the deities is performed to ward off the evil done by the death and to get rid of suffering caused by the messenger of death news.

Tripura is a land of twelve sacred rivers and twelve holy mountains. The Tipras along with other tribes are extremely dependent upon the rivers and the mountains for which the propitiations are made to them in every year during the Ker pūjā. In the courtyard of the Ker pūjā, the symbolic representations of the rivers are made in a peculiar way. It has been examined that the twelve clod of earth are kept on them whom are adored as the deities of rivers 'Tuichha matai'. In front of these lumps of earth, twelve long pin of stick of green bamboo are planted in the ground which are fastened with the thread of cotton. Each of the cotton thread is tied with a piece of cotton. These bamboo strips represent the mountain deities of the Tipras whom they are called 'Chinui hapang matai'. In the same way these deities have to be propitiated by killing he-goats, pigeons and eggs.

Last of all, the *Chantai* with the help of the Galim serves wine and Longi (rice beer) to each and every deities worshipped there and he leaves the place. After the departure of the *Chantai*, the Galim conducts the worship of Balang. It is the deity of the forest. The symbolic representation of the deity along with his consort seems to be a wounderful creation of an indigenous artistic priest Galim. The materials required for the construction of the symbolic representations of the deities is as follows:

1) The bamboo strip which has perforated the pieces of turmeric measuring 28 cm. in height.

2) The rope of bamboo cane which are tied with cotton thread along with cotton.

3) The skewers of bamboo in which the bows are attached at the lower portion.

4) The small bamboo slips pointed at both the sides.

The Galim with the aid of these articles constructs two simiıar symbolic representations of the forest deities. Chanting the *mantras* the Galim sacrifices the pigeons as the offerings to the deities. Thus the worship of the deities in the morning is ended. In the afternoon, just before the evening, one of the assistants of the *Chantai* taking the symbolic representations of Thumnairog and Banirog places them on his shoulder and he holds the symbols tightly. It is a very notable incident that the bearer of the symbols is carried by the another assistant priest on his back and he moves towards the main gate of the palace compound. On the middle of the road, these deities are worshipped by sacrificing the pigeons and wine but the deities are kept on the shoulder of the assistant priest who have to be remained also on the back of the aforesaid assistant like a child.

In the corner of the Jagannath dighi near the main gate of the palace an area of land is cleaned. Two bamboo poles measuring 2 mtr. in height are planted in the ground when a bamboo pole is tied to them horizontally. A bamboo step is placed over the tops of the two bamboo poles hemispherically. Below this bow-shaped portal, two lumps of earth are made digging the holes there. The symbols of the deities are placed on the ground in front of these lumps of earth which are supported by the portal. A bag of dried rice and eggs is hung from the right side of the portal.

The ingredients of the worship of these "Nagray" (guests) deities consist of Vermilion sprayed eggs, two earthen post containing full of undried rice, banana, batasa, turmeric pieces, two ducks, two bottles of wine, cotton thread of red and white colour, preached rice, mustard seeds, cotton, two earthen pots full of water.

Among the leaves, these are to be mentioned.

Chhan, Banana, Chatir, Dumra, Laridam, Chākmā

Besides, the skin of the Kanak tree is also needed for this ritual. The chief priest *Chantai* remains absent during the Nagray pūjā. The chief assistant of the *Chantai* taking a small picher contained full of water seats on the Asana of Banana leaves. First of all, he divides the ingredients into two shares equally and places them in front of the symbols of the deities. In the same time an *Ochai* places a slip of bamboo over the another slip and begins to rub - repeatedly. This kind of continuous rubbing produces holy fire and the lamp of the pūjā is lighted by it. However, the ingredients consist of the leaves and skins of trees are amalgamated by the assistant priest on the banana leaves and the bamboo pole, the symbolic representation of Banirog is placed on these articles and the symbol of the deity is tied with the white thread of cotton. In the same way the symbol of Thumnairog is also tied with the red thread of cotton. Now, the symbols of the deities are placed in the holes and planted properly in the ground and many bamboo strips are also sticked around the two symbols. It has been observed during our stay in the sanctuary with enthusiasm that the empty egg shells are kept on the tops of the bamboo splits. After this type of religious practices, the *Ochai* fastens the structural symbols of the deities and the planted bamboo strips with the red and white cotton threads. The *Ochai* chants the *mantras* and he drops water on the symbols of the deities. Two ducks are brought near the *Ochai* in which one of them has vermilion sprayed on its head and beak. The *Ochai* chanting the *mantras* half cuts the neck of the duck in the traditional way. As soon as the sacrifice is over, the *Ochai* sprinkles the blood on the symbols of the deities and serves wine to the deities according to ancient custom.

Next, we have found that the *Ochai* forecasts the results of the Ker puja, if the reading is auspicious, the Ker pūjā should have to be arranged again. The fire produced by the rubbing of two pieces of bamboo splits, is received by the citizen of Agartala and they keep the sacred fire in their houses with a hope that it will bring, no doubt, good fourtune to them as the blessing of the deities. The distinctive characteristic of the Ker pūjā is that it has not been influenced by the other religions. The Ker pūjā is held from an unrecorded period for the safety from diseases as well as to protect the state from the crude hands of death.[44]

About the Ker pūjā Dr. Kartik Lahiri says "One of the occasion of Ker puja which is a royal but tribal, a bamboo is erected, and to chanting of *mantras* (a king of spell), the top of the bamboo is laid to touch the ground."[45] But Priyabrata Bhattacharya opposed this opinion. According to him such type of miraculous event of erected bamboo might not been practiced by the *Chantai* during the Ker pūjā. In this connection Kaliprasanna Sen observed that the principal part of the Ker pūjā includes the worship of "*Nagara*" (city) from which the term "Nagrai pūjā" comes into light[46]. But this opinion is not free from doubt because on the linguistic ground the Kakbark word stands as "*Nagray*" in place of "*Nagrai*" which means the guest in English or *Atithi* in Bengali[47]. Moreover Mr. Sen has sought to prove that the Ker pūjā reminds us as the newly creation of the nature[48] which is also a controversial remark. Actually from the anthropological point of view the Ker is not related to the creation only, the chief aim of this ritual is to receive blessing from the supernatural forces for security of the peoples of Tripura from the natural calamities and havoc of death. In other words it may be suggested that the Ker pūjā is performed to save the creation from the dangers made by the evil spirits and to preserve the creation of the nature properly.

Garia Pūjā

Garia is the natural benevolent spirit of the household who looks after the increase of production. There are differences of opinions among the scholars regarding the identity of the Garia. Some consider Garia as form of Ganeśa. Some consider it as form of Narasimha, while others took it as a form of Śiva. There are reasons to regard Garia as Narasimha or Śiva. Narasiṁha is considered to be a very powerful God by Tripuri and some other tribal communities. He is supposed to be the destroyer of evil forces. Many utter his name when in danger or in fear. So Garia the protector, is naturally looked upon as Narasiṁha.

Śiva is the God of agriculture and famous for his unsocial ways and that strange aloofness. Garia too has these traits of character. Garia pūjā is held on Mahabishu day, the last day of the Bengali month of *Chaitra*. This day is considered as an auspicious day from the religious point of view to the non-tribal Hindus of this area also. Moreover, the most popular form of Śiva worship, the Charak pūjā is also held about this time in this region. Besides, the trident which Śiva holds in his hand is also implanted before the image of Garia. Perhaps these similarities gave rise to these ideas of equaling Garia with these deities. But still others think that Garia is Garia and it is futile to identify him with any other deity. Both the Tripuri and the neighbouring non-tribal Hindus are polytheistic by nature. So as a result of interaction in many cases the Tripuri deities whose nature and functions appeared similar to those of the deities of the neighouring non-tribal Hindus got the name of the more familiar non-tribal deities.

The Tipras worship 'Garia Rājā' as the powerful nature deity who provides life, wealth, fertility and strength of war. On the whole, Garia Rājā represents the character of our benign nature and he always does good to us. The rites and rituals of the Garia pūjā seem to have a peculiar blending of naturism, animism, fertility cult and animatism. In the anthropological point of view, the tribal religion consists of beliefs and rituals, beliefs are static while rituals are dynamic.[49]

There is no permanent place or temple dedicated to this deity. The pūjā is performed in the open courtyard. The Garia is very dear to them and the pūjā is performed socially. The Garia pūjā begins usually in the spring season on the last day of the month of Chaitra and continues for about seven days. But it has been observed that the Tipras generally worship the diety Garia on the last day. According to the instructions of the *Ochai,* the house holder brings the upper portion of a bamboo pole along with its branches and leaves and plants it in the north or east side of his courtyard. Afterwards, a beautiful garland is fastened to it which is prepared by the cotton thread along with the flowers of cotton thread. A newly made "*Risa*" tied to its upper portion which contains some paddy and rice within its fold, a few bamboo poles small in size are also planted round the symbolic representation of the deity. Thus, it appears that the practice of planting a slender bamboo pole, with branches and leaves to make the symbolic representation of the deity, is the characteristic manifestation of animistic belief where the bamboo pole itself is worshipped in its natural form as Garia.

It is important to note that the bamboo tree occupies the same high position as enjoyed by the bel tree. It possesses the additional merit of warding off the evil spirit[50]. The bamboo pole is decorated with a piece of new cloth and worshipped[51] during the *Pousha Sankerantī* in Bengal. A faithful example of West Bengal like the Garia pūjā, a slender bamboo pole with the branches and leaves is also adored in the Gambhira festival[52]. In the north Bengal bamboo is worshipped as the village deity who is believed to be the caretaker of the agricultural fields, cottage industries and villages[53]. The leaves of bamboo are in use during the worshipping of *Ṣasthī* Goddess who grants long life and children to the Bengalees even to day. The Gāros and Kacharis also worship the bamboo pole after planting it in the ground. In Uttar Pradesh Churait is a female evil spirit who is believed to live in the groves of bamboo. It is found that the branches of bamboo are used in removing the bodily pain[54].

The ingredients of this pūjā consist of paddy, undried rice, cotton, cotton thread, Garland of cotton thread, *Risa,* small earthen pots, eggs, fowls, chickens, *longi* (rice-beer) and wine etc. The *Ochai* taking a water pot (*ghati*) made of brass sprinkles in water on the symbol of the deity and he is chanting *mantras*. The *Ochai* takes two banana leaves or jack fruit leaves or two bamboo slips in his hand and throws them in the air to know the result of the said puja. If a leaf falls flat on the ground and the remaining one falls on its back, it is a good result. This kind of tossing is called 'Patharna'[55].

When 'Patharna' is observed and ended with a good sign, the *Ochai* sacrifices the fowls and chickens according to the traditional custom and the blood of the animal is sprayed on the banana leaf in front of the symbol of deity. Afterwards, the heads of the fowls along with a piece of meat cutting from the neck are also placed on the banana leaf in the name of deity. Thereafter, cutting the rectum of the fowl the *Ochai* examines the entrails if it is in good condition or not. If it is found good, it may be assumed that the result of the pūjā will bring welfare to the house holder.

There is a taboo associated with the Garia pūjā. During this ritual no body is allowed to cross the shadow of the symbolic representation of Garia. It is feared by the devotees that this kind of action will displease the deity[56]. Then, at about 3 P.M. the ceremony of "Yakung Chhurua" (feet washing) begins for the welfare of the inmates. The eggs and chicken are dedicated to the deity for his pleasure and appeasement[57]. It may be called a poultry rite like the "*Kukkuti brata*" of Bengalees. Moreover, the fowl is a symbol of fertiiity and the egg is greatly loved by the tribal deity because "an egg is like a virgin whom no one has touched or a pregnant woman who hold two souls at once." Therefore, sacrifice of eggs to the God is a common rite among the tribes of India as well as the tribes of Tripura also. It is believed by the tribals of the universe that any egg can cause maternity, crops and increase life strength. An egg symbolies fertility cult and sex which is why the Tipras perform 'feet washing' ceremony as a poultry rite during the Garia pūjā.

After the performance of egg offering rite, the inmates of Garia start to carry the symbolic representation of Garia which is specially prepared for the purpose only. The *Risa* (covering of female breast) is taken from the original symbol and some cotton, paddy and rice etc. are kept on it and three knots are tied in order to make it a baggage. Then, the baggage is hung on the top of a spear which is called "kol"..As the representative of the deity, the kol is to move from one house to another in the selected village or para. The inmates are mostly young stars whom are found singing, dancing and playing the drums. The songs are generally chorus in nature and extremely erotic in character but the songs are melodious and rhythmic also. The householder receives the inmates of Garia and pays reverence to the deity and the fowls and eggs are offered to Garia by him. The inmates of deity are also offered money, cloth, egg, wine and fowl according to the financial condition of the householder. The inmates of deity serve the blessing to the householder on behalf of the deity Garia. The symbol of Garia, generally, is immersed at the end of seven days and seven nights to the river. But "Kol" is not taken for immersion. From the ritualistic point of view, it has been found that the worship of Kalaia is observed strictly following the animistic rites and practices. Kalaia seems to be the soul of dead who is supposed to associate with the tree cult. Abdul sattar says, "the most notable tree worship is the Kalaia pūjā. This pūjā is rendered in a very solemn manner, the worshippers have to shave their heads and place wine and other ingredients near the altar".[58] Kalaia is the spirit of ancestor whom the Tipras offer fowls, eggs etc. to please the deity. It is an idea of the animistic belief and this kind of ancestor worship is an archiac form of tribal religion. In the Kalaia pūjā, the *Ochai* has to observe some taboo and he has to be abstained from all foods, even not a single drop of water.

The Mwytamwng Pūjā (Worshipping of River / Stream)

The pūjā which is held in the village is called Luku Samwng. The Kakbark word Luku Samwng is derived from the words Luku = Village council + Samwng = works. So it means the work of village council. As buffalo is not sacrificed in this puja it is not called luku mwytamwang. Here importance has been stressed on the work of the village council than the sacrificed animal.[59]

Nakhung Samwang (Household Pūjā of Water)

It is not a compulsory pūjā for the family members. The word Nakhung has been derived from the words nag meaning house and samwng meaning work / function[60]. So Nakhung Sumwng literally means the function of a family. But here Nakhung Samwng means the worshipping of the deity of water by a household. Here two male goats are sacrificed. In this pūjā the animal to be sacrificed is more important.

Saon Pūjā

This pūjā is performed by the hada for the welfare of the people of their community. In this pūjā they pray to the Goddess of paddy to protect the country from scarcity.[61]

Agan Pūjā / Balang Kateramā

This pūjā is done by the hada[62] for the welfare of those who go into deep forests for the purpose of cultivation. The worship of Sangrangamā is mainly performed in this pūjā. The name of the puja Balang Katerama may be derived from the Kakbark words Balangni kiri - Karani Kateromoni (Bologni = of the forest + Kiri = fear + Kara = hesitation + Kara = removal + Ramani = giving)[63] meaning removal of the fear of the forest.

It this pūjā a live pigeon is buried in the ground outside the boundary of the village which is known as Khibwtharmani. This is also done with a view to remove fear as Khibwtharmani (Khi = fear + bwtharmani = killing) means killing of fear.[64]

Chaitra Chayngwra

This pūja is performed to protect the villagers from the attack of various diseases like cholera, pox etc which generally takes place in the month of Chaitra. It is believed that in the month of Chaitra, the evil spirits make fun (Chayngwra) with the people through these diseases.[65]

The Nagsu Mwtay Pūjā

Nagsu is not a common household deity of the Tripuris. The term Nagsu Mwtay (Nag = House + su = corner + Mwtay = God) means the Goddess of house.[66] It is considered as a female deity. It is believed that in some cases a woman is possessed by the Nagsu and she receives puja of the Nagsu Mwtay as a medium.

The Nagsu pūjā is performed on the day of the Garia pūjā only in those homes where Nagsu exists. The pūjā is officiated by an *Ochai*. All *Ochai* do not know the *mantras* of this Pūjā. The *Ochai* constructs a Yafwra (a bamboo cane made small square sized platform with small holes on it). After the completion of the pūjā the Yafwra is placed on the grilling of the roof at the south east corner of the house and the old one is immersed in water. The south east corner of the house has a special significance among the Tripuris. Generally oblation is offered to the Nagsumwtay but animals are sacrificed if the *Ochai* feels the necessity.[67]

When a man has sudden attack of diarrhoea, vomiting, headache etc. he promises gifts to the Nagsu. In such cases he offers something to the woman possessed by the Nagsumwtayes. It is believed that with the acceptance of the offering by the possessed, the patient will recover. The offering may range from a banana to sugarcane etc.

The Sangatran Pūjā

The Sangatran is a benevolent female deity. She is worshipped to get relief from all problems and sufferings like to rediscover a lost article, to win a case at the court, to get back a lover, to have a child etc.[68] In this puja the worshipper promises an offering to Sangatran.

An earthen cone represents this diety. The Puja is performed by the worshipper himself. In this pūjā the tale of Kamalapati is recited on a Sunday. The tale of Kamalapati deals with the glory of the Sangatran and how Kamalapati was relieved from her suffering. Generally a Naibadya is offered in this Pūjā. But a sacrificial is also done if the worshipper promises it to the Sangatran. In case of such a happening the *Ochai* officiates the Pūjā.

The Kuwaychanayma Pūjā

Kuwaychanayma is a malevolent female deity. This name is derived from the Tripuri word Kuway = betel nut or mixture of betel nut and betel leaf + Chawani = one who eats + ama = mother.[69] As offering of Kuway is a must in this puja the deity is known as Kuwaychanayam.

This pūjā is performed if the *Ochai* prescribes the propitiation of Kuwychamayma to a patient suffering from a disease sent by her. She leaves the patient alone only, if she offered the coveted dish. Some people promise an annual propitation to the Kuwaychanayma. In such cases the puja is performed on the day of Mahastami (during the period of Durgā pūjā). The *Ochai* officiates the pūjā. The pūjā is held in one corner of the village.

The Daykang Bwrwyrag Pūjā

This pūjā is also performed to get rid of a patient of the Swkal. This pūjā is performed if the *Ochai* feels the necessity of it. Unlike the Harmuthu pūjā it is performed at the Daykang the border of the village.[70] The *Ochai* gives the name of the animal to be sacrificed to propitiate the Swkal or the Bwrwyrag. The flesh of the animal to be taken by the *Ochai* and his party at the spot of the puja and it can not be taken to house. At the end the pūjā the *Ochai* tells the result of the puja to owner of the house.

Construction of images of customary Deities

The images of the traditional deities of the Tripuri, Jamatia and others tribes are made of bamboo instead of clay. Bamboo plays a vital role in their religious functions. Their inherent craftsmanship is evident from the art of construction of these images. The bamboo is as important to the tribal community of Tripura in their traditional puja as it has been in their day to day works since time immemorial. In fact, bamboo is an essential element in the life of tribal community since birth to even after death.

The green bamboos are first cut into pieces and then designed for making the images of various deities according to their custom. The structures and designs of various deities differ to a great extent. There are specific designs in constructing of specific deities.

Besides this, there are specific customs in the arrangement of the bamboo sticks for specific deities. The *Ochai* is the only authorized man to give necessary instructions regarding the structure of the images and arrangement of bamboo pieces in pūjās of various deities.

The various types of bamboo made images and other articles which are generally required in their traditional pujas are [71] :

1) Wathap 2) Dip 3) Lankhang Chufang 4) Tharuma 5) Nakri

6) Khulong 7) Charthangmani 8) Yakbar 9) Thampa etc.

A short description of the above mentioned articles are given below :

1. Wathap : The altar which is made of bamboo for the performance of puja is known as Wathap in their language. The term Wathap has been derived from the words WA (bamboo) and bathap (means nest of the birds). The platform of altar of a deity is known as Wathap as they are made of bamboo. The Wathap is required in the performance of Lampera pūjā, Thunairag Bonirag pūjā, Bolongwwamani pūjā, Bwasa pūjā etc.

Construction : The Wathap is constructed with six (three pairs) green bamboo sticks of one cubit length. In its construction, two pairs of bamboo sticks are fixed on the ground at a distance of about one cubit and the another pair of sticks are tied to the upper portion of the two pairs of sticks which were fixed on the ground earlier with bamboo cane. These bamboo sticks are designed by the *Ochai* according to custom with the help of a Scyth. The holes at the top of the bamboo sticks are covered with bamboo leaves.[72]

2. Langkhang / Chufang : The Langkhangs and Chufangs are used in all pūjās. During the time of pūjā, the deities are offered water and rice beer (Chuak) through these Langkhangs and Chufangs. These are made of two green bamboo pieces in such a manner that they may contain water and rice beer. The bamboo made container which is used to offer water to a deity is called Langkhang and the Container which is used to offer rice beer to a deity is called Chufang.[73]

3. Dip : In making of a Dip, a bamboo piece of a certain length is first of all stripped vertically into two flat pieces and then one flat strip is designed in its both sides.[74] The designs of this bamboo strip are fashioned to look like flower and are called *Matra*.

It may be noted here that different number of *Matras* are made for different deities. As for example, the dip which is required for Swkaljwk Mwtay or Bwrwyrag puja must have nine *Matras* (flowers). But in all other Pūjās Five *Matras* of a Dip are required.

4. Khang : It is made of bamboo strip which has designs on both sides and bent into arcs. Both the ends of this bamboo strip are fixed on the ground. This Khang[75] is required for Sangrang pūjā, Gaṅg pūjā, Ker pūjā, marriage ceremonies etc.

5. Tharuma : It is bamboo piece of one cubit length and it is fixed on the ground before the image of the deity.[76] The hole of this bamboo piece is covered with bamboo leaves.

6. Khoulong : It is a small sized bamboo made basket which is required only for the purpose of Burasā pūjā.[77]

7. Nakri : This pūjā is done in the month of *Chaitra* (March - April) for the welfare of the village.

The image of the Nakri can be made in two ways. Generally, a Muli (a variety of bamboo) bamboo piece of a certain length is designed according to the instruction of the *Ochai* and a small quantity of cotton is tied to the middle part of this bamboo stick and is fixed on the ground.[78] There are also certain restrictions regarding the use of thread. In the performance of the Burasā pūjā - both black and white coloured thread can be used.

On the other hand, a Nakri can also be made by fixing Jhum cotton on a branch of a Dexaram tree. Both white and black thread can be used in this type of Nakri.

8. Charthangmani : The Charthangmani is made during the time of Gang pūjā to satisfy Twikhulumani (Goddess of water). In its construction four bamboo pieces are fixed on the ground first and then six flat bamboo pieces are arranged at the top of these four bamboo poles. At the centre part of the bamboo poles, one platform is also made with flat bamboo pieces which is called 'Changni.[79]

9. Thapna : The two flat bamboo pieces which are fixed on the two sides of the Charthangmani are called thapna.

A

Religion of Buddhist Tribes, the Maghs and the Chākmā

In Tripura where Hinduism is a religion of the majority people including tribal and non-tibal communities but the Maghs are in a certain sense Buddhists excepting a very few who profess after Hinduism or Christianity.[80] It is significant that the Maghs are said to be Buddhists but they still contine some of their primitive pūjās and festivals. The Primitive forms of religion along with Buddhism seem to influence over them, but it is a real fact that what is dominant is their traditional indigenous religious culture, on the other hand, the traces of Hinduism along with its Gods and Goddesses have been found in their day to day life also.

The Maghs are the universe with spirits. These are involved in their religious rites, ritual and rivalries.[81] Side by side with the Buddhist priest, there exists the tribal priest of the animistic faith who is called *Ojhā* in Tripura.

The Maghs have their nature deities and certain offerings are set aside for each deity. The propitiation of Chug-Mung-Ley is usually made around the marriage ceremony of the Maghs.[82] The offerings with the *mantras* and sacrifices of a pig and five fowls have to be made to the deities by the *Thangpārā* or *Ojhā*.

The Magh religion is an unique religion and is expressed in rituals both at the family and communal levels. The mortal remain of a Magh is cremated after observing funeral rites of offering food and water. Obsequies is performed with great pomp and festivals. The priest holds a service for the dead. He meditates and prays for spiritual salvation of the atman. According to one's capacity food and water are given to the priest when the corpse is taking to the *pyre*. At least the nearest relation sets fire to the *Pyre*. After seven days some rituals in the form of the *Sraddha* are held for the good of the departed when the priest and other people are treated with entertainment.

The common deity of the *Kakbark* speaking tribes who is called Budadevata is worshipped by the Maghs as *Chicki*. It is believed that *Chicki* is the deity of forest.[83] During the Gaṅgā Pūjā, a great festival of water is celebrated which is some what akin to *Holi*.[84] They also worship the deities, but the characters of which are not similar to the Fourteen deities of the Tripuras.

Religion of the Chākmā tribe

In the matter of belief and practice, the Chākmās are not very different from the other tribal communities of Tripura and they are called Buddhists only because they can not be known under any other religious nomenclature now-a-days.

They have borrowed some Hindu customs, beliefs, Gods and Goddesses and Brahmanism is still traceable in their religion even today. At present the Chākmās subscribe to the *Saṅgharājā Nikaya* of East Bengal Buddhism.[85] Buddhism of the Chākmās had been quite different from orthodox theravada before the reform initiated by the *Saṅgarājā Saramedha Mahāthara*. The Chākmās have their traditional priest who is called lorhi or Roubee. These lorhis are to day considered a lower order of Buddhist priests in relation to the *Bhikhus* but they still perform traditional religious rites. According to H.H. Risley, animism is the highest factor in the religion of the primitive tribes and the Chākamās are not exception.[86] They worship the super natural forces of nature as the nature deities to attain desirable success. Their religious cults are combinations of ancestor worship, worship of nature deities and spirits. Before they were merged into the stream of Buddhism the countless deities of Hinduism held their sway over the *Chākmās* mind, but later advancing Buddhism had thrown many such deities of the pedestal.[87] At present, Śiva, Kālī, Lakshmī, Saraswatī and others are adored.

The nature deities such as the Sky, the River and the Earth are paid reverences at the time of beginning of all their rituals as Chu-Ngu-Lang, Parameswari and Bajamonatti respectively.

Chu-Ngu-Lang-Pūjās

The offering to chungulang can be made at time for getting a child, marriage, increasing harvest or for any social gain or growth. It has been found that the rites of this pūjā vary according to the character for which it is performed. The *Ojhā* is informed by the house-holder in the previous evening to perform the pūjā. The next morning the priest generally appears to the house-hold where the pūjā is being celebrated. He asks for a bamboo structure called *Changari* to be raised with seven parts of bamboo strips.[88] In addition to that two small baskets are placed near the *Changari* one containing rice and the other paddy. It has been found that the casks of wine are also served there. The Lorhi changing, the *mantras* begins the pūjā and three pigs and a roster head, are boiled, laid up on banana leaves and kept in the *Changari*. The adoration of *Parameswari* is also performed during this time. The offerings of this ritual is similar to the *Chungulang* pūjā. The Chākmās imagine *Parameswari* as mother earth being the wife of *Chungulang*.

Vadya Pūjā

The Vadya pūjā of the Chākmās is observed in which they serve rice to the souls of their ancestors. In every village dominated by the Chākmās, there occur the Vadya pūjā. Generally, the family which takes initiative the Vadya pūjā counts the souls of its ancestors up to the third or fifth remove. On the selected day the new pyres are constructed for all the souls presence of the Lorhi.[89] The offerings for each ancestor consist of a dish of rice and curry and also sweets. These offerings are prepared on a wide patch of earth in the dense jungle and the relation of the souls have to be remained present at the time of ceremony. The Lorhi Chants, the mantras from the scriptures. "During his recitation he coaxes the souls of fly back across the frontier of death to partake the food served out to them. The flies and insects which may settle on the food must be thought to be souls of the dead reborn in the shape of insects on account of divine retribution. In that case there is a prescribed redemptive rite to expiate the sins of the condemned souls".[90]

Dharmakam or Jadipūjā

From the religious point of view the Dhārmākam pūjā or the Jadi Pūjā is an extraordinary ritual, the success of which totally depends upon a number of miracles. The lorhi performs the pūjās outside the village generally in the dense part of the jungle because an uncanny sylvan semi-darkness and solitude are required for this ritual.[91] On the appointed day rice is cooked by a person who has to observe some ritualistic in which the cook is not allowed to talk or the entrance of any one to this area is strictly prohibited. Then the cooked rice is stuffed into a banana leaf packet and carried to the venue of the pūjā. The other offerings of the Jadi pūjā consists of coconut, banana, sugarcane and sweets. Stremers are improvised by tieing shred of cloths on bamboo spikes and put on a loft. As the priest starts the pūjā by reading from the *Dasaparami Tara,* a faint streak of smoke will be seen rising from the capsule. The smoke signifies that the God has been pleased and graciously accepted the reverence of his mortal devotees. Every one will then prostrate themselves in salutation to the invisible deity.[92] Like the other pūjās, the Lorhi sacrifices fourteen roosters and a pig. After a few minutes incidentally a spider will appear from an unknown place and spin a web around the rice filled capsules which indicates that the pūjā has been accepted by the deity.

Thanmana Pūjā

One of the most characteristic trait of Chākmā religion is the observation of Thanmana Pūjā or Gaṅgā pūjā in the month of January. The nature deity of water has been identified as Gaṅgā who is similar to Tuimā of the *Kakbark* speaking tribes of Tripura. This ritual is to be held for aiding Jhum cultivation or increasing its yield in which the educated elite and the *Bhikhus* do not take active part. It is performed by raising subscription from all villagers. On the selected day, the pūjā is celebrated on a river by constructing symbolic representations of the deities. Two bamboo made pedestals one high and another low are made on knee deep water of river according to the rank and position of the deities. The bigger pole represents for the bigger deities like Gaṅgā, Baitra, Than, Chella, Bajammatti, Parameswari, Bhut, Rakhyoal and Thammang and the smaller one is for the deities like Chekong, Maji, Shiji, Baradhan, Kālī Jundur, Aanesha, Laojya, Thakur, Hatya who are supposed to be smaller.[93] The pedestals are four sided and raised on four main pillars of bamboo with a few supporting props.

The tops of the pillars are over-hung with images of an ear of paddy and the other posts are spiked with images of cotton. At the middle of the pedestal clod of earth is kept which has to be collected from the Jhum cultivation. The clay lamp is decorated with the ear of paddy, cotton and a few flowers. The priest chanting the *mantras* starts the ritual by sprinkling water on the pedestal. As soon as chanting of the water on the pedestal and chanting of the *mantra* is over, the deities have to be propitiated by sacrificing goats, pigs, rooster and pigeon etc. Traditionally, the neck of the animal has to be completely severed in case of greater deities and generally, in case of lesser deities, the neck of the animal is half-cut. Then the priest sprinkles the blood over the altar and the ritual is rounded off with a big feast in which the whole village takes part.

Bur Para Pūjā

The *Burpara* pūja[94] is rendered to propitiate a nature deity for the well being of the family. According to the prescription of the Lohri all the family members go to the river *Ghāt* and wash their head for purification. The ingredients of the ritual consist of flowers, gold silver and iron.

Pūjā associated with birth

The Gaṅgā pūjā is performed for the welfare of the mother along with her baby who will born in future.[95] The Pūjā *Bhut* is also arranged in some villages. Another important ritual is called the *Barabara* pūjā which is celebrated for the safe delivery of the mother. For the welfare of the pregnant woman an unique pūjā is observed by the river side in which a hut is build, in front of the hut a pitcher with a betel nut dipped into it. One end of a thread is tied round the neck of the pot and the other end is tacked to the door of the house. Then the pot is brought in contact with the forehead of the women seven times. The woman along with the pot is then taken to the hut of the river side where certain prescribed rituals take place.

Back home, they keep the pot carefully and offer a feast by killing a pig. The *kuja pani* pūjā is connected with a new born baby.[96] One month after the birth of a child the Dhatri performs this ritual in which she takes the mother to the river-*ghāt* for purification by holy water.

Bijhu festival

Bishu or *Bijhu* is the most significant and holy festival in religious point of view and it is started in the last day of *Chaitra,* continues for 3 days. It has been found that no body of the Chākmā community works for their bread on the occasion of *Bijhu festival.*[97] An important ritual is called '*Phool Bijhu*'. The last day of the festival is called '*Gecha-pacha*'. The Chākmās collect the vegetables, leaves of trees and roots from the forest in the sacred day of *Phool Bijhu.* Next day they rise early in the morning and after having bath from the river both the boys and girls come to the house to release the household domestic animals from captivity and necessary foods are offered to the animals. The virtuous people gather round the temple and start to chanting the name of Lord Buddha. Afterwards, these people enter the temple and pay due offering to Lord Buddha. "*Gecha pacha*" is celebrated on the third day. The fouls and pigs are killed for the feast in which the friends and relations take part. The songs and dances of the Chākmās are essential accompaniments of the festival which now a days continues for a week.[98]

Lakshmir Pūja

Significantly while the Chākmā are Buddhist, their culture have Hindu influence. The Hindu deities like Śiva, Kālī, Lakshmī and Sarasvatī are still worshipped by the Chākmās. The Chākmās have a remarkable religious scripture called *Lakshmir pālā* which is sung whole night long. A special adoration of Lakshmī, Kālī and Biyatra is observed in the next morning in which the symbolic representations of the deities are constructed with the help of bamboos. Animal sacrifices and *Naivedya* are very essentials for the pūjā. They believe, this pūjā is the meant of getting wealth and prosperity. But it should be remembered that she is not similar to the Goddess Lakshmī of Brahmanical Hinduism. The Lakshmi pūjā is rounded off with a big feast. The other important Buddhist traditional inters and rituals are *Hajar, Baatis, Thamington, Dhanpang, Ayapuja, Langtarai* pūjā, *Ekatara* pūjā, *Halpalani* pūjā. Besides, the *Fagiri* pūjā is also observed to get rid of the terrible activities of from ferocious tigers and the *mantras* from the sacred '*Agartare*' (holy creed of Buddhist Chākmā) are chanted.

B

Pūjās, Rituals and other Religious Influences on the Tribal Community

Besides their traditional deities and other magical religious functions which are officiated by their traditional priests, the tribal community of Tripura also perform many pūjās and religious functions, according to the almanac which are borrowed by them from their neighbouring castes and communities. This is the result of their long days of acculturation with their neighbouring religion of other communities.

The Tripras of Tripura are strong followers of Vaiṣṇava *dharma* and Śakta *dharma* and they have simple devotion to Brahmanical Gods and Goddesses. In fact, through the centuries many of the Tipras have been drawn into the main stream of Brahmanical way of life along with its pantheon. It is believed that the religion and culture of the Bengali-speaking people had come to enjoy an advantage and to live side by side with the indigenous culture of Tripura community resulting in cultural exchanges.[99] It was Hindus' sacred scriptures, their epics and purāṇic myths and legends and their social and religious systems which modified the religious beliefs and practices of the Tipras. As a result, they began to engage the Brāhmaṇa priest for the performance of śāstriya pūjās on the one hand and the Ochai on the other, the late preserving the old Gods and rites, "These are the custodian of Tripras religious, a dual arrangement which is still in vogue."[100]

The worship of house deity Śrīlakshmī has a great impact on the religious life of Tripras. During Lakshmī *pūrṇimā* they worship the goddess with image similar to other caste of Hindus.[101] The worship of Mahādeva is, however, most wide spread among the men and women folks of Tripras. Some of them observe the holy night of Śivarātri. The worship of Kālī is no less popular. Besides, they worship the Goddess Tripurāsundarī, Lakshmī Nārāyaṇa, Jagannātha and so on. The goddess of Sarasvatī is paid honour by the Tipras at the time of Śrī Pañchamī. The popularity of Durgā pūjās is most important in the life of Tripras in which they take part with great devotion. There are festivals where the Tipras participate together without making any hierarchical difference. They all enjoy to the Holi, Diwali, Rathayātrā etc. A large number of Tipras on many occasions have been visiting the temples and accompanying religious functions.

The Jāmātias have their tribal religion much modified by Brahmanism. It is significant that majority of them are Hindus, but there are many pre-Hindu religious pūjās and rites among the Jāmātias. They are classified into two sects, Vaiṣṇavas and Śāktas. They like to go on a pilgrimage every year and often visit sacred placed like Kasī and Vrindavan, etc.

The Vaiṣṇavism practiced and professed by the Jāmātias, has certain conspicuous features, quite distinct from those of the Vaiṣṇavism as practiced in Āssam. This may partly be due to the personality of Śrī Chaitanya and his followers called Goswāmins. In fact under the proper guidance of the Goswāmins they started Hari Saṁkirtan and began to wear *Tulsi mālā* and started to bear *Tilaka* of sandal-paste in which represented their devotion to Viṣṇu.'[102]

The Śāktas use a dot of sandal paste in red or vermilion as symbol of Śāktism. It is evident that the pujās and religious rites of the Jāmātias are performed by their traditional priest along with the Brāhmaṇa priest. They worship the goddess Durgā, Tripurāsundarī, Kālī, Sarasvatī, Gaṅgā, Lakshmī, Śiva, Śani, etc.

Majority of the Noatiās are Śāktas. While a good number of the Noatiās is found to lead a life of Vaiṣṇava mendicants. They believe that sacred duty is to set out on pilgrimage every year like Hindus to pay homage to their beloved Gods and Goddesses. The Brāhmaṇa priests are appointed to perform the worship of Kālī, Lakshmī and other Sastriya Pūjās.

Generally, the Riangs believed in the Śākta Cult but at present some of them are followers of Viṣṇu and Christ. The worship of Brahmanical deities like Kālī, Śiva, Lakshmī, Durgā are traceable among them.

Although the Chākmās are basically Buddhists, so all the Buddhist Pūjas are fixed by local calendar. The Chākmās celebrate Bijhu festival, in which Lord Buddha is worshipped to achieve their different needs of life. All the full moons are identified as very sacred to the Chākmās in which they offer ingredients to their beloved deity.[103] The Chakrabuha pūjā[104] is observed to the full moon of the month of Baishākh, Asaḍh and Āswin. A circular enclosure is raised with hedges providing for only two accesses.

There is a *dais* at the centre on which sits the priest. His devotees sit round him triumphantly chanting the name of Lord Buddha.[105] In addition to that, a ceremonial ritual Thaming Tang is celebrated in which rice mixed with turmeric is heaped on a platter like a mountain. The other ingredients required for the Thaming Tang are vermillion, sandal wood, betel-nut, etc.[106]

The Maghs have given a religious importance to full moon. Generally, all their festivals are observed during full moon. The full moon in the month of Magh is called *Tabunglabre* when they pay homage to lord Buddha. In addition to this festival *Thinziana festival* also is celebrated. Śani, Kālī and Gaṅgā are also worshipped by the Maghs.[107]

C

Religious Mantras of Tribal Community of Tripura

The belief of the supernatural deities has compelled the tribal people of Tripura, to create the *mantras* for the satisfaction of their desires. The *mantras* of the tribal communities may be divided into the following:

1. The ritualistic *mantras* in times of pujas and prayers;
2. The *mantras* for the shamanistic activities;
3. The *mantras* for the occultism.

The *mantras* recited in the various activities of the tribal people of Tripura, have not found written in the realm of tribal world except the Chākmā tribe. The Chākmās write their *mantras* in corrupt Burmese script as well as Bengali script for the purpose. The *mantras* are very essential for the purpose of the black magic, jugglery, worship of Gods and Goddesses, incantations and cure of diseases. A special kind of *mantra* is applied as a method of curing various diseases and also for transmission of diseases towards the end of the enemy. The tribal priest called Ochai learns the holy spell or *mantras* from his *guru*. The *mantras* are transmitted orally from generation to generation, with changes, modifications, additions and alterations according to the need of the society. So, in the absence of a written code, the *mantras* vary according to the memory and individual faculty of speech of the Ochai. The post of Ochai is not hereditary and there is no priestly class or caste who performs the rituals of the tribals.

However, the *mantras* are kept well in the memory of the Ochai confidentially. The king, the dwellers of town and the non-tribals are not allowed to learn the *mantras* of the tribal communities. The priests strictly follow the principle of secrecy of the holy *mantras* and it has been observed that the *mantras* are not loudly uttered. The ritualistic *mantras* are rhythmic and sweet to hear.

The *mantras* are generally in form of verse consisting of several stanzas in the respective mother dilect of the communities in which the Ochai is belonged. In case of the Chākmās, the *mantras* are found written from the beginning of their script. The Ojhā of the Chākmās is called Vaidya who seems to utilize the *mantras* for the purpose of pūjā and the treatment of diseases as a shaman. It appears that the *mantras* of the Chākmās are influenced by the Hinduism and Buddhism. It is a fact that some mystic words are added with the *mantras*, the meaning of which are not clear to anybody. The following *mantras* which are belonging Kokbark's-speaking tribe and subtribes of Tripura are[108] :

a) Tripura/Tipra; b) Riāng; c) Jāmātiā; d) Noatiā, e) Rupani; f) Koloi; g) Uchoi h) Murāsing

Kakbark mantra

a) An extract drawn from the *mantra* of the Lampra pūjā[109] as uttered by Ochai has been given below along with its English translation.

1. *Ang Hiya dan Sakha*
   Siri Akatha, Siri Bikatha
   Ama Twybuk, Ama Sangrang
   Niragsi Ma Fayjanay

Uttar Tanglbw, dakkin Tanglbw
Pube Tanglbw, Paschim Tanglbw
Rajsinghasan Rokha
Achak Faybay Jadi
A takle achok faybay jakha ba
niragna Chaswmay Rojakha
nung swmay Rojakha
Yasu-Jaknay twy Rojakha
Yasu Bay jaisidi.
(Twy kisa kisa Hawo lu khwayuwy Yaksu Rwkha)
A takle yasu bay jákha be
Nwsa Fana (Bwmwng) kwrwyja Twtay Fanw.
Bikhwra khangwra jafanw niragna
Khulumasayawani banguwy
Niragna Suri Sajawani Banguwy
Nirangi Thani Kisa kay Jawani banguwy
Niragni Thani Mansa Jawni Banguwy
Chgajaya Tutay fanw
Niragna Mayrum Kisa Ram bafal (Thaaylwy) Kisa
Batasa Kisa Khwlay Jaguwy
Chaswamay Rojayaguw
Chaswamay Rojajaguw
A Thaguw Thagya Fanw
Chaja Baykha
Atakle Chabay Jakha Nungbay Jakhaba
Yasu Bay Jasidi
Bukhuk su Bay Jasidi
A Takle yasu bay Jakha be

Bukhuk su Bay Jakha Ba

Swrasa Fale Leyngla Long Bay Jadi

(Pasa/Chaswmay Raranany Tey Bani Nag Baragragni Hammari Nuyuwy Mwthary Ragni Thani Ochaini Kabakmwng Kaymwng Tey Samwng)

Dau A Danda Kwrwy Dasa Kwrwy

Ayakwrwy Achi Kwrwy

Kungtwy Kwrwy, Mwktwy Kwrwy

Hener Kwrwy Sakron Kwrwy

Akasa Kwrwy Khasa Kwrwy

Baban Kwrwy Rway Kwrwy

Kulun Kwrwy Kwma Kwrwy

Rajdanda Kwrwy Debadanda Kwrwy

Khwlayuwy Tang Rajadai, hwnwy

kabakjani Banguwy,

Nwsa Funani (Bwmwng) Banguwy Ang bachuw (Twy Ma Lunay)

Dau A Takle Nws a Fanani (Bwmwng) banguwy

Ayuk Tabakha Jan Tabakha

Dhan Tabakha Jan Tabakha

May bw Tabakhe Khul bw Tabakha

Dau Nwsa Fanana Kasang Khwngchurwy Lakruwy

kebeng Faklay Taranwy

Naksing Siniya Chauyaalok Nakhawo

rimwing Siniya Ribagruwy

Chamwng Siniya Chwauwy

Ayuk barey Thaluk barey

Dhan Barey Janbarey

Ayuk Kwchang Thaluk Kwchang

Jala Jala Mal Mal Khwlayuwy

Tinini Sasimi Tangrojadi Dak........ Baba

(Mayrum Agnauwy Sema anylaha/Thikana Naylaha)

A Takle chabaykha Najgbaykha Tei

Le Bw Leynla bayjakha Ba

Je Ṇirag Thaṅgwan Muchak Thini

Thangbay jasid;

(Twy Kisa Kisa Lu Khwayuwy biday Robay Kha)

Translation in English :

The Ochai Utters :

These are not my words,

Śrī Akatha, Śrī Bikatha

Masangrangma and Matwaybuk.

Please to make an appearance;

be you in the east, be you in the South

The throne has been laid out for you

Please to take a seat.

For your pleasure, I have placed food and drinks

and water too, for washing your hands please to wash them.

(The priest now pours some water on the earth and performs certain acts to signify the washing of the hands)

Alright its over now

when your son (here the worshipper)

albeit poor and of humble origins,

Incapable of great pomp and show

pays his obeisance

in order to invoke you

And place before you

Some requests, some prayers.

Though he can hardly afford it

Offers you some rice, a few bananas

please to partake a little of the humble offerings.

(The priest carries out certain acts which signify the terminal of the meal)

Now that you have finished your food

please to wash your hands.

(The priest again carries out certain acts)

Now I pray you, indulge in some rest.

(In order to increase the general welfare of the house-holders, the priest propitiates and pleads with the deity)

God that never deals a bad blow

Keep him forever free from pain and disease

Please see to it that there is never cause to weep wail or suffer from stomach disorder or cold or languish in fever.

I pray to you, O omnipotent God,

On behalf of your son,

Proceed over this household

Keep it forever free from your wrath and shield him from the kings displeasure

(Water is scattered on the ground)

Grand him a long, healthy, happy life

Wealth in quantities large

Let his family members augment, prosper

Replenish his stock of cotton and care of corn

Now, let your son possess such a physique

That his head brushes with the roof-top.

His breath be equal to the beam of his ceiling

Let his house stock so much food and clothing

That he cannot even keep take on them

Give mental peace that he may dwell

Happily from the day onwards, O God.

(The priest meditates with a handful of grain and satisfies himself as to whether the result is favourable or not.)

Now comes the bidding farewell to the deity bit.

The priest Utters:

Now that you have partaken of the refreshment

Rested, you can return to your original

dwelling place or any where you choose.

(Farewell is bid by scattering some water on the ground.)

2. *"Hangnai Danganai Chiri Adung Balas*

Akhataa Bikhata Tuittuibu Kolakshi Raja

Dung Balae Nasu Nasu Hamayahai

Tangnai Tuibak Laktai Aiuga lagay,

Tangnani Helanni Aiugo Onanay Tang Thun Dangnay"[110]

Meaning : Let the couple so and so be laborious and happy in their married life by the blessing of AKHATA and BIKHATA and KOLAKSHI RĀJĀ. Let their life be as long as river and unaffected like and undecaying stone.

3. *"Anha Shri Ikhitra Bikhitra Raja,*

Taibuk Kolakshi Raja,

Dang Balinasu nasu Hamaya Hai Tanganal Taibuk logtui Ayugo Lokgay Tangnani, Lalangni Ayuk Ngay Tang Thum—Dhaksai"[111]

Meaning : Ikhitra, Bihhitra and Kolakshi Rājā, let his life be as long as river, as long as the stone—a man.

4. *"Okapuma Hreng Pathin Maman Damre Deshi Hairse Damrang Ongreng Damreche" Okapuma Reng Damresu Desea Haichha Raja Hairchhe Raja, hairchhe Damresu pathein maiman*[112]

Meaning : O my king and the god of king, do good to human, country, kingdom and our community, let the life of king be unaffected by death.

5. *Achuk Faidi bacha Phaidi*

   Mwkhang Ta Khedi, Khorang Ta Khedi

   Achuk Phaidi Bacha Phaidi

   Yaksudi yakong sadi

   Randchak-Ni khampali-O Achukdi

   Rang Chak - Nj Khrio, Purhai-Ni Bati - O Chadi.[113]

Meaning : Please come and sit, do not cast any look to this side, stand up, do not utter indecent words, and take your food placed on the golden and silver cups.

6. *"Bamoinha-Le, Gangokha-Le*

   Taktwi Sema Nai-O

   Okchai Ha-Le Khama Ha-Le

   Komala Ha-Le Komotha Ha-Le

   Per sema Nai-O Tor Sema Nai-O[114]

Meaning : We are illiterate people, we can not read and write; So from an observation of the dropping of a pair of leaves, we come to know whether you have come or not.

7. *Ama Mainokma Nsu—Fang*

   Hamya tong ba chaia Tong ba

   Maising Kongrai vasa musa

   Bukhri Khuidi Sikhri Khudi"[115].

Meaning : O Mother Mainokma, the house holder Mr. so and so has been suffering from cough and cold in the winter and from the eye disease in the rainy season-removc all these, he prays for your blessings.

8. *Nausa Falna-O Toumani Bagoui*

   bumugn Khurbai Bousak Khurfai

   Chhili Khaioful Bili Dhai-fai[116]

Meaning : The name of your son is Mr. so and so, why you have created a disease in the body? Please save us from all diseases in world. You are our king.

9. *Nausa Falna Yak-Ni Da Faloui*
Chang-Ni Rifaloui Chama Rou-O
Nungma Rau-O, Rangchak bati Rufai Bait.
Yachak Chadi Hkuk Chak Chadi
Yak Sudi Khuk Sudi.[117]

Meaning : Your son Mr. so and so having disposed the chopper of his hand, clothes of his waist, has collected all necessary articles of offerings for you. Please take the food placed on the golden cup and silver cup.

10. *"Asuk Him Khoulai Bini Hamaya Tangmani*
Chaya Tancmani Moukie Tangmani
Kungle Tangmani, Kulom Tangnani
Kousa Tang mani, Hani Kano-O
Tai-Ni Busub-O, Taibuk Kousatai
Taikha Kousa Tai srung srung prung purng
Suoi Tlangdi rogoy Tlangdi Ballai, dakshal"[118]

Meaning : You wipe all of his misfortunes and while returning carry all contemps. You save from the all evil spirit of our society. You also wipe the Swkal from our community because you are king of god.

11. *Anu Pokhi Raja*
Subroy chang ouichhe Baruya chang ouichhe.
Nojma Kouchamung Naufa
Koucha Mung Horo oung
Out Horo-Ha Tanjakgo
Bal Oung-Oi salok
Rajago Ochai Papo
krwi Barua Papo
Krwinini Na Moui-Ho
Khitung Kha Tlanodi Ballai[119]

Meaning : O bird, your mother and father have been accepted the sacrificial ruling of Subroy Rājā from generation to generation. You may be slaughtered any time of a day and night. The Ochai and his assistant Baruya can not do any inauspicious act. Your tail is tied with sin, while returning carry all sins; I am not responsible for this.

12. *Ah Bagbol Raja*

    Moongma Kwchacha Mangmo

    Noonpha Kwchcha Namgmo

    Noong-no tain nai

    Aboni ang Daya Krwi

    Angls susao Saimain Ya

    Angle Ya oha-O main-Ya[120]

Meaning : O he goat, you will be satisfied today. Your mother and father promised for this. I have no responsibility; my assistants are not responsible also. Do not curse us.

13. *Phoin he Klai Boatu pung nai*

    Tho Ka Klai bo khari Pung nai

    Yachak Chaid Khuri chak chadi[121]

Meaning : A single piece of meat is sufficient for the fullness of a pin of bamboo to hold meat spices together, and only a single drop of blood is required to fill completely the vessel. You gladly take food and drink with the help of your hand and mouth.

14. *Noong chamung Main-Da*

    Nung Nung Main-Dw

    Noosa Polna humya Chaya

    Chaiklai Khuidi Makhlai Khuidi[122]

Meaning : You are entertained with food and drinks. The disease of your son Mr. so and so is to be washed down away by you. You are king of god. Only you save the boy from the disease, please, do it.

15. *Cha phio he nan phi ha*

    Noosa Folna-No Bakya Chaphi-ha

Nini habi ha-O Nokha ha-O

dasa Dordo Tuin-nang Thang-di

Mikhlai Thang-di Bakhlai Thang-di

Aro to Tong di[123]

Meaning : You have entertained. You have blessed Mr. so and so. Now you go back to your residence (land of gods). Do not stay here, while returning carry all misfortunes.

Chākmās mantra

There are various kind of *mantras* of Chakma tribe, recited in the Shamanistic purpose. Some *mantras* are also applied against the enemies and to ward off the evil eye and cure the patient from sufferings. The Chākmās make use of river water during the purification ceremony of any individual when the Ojha spells the *mantras* in the dialect of the Chakma[124] follows :

16. *Dere gaṅgā kere pani*

Abjumanei Suddha gari

Suddha gari Padhang Ghar

mar mang bebir put shibsankar.

juro chhara Jure pani

Dere gaṅgā dere pani

Surang garang urang mani

Sujang nale varang pani

Dere gangadere Pani

Abujmanei suddha gari

Suddha gari Padhang Ghar

Mar nang debir pur Shibsankar.

Shil bhangi pather garang

Pathar bhangidarga garang.[125]

Meaning : O, mother Gaṅgā, the son of Goddess, Shibsankar prays to you for water, so that he may purify the silly human beings. The water of the rivulet is cold. O mother, I shall draw water from the flowing brook, please allow purification, I am the son of Goddess, my name is Shibsankar, I pray to you for the grant of my solicitation.

17. *Ung Uttarettum anilung phul*

    Nange Niranjan,

    garokhanahte dila Phul

    Garlung jattan

    Dela tare

    Nadele mare

    Satgang sajuri

    (Falner) dwi-charanat parhe

    Unung swaha Pua.[126]

Meaning : The follower brought forth from the north is called Nirañjan (pure). This flower has been obtained from Gorakh Nath. It has been kept carefully. One gets life at the sight of it, if not death is inevitable. Let the person be and hypnotized bend down to the lady love. I transmit this hypnotic words for the purpose.

18. *Shil bhangi pather garang*

    pather bhangi darja garang

    Durja pani huje tulong

    Sajang nale bharang pari

    Abuj manei suddha garang

    Shuddha gari padhang ghar

    Mare nang Debri put Shibasankar.[127]

Meaning : I shall create a sea by crushing the stones. I shall turn all habitations in to a watery surface. I shall draw water from the flowing brook. I shall purify the silly human beings and send them to their respective houses. O Mother, I pray to you for the grant of my prayer.

19. *Ung-Utha Larang mularang*

    Bayu grang their

    Phalner Ulmatya mana

Gange garng
Jwilba toanse thidhi garang
Gaṅgā bhagirathi
Thengtale thidhi garang
Mada Bajunmati
Nabhimule thidhi garang
Burma Ujal ghar
nasikate thidhi garang
padan dui Shar.
Chaksu madhue thidhi garang
Dui Kalachan
Karnamule thidhi garang
Chaitanya Gojen.
Mulumette-thidhi garang
Ekachakra ghila
Dui haste thirdhi garang
Engila Pingila
Dui padi thidhi garang
Susarmma Gandhari
Dhari aaghe Mahaprabhu
Ei chare nari
Kaya charmadhari aaghe
Bishnu Naranjan
Rakta mangsa dhari aaghe
Deva Birochan
Ketu-Durga dhari aaghe
Shakti tribhuvan
Bhenu bhenu badya baje

Nikunga bhavan
Ungkar susari Gaṅgā
Ungkar Suya!
Ungkar bhagirathi Gangda
Ungkar Suya!
Ungkar bhagirathi Gaṅgā
Ungkar Suya!
Ungkar jannhabi Gaṅgā
Unkar Suya!
Ungkar shiba jal Gaṅgā
Ungkar Suya!
Miran hok th tan hok thir
Ungkar Suya![128]

Meaning : A considerable quantity of water is sanctified by means of uttering the prescribed mystic words cited above for the removal of fever.

20. *Ung Phul aason phul bajan*
Phuler jay jagar,
Ei phul paridyanagar
Phalni na long gha duyer
Khuwai aanang-ben duyer
ben duyorate dile bari
Satgang sajuri
Phalni e Yek mar charanta Pari.[129]

Meaning : The mystic *mantra* cited above is uttered by the Chākmā Ojhā on a flower aimfully for the purpose of hypnotization of any body as requested by some one from his community.

21. *Ung shibeng pudi kajal pudi*
Sat-phudure ma

Ki puge chara kare
Andhar ratri ga
Marija phuddye
Marija[130]

Meaning : A quantity of wine is sanctified by means of this *mantra* for the purpose of destroying the insects from the plants.

22. *Umg ore ore padma*
Mahadeer Jhi
Deb nange Kam
Ganar bana Ki?
Sumeru rupasi padma
Kam nei ghuraghuri
Karma dile dwani aar
Muri dilung bhat bari
Mahadeve dile bar
Padmaya gare ra.
Phalner kalkuti
nimijat Kadi jha.[131]

Meaning : This mystic *mantra* is applied by the Chākmā Ojhā to cure a person from snake-biting.

References

1. Gonda, J. *Die Religionen Indiens,* Vol. II, Stuttgart, 1963, p. 11.
2. Eschmann, A. "*Hinduisation of Tribal Deities in Orissa*" in the book on the cult of Jagannāth and the Regional Tradition of Orissa, New Delhi, 1978.
3. *1901 Census Report of Tripura* (Reprint 1995), Agartala, p. 16.
4. *Tripura District Gazetteers,* Agartala, 1975, p. 129.
5. Bhattacharjee, P. N., *Jamatia Folklore,* Agartala, 1995, pp. 120-122.
6. Delton, E.T., *Descriptive Ethnology of Bengal,* Calcutta 1872, pp. 109-113.
7. Sengupta, Sankar, *Tree Symbol Worship in India,* p. 8.

8. *Ibid.*, p. 133.
9. Deb Barman, Debapriya, *Treatise on Traditional Social Institution of the Tripuri Community,* Agartala, 1980, p. 55
10. *Ibid.*, pp. 27-28.
11. *Ibid.*, p. 16.
12. *Anglo-Kakbark Dictionary,* Agartala, 1996, pp. 93, 153.
13. Satter, Abdus, *Tribal Culture in Bangladesh,* Dhaka, 1975, p.60.
14. Crooke, William, *Religion and Folklore of Northern India,* London, 1896, p. 57
15. *Anglo-Kakbark Dictionary,* pp. 59, 98.
16. Bhattacharjee, Priyabrata, *Tribal Pujas and Festival in Tripura,* Agartala, 1994, p. 35.
17. *Ibid.*, p. 41.
18. Bhattacharjee, P.N., *op. cit.*, p. 148.
19. Bhattacharjee, Priyabrata, *op. cit.*, p. 42.
20. *Ibid.*, p. 43.
21. *Ibid.*, p. 44.
22. *Ibid.*, p. 43.
23. Satter, Abdus, *op. cit.*, p. 33-63.
24. Bhattacharjee, Priyabrata, *op. cit.*, pp. 44.
25. Deb Barman, Debapriya, *op. cit.*, p. 15.
26. *Garia,* Directorate of Tribal Research, Govt. of Tripura, pp. 20-21.
27. Deb Barman, Debapriya, *op. cit.*, p. 52.
28. *Ibid.*, p. 53.
29. *Ibid.*, p. 54.
30. *Ibid.*
31. Das, Sudhir, *TUI-A* Quarterly Research Journal of Tripura Life & Culture, Vol. IV, 1996, Agartal, p. 18.
32. Bhattacharjee, Priyabrata, *op. cit.*, pp. 54-55.
33. Bhowmik, Dwijendralal, *Tribal Religion of Tripura,* Agartala, 1997, p. 16.
34. Bhattacharjee, Priyabrata, *op. cit.*, p. 49.
35. Ganchoudhuri, J., *Tipras of Tripura* (unpublished thesis), Calcutta University, 1978, p. 366.
36. Bhattacharjee, Priyabrata, Other Religious History of Tripras on the background of Kharchi pūjā, in *Proceeding vol. 6th Session North East History Association,* 1985, p. 100.

37. A piece of cloth to cover the breasts of the Tribal girls of Tripura.
38. Sen, Kaliprasanna, *Śrī Rājmalā,* Vol. I, pp. 10-14.
39. Bhattacharjee, Priyabrata, *op. cit.* p. 100.
40. Chatterjee, S.K., Kirata-Jano-Kriti, *JRASB,* Vol. XVI, N : 1, 1950, pp. 218-220.
41. Singha, Kailash Ch., *Rājmalā Bā Tripurār Itibritta,* Agartala, p. 23.
42. Bhattacharjee, Priyabrata, *op. cit.,* pp. 54-55.
43. Deb, Dasharat, *Kakbark Chhouroung,* Agartala 1977, p. 70.
44. Tripura, Ahindra Lal, *Tripura Samthita,* Agartala, 1996, p. 56.
45. Kartik, Lahiri, *Temple of Tripura,* Calcutta, p. 9.
46. Sen, Kaliprasanna, *op. cit.,* p. 145.
47. Deb, Dasharat, *op. cit.,* p. 70.
48. Sen, Kaliprasanna, *op. cit.,* p. 145.
49. Bhattarjee, Priyabrata, *op. cit.,* p. 36.
50. Sengupta, Sankar, *op. cit.,* p. 89.
51. *Ibid.,* p. 134.
52. *Ibid.,* p. 134.
53. *Ibid.,* p. 134.
54. *Ibid.,* p. 9.
55. Directorate of Tribal Research, *op. cit.,* Agartala, 1976, p. 23.
56. *Ibid.,* p. 10.
57. *Ibid.,* p. 11.
58. Satter, Abdus, *Iss,* p. 291.
59. Bhattacharjee, P.N., *op. cit.,* P. 143.
60. *Ibid.,* p. 144.
61. *Ibid.*
62. The traditional supreme council of the Jamatias.
63. *Anglo-Kakbark Dictionary,* pp. 89-90.
64. Bhattacharjee, P.N., *op. cit.,* p. 145.
65. *Ibid.*
66. *Anglo-Kakbark Dictionary.* p. 76.
67. Bhattacharjee, P. N., *op. cit.* p. 145.
68. *Ibid.,* p. 146.
69. *Anglo-Kakbark Dictionary*, p. 105.
70. Bhattacharjee, P. N., *op. cit.,* p. 148.
71. *Ibid.,* p. 157.
72. *Ibid.,* p. 158.

73. *Ibid.*
74. *Ibid.*
75. Dev Barman, Debapriya, *op. cit.,* p. 52.
76. Bhattacharjee, P.N., *op. cit.,* p. 159.
77. *Ibid.*
78. *Ibid.*
79. *Ibid.*
80. Deb Barman, S.B.K., *The Tribes of Tripura, A. Dissertation,* Agartala, 1986, p. 43.
81. Sattar, Abdus, *In The Sylvan Shadows,* Dhaka, pp. 237-38.
82. *Ibid.,* p. 242.
83. Deb Barman, S.B.K., *op. cit,* p. 43.
84. *Ibid.,* p. 43.
85. Bechetr, H., The Chākmās, a Buddhist communities in Bangladesh in *Jagjjyoti, Buddha Jayanti Annual,* 1973, p. 3.
86. Satter, Abdus, *op. cit.,* p. 273.
87. *Ibid.,* p. 277.
88. Satter, Abdus, *Tribal Culture in Bangladesh,* Dhaka, 1975, p.50.
89. *Chākamā,* Directorate of Education, Agartala, 1975, p. 25.
90. Satter, Abdus, *op.cit.,* p. 389.
91. *Ibid.,* p. 390.
92. Satter, Abdus, *Tribal Culture in Bangladesh,* p. 52.
93. Satter, Abdus, *op. cit.,* p. 302.
94. Chākma, *op. cit.,* p. 22.
95. *Ibid.,* p. 12.
96. Chākmā, *op. cit.,* p. 22.
97. *Ibid.,* p. 23.
98. Bhattacharjee, Priyabrata, Tripura Jatiya Utsav Bishu ebang Bijhu, *Dainik Sambad,* 1st Baishak, 1393, BS.
99. Bhattacharjee, Priyabrata, The religious history of the Tipras on the Background of Kharchipuja, in *proceding volume of 6th North Eastern India History Association,* 1985, p. 99.
100. Chatterjee, S.K., *Kirat-Jana-kirti,* Calcutta, 1974, p. 136.
101. Deb Barman, Devapriya., *Treatise on Traditional Social Institutions of the Tripuri Community,* Agartala, 1983, p. 49.
102. Bhattacharjee, P.N., *The Jāmātias of Tripura,* Agartala, 1983, p. 56.
103. Satter, Abdus, *In The Sylvan Shadows,* p. 388.

104. *Ibid,.* p. 388.
105. *Ibid,.* p. 388.
106. *Ibid,.* pp. 388-89.
107. Dev Barman, S.K.B., *The Tribes of Tripura, A Dissertation,* Agartala, 1986, p. 43.
108. Chattopadhaya, Subash, *Kak Bark Bhashar Likhito Rupe Uttaran,* Calcutta, 1972, p. 1.
109. Bhattacharjee, P.N., *Jāmātiā Folklore, A Sociological Study,* Agartala, 1995, p. 153.
110. Bhattarjee, Priyabrata, *Tribal Pujas and Festivals in Tripura,* Agartala, 1994, p. 125.
111. *Ibid,* p. 126.
112. *Ibid,* p. 126.
113. *Ibid,* p. 127.
114. Kakbark *mantras* collected personally from Ochai Ahindralal Tripura, Latiachara, West Tripura.
115. *Ibid.*
116. *Ibid.*
117. This Kakbark *mantras,* collected personally from *Ochai,* Nandadulal Tripura, Dhumachara, Tripura.
118. *Ibid.*
119. Bhattacharjee, Priyabrata, *op. cit,* pp. 129-130.
120. *Ibid,* p. 130.
121. *Ibid,* p. 131.
122. *Ibid,* p. 131.
123. *Ibid,* pp. 131-132.
124. (a) In the central portion of the Chittagong Hill Tracts in the Chakma chief's circle, situated in the country round the Kharnafuli River, broken dialect of Bengali, peculiar to the locality, and of a very curious character is spoken. It is called Chakma, and is based on South-Eastern Bengali, but has undergone so much transformation that it is almost worthy of the dignity of being classed as a separate language. It is written in an alphabet which allowing for its cursive form, is almost identical with the Khemer character, which was formerly in use in Cambodia, Laos, Annam, Siam and at last the Southern parts of Burma.

    Lingustic Survey of India/Vol. V/part I/1968.

    (b) They are undoubtedly a branch of the Mongolian family and have migrated to their present habitat from Arakan. Owing to close contact with the Bengali speaking people of the plains they have considerably changed their native language and now speaking a mixed form of speech.

—*Journal and Proceedings of the Asiastic Society of Bengal* (New Series) Vol. XXVII/1931.

125. It has been collected from Nirangan Chakma, Information & Culture Department, Govt. of Tripura.

126. *Ibid.*

127. It has been collected from Suren Deb Barman, Education Department, Govt. of Tripura.

128. *Ibid.*

129. *Ibid.*

130. Bhattacharjee, Priyabrata, *op. cit,* p. 136.

131. *Ibid.*

BIBLIOGRAPHY

I. Original Sanskrit Texts : Literary

Atharva Veda trans., W.D. Whitney, Cambridge, Mass, USA, 1905.

Bhāgavata Purāṇa, ed., Swami Dhananjaya Das Tarka Vyakarana Tirtha and Nrisimha Das Basu, Nimbarkasrama, 1930.

Bhaviṣya Purāṇa, Bombay, 1910.

Brahma Vaivarta Purāṇa, ed., P. Tarakaratna, Vaṅgavasi Edition, Sak. 1827.

Bṛhat Saṁhitā of Varāhamihira, ed., and trans., by Subrahmanya Sastri and M. Rama Krishna Bhat, Bangalore, 1947.

Devī-Purāṇa, ed., P. Tarakaratna, Vaṅgavasi Edition, Calcutta, 1302 B.S.

Harivaṁśa Purāṇa, ed., and trans., by M.N. Dutta, Calcutta, 1897.

Kubjikā Tantra (Patala VII), Manuscript No. 3178 (T.S.S.B).

Liṅga Purāṇa (L.P.), ed., P. Tarkaratna, Calcutta.

Mahābhārata, ed., P. Tarkaratna, Calcutta, 1910.

Matsya Purāṇa, ed., P. Tarkaratna, Vaṅgavasi Edition, Calcutta, 1910.

Rig Veda Saṁhitā, Vedic Research Institute, Poona, 1946.

Śatapatha Brāhmaṇa, ed., Weber, Leipzig Otto Harrasso Witz., 1924.

Skanda Purāṇa, ed., P. Tarkaratna., Calcutta.

Taittiriyāraṇyakaṁ, ed., R.L. Mitra, Asiatic Society of Bengal, Calcutta, 1872.

Varāha Purāṇa, ed., Hrishikesa Sastri, Calcutta, A.S.B, 1887.

II. Other Literary Works

Ain-i-Akbari II, Abul Fazal, trans., and ed., by H.S. Jarret, Calcutta, 2nd edition, 1949.

Baharistan-i-Ghaybi, Mirza Nathan, ed., and trans., Borale, M. Gauhati, 1936.

Rājmālā, ed. Education Directorate, Govt. of Tripura, Agartala, 1967.

Śrī Rājmālā, Sen, K.P. (ed.,). (I-IV), Agartala, (1926, 1927, 1931, 1932).

Tripura deśara Kathār Lekha, Bairagi, Arjunadasa and Ratna Kandali ed., and trns., Bhuinya, S.K., under the title, Tripura Burunji, Gauhati, 1938.

Secondary Works

Alam, A.K.M. Shamsul, *Maināmati,* Dacca, 1975.

Allan, J.,*Catalogue of the Coins of Gupta Dynasty,* London, 1914.

Benerjea, J.N., *Development of Hindu Iconography,* Calcutta, 1956.

Benerjea, J.N., *Pañchopāsanā,* Calcutta, 1960.

Benerji, Adris, *Temples of Tripura,* Varanasi, 1968.

Bhattacharjee, P.N., *Jamatia Follklore, A Sociological Study,* Tribal Research Institute, Govt. of Tripura, Agartala, 1995.

Bhattacharjee, Priyabrata, *Tribal Pujas and Festivals in Tripura,* Tribal Research Institute, Govt. of Tripura, Agartala, 1994.

Bhattacharjee, Priyabrata, *Tripurar Dev O Devi* (in Bengali), Agartala, 1987.

Bhattacharya, Haridas, *The Foundation of Living Faith,* Vol. I, Calcutta, 1938.

Bhattacharyya, Dipak C., *Tantrik Buddhist Iconographic Sources,* New Delhi, 1974.

Bhattasali, N.K., *Iconography of Buddhist and Brahmanical Sculptures in the Dacca Museum,* Reprint, New Delhi, 1974.

Bhowmik, Dwijendralal, *Tribal Religion of Tripura,* Agartala, 1997.

Chatterjee, B., ed., *Culture of Bengal through the Ages,* Burdwan, 1988.

Chatterjee, Rama, *Religion of Bengal,* Calcutta, 1985.

Chatterjee, S.K., *Kirāta-Jana-kriti,* Calcutta, 1974.

Crooke, William, *Religion and Folklore of Northern India,* London, 1896.

Dalton, E.T., *Descriptive Ethonology of Bengal,* Calcutta, 1872.

Dani, A.H., *Pre-History and Proto History of Eastern India,* Calcutta, 1960.

Das, Ratna, *Art & Architecture of Tripra,* Tribal Research Institute, Agartala, 1997.

Deb, Dasharat, *Kakbark Chhouroung,* Agartala, 1977.

Deb Barma, S.C., *Tripura Smriti,* (in Bengali), Calcutta, 1927.

Deb Barman, Devapriya, *Treatise on Traditional Social Institution of Tripura Community,* Tribal Reasearch Institute, Agartala, 1980.

Deb Barman, P.M., *Unakoti Tirtha* (in Bengali), Agartala, 1921.

Deb Barman, Rajendrajit, *Gariya Puja,* Agartala, 1976.

Deb Barman, Binoy, *Anglo Kakbark Dictionary,* Agartala, 1996.

Deb Barman, S.B.K., *The Tribes of Tripura — A Dissertation,* Tribal Research Institute, Agartala, 1986.

Deb Baraman, S. Bikram, ed., *1901 Census Report of Tripura,* Tribal Research Institute, Agartala, 1995 (Reprint).

Dev Sarma, Chandradaya, *Silalipi Sangraha,* Agartala, 1968.

Directorate of Education, ed.,*Chakma,* Govt. of Tripura, Agartala, 1975.

Dutta, Jyotish, *Bhumi Lekhya Pattrer Aloke Tripurar Bhumi Byavasthā,* Directorate of Higher Education, Agartala, 1987.

Ganchoudhuri, J., *Tripura : The Land and Its People,* New Delhi, 1980; *The Riangs of Tripura,* Directorate of Research, Agartala, 1983; *Tripras of Tripura* (unpublished Thesis) Calcutta University, 1978.

Getty, Alichary, *Gaṇeśa monograph on the Elephant Faced God,* Oxford, 1936.

Gupta, Kamalakanta,*Copper Plates of Sylhet* I, Sylhet, 1967.

Habibullah, A.B.M., e.d, *Nalinikanta Bhattasali Commemoration Volume,* Dacca, 1968.

Hunter, W.W., *A Statistical Account of Bengal,* Vol. VI, Reprint, Delhi, 1973.

Jash, P, ed., *The Development of Mother Goddess Worship,* Visva-Bharati Research Publication, Santiniketan, 1987, *Society and Religion in Ancient India* (*Sudhakar Chattopadhyaya Commemoration Volume*), Calcutta, 1984.

Jash, P., *Glimpses of Hindu Cults and Culture,* New Delhi, 1997; *History and Evolution of Vaiṣṇavism in Eastern India,* Calcutta 1982;

History of Śaivism, Calcutta, 1974;
History of the Parivrājakas : Śankarācārya, Delhi, 1991;
Some Aspects of Jainism in Eastern India, New Delhi, 1989.

Khan, F.A., *Maināmati,* Karachi, 1963.

Lahiri, Kartik, *Temple of Tripura,* Calcutta, N.D.

Law, B.C., *Historical Geography of Ancient India,* Paris, 1958.

Lewin, T.H., *The Hill Tracts of Chittagong and the Dwellers Therein,* Calcutta, 1869.

Majumdar, N.G., *Inscriptions of Bengal, III,* Rajsahi, 1929.

Majumdar, R.C, ed., *History of Culture and Indian People (I-VI),* Bombay; *History of Bengal, I,* Dacca, First edition 1943, 2nd Impression 1963.

Majumdar, R.C., *History of Ancient Bengal,* Calcutta, 1971.
Bānglādeśer Itihāsa, Calcutta, 1317 B.S.

Marshall, J., *Mohenjodaro and Indus Valley Civilization,* London, 1931.

Mecutchion, David, *Late Mediaeval Temples of Bengal,* Calcutta.

Menon, K.D., *Tripura District Gazetteers,* Govt. of Tripura, Agartala, 1975.

Morrison, B.M., *Laimai—A Cultural Centre of Early Bengal,* New York, 1977.

Mukherjee, B.N., *External Trade of Early North Eastern India,* New Delhi, 1992.

Mukherjee, Bikash, *Religious Centres of North India,* New Delhi, 1993.

Mukherjee, S.C., *Study of Vaiṣṇavism in Ancient and Medieval Bengal,* Calcutta, 1966.

Mukherji, R. and Maity, S.K., *Corpus of Bengal Inscriptions,* Calcutta, 1967.

Mukhopadhyay, Sukhamay, *Banglar Itihaser Duso Bachar,* Calcutta, 1966.

Niyogi, P., *Buddhism in Ancient Bengal,* Calcutta, 1980

Paul, P.L., *Early History of Bengal, II,* Calcutta, 1939.

Roy Chowdhuri, M.R., *Tripura Through the Ages,* New Delhi, 1983.

Roy, M.R., *Sources of the History of India,* Vol. IV, Calcutta, 1982.

Ray, N.R., *Brahmanical Gods in Burma*, Calcutta, 1932; *Bāṅgālir Itihāsa : Adiparba*, Reprinted, Calcutta, 1959.

Sarkar, J.N., ed., *History of Bengal, II*, Dacca, 1972.

Sarkar, J.N., *India Through the Ages*, Calcutta, 1951.

Sattar, Abdus, *Tribal Culture in Bangladesh*, Dhaka, 1975.

In The Sylvan Shadows, Dhaka, N.D.

Sen, Benoy Chandra, *Some Historical Aspect of the Inscriptions of Bengal*, Calcutta, 1942.

Sengupta, S., *ed., Tree Symbol Worship in India*, Calcutta, 1965.

Sengupta, S., ed., *Tripura Prasanga*, Agartala, N.D.

Singh, C. and Nath, Prem, *Hindu Goddesses*, New Delhi, 1995.

Singha, Kailash Chandra, *Rajmala Ba Tripurar Itibritta*, Agartala, N.D.

Sircar, D.C., *'The Śākta Pīṭhas'*, Delhi, 1973;

Select Inscriptions, Calcutta, 1965.

Tripura, Ahindralal, *Tripur Samhita*, Agartala, 1996.

Williams, Monier, *Religious Thought & Life in India*, London, 1883.

INDEX

Tughra style of Arabic writing on the coins of Sultans of Bengal 165